Re-distribution of Authority

A Cross-Regional Perspective

Edited by
Jeanie J. Bukowski and Swarna Rajagopalan

Westport, Connecticut
London

Library of Congress Cataloging-in-Publication Data

Re-distribution of authority : a cross-regional perspective / edited by Jeanie J. Bukowski
and Swarna Rajagopalan.
    p.   cm.
  Includes bibliographical references and index.
  ISBN 0–275–96377–2
  1. Local government—Cross-cultural studies.   2. Administrative and political
divisions—Cross-cultural studies.   I. Bukowski, Jeanie J., 1964–   II. Rajagopalan, Swarna,
1964–
JS78b.R44 2000
321.02′3–dc21   99–059848

British Library Cataloguing in Publication Data is available.

Library of Congress Catalog Card Number: 99–059848
ISBN: 0–275–96377–2

First published in 2000

Praeger Publishers, 88 Post Road West, Westport, CT 06881
An imprint of Greenwood Publishing Group, Inc.
www.praeger.com

Printed in the United States of America

The paper used in this book complies with the
Permanent Paper Standard issued by the National
Information Standards Organization (Z39.48–1984).

10 9 8 7 6 5 4 3 2 1

Dedicated in loving memory to Myrtle M. Danner, Dr. Walter E. Heston, and P. M. Rajagopalan, for all that they taught us.

Contents

Illustrations

Preface

This project began as, more than anything else, an exercise in friendship. While completing the doctoral program in political science at the University of Illinois at Urbana–Champaign, the editors discovered a true sign of friendship and camaraderie: the willingness to read endless drafts of each other's dissertation chapters. And in those exchanges, they also began to observe, much to their initial surprise, parallels in their work. Despite the fact that Swarna was dealing with issues of state building in South Asia, and Jeanie was looking at multilevel governance in southern Europe, they noticed similarities in the causes and consequences of both phenomena, across the two vastly different geographic regions. Moreover, in discussing these similarities, they began to realize that the very different sets of literature they were using to approach their respective questions in their respective regions also yielded similar explanations. So they began both to lament the fact that so many useful bodies of literature seem to ignore or talk past each other, and to wonder if the same sorts of similarities that they were seeing in South Asia and southern Europe would also be present in other states and areas of the world.

This book addresses these concerns. It redefines the phenomenon described varyingly as decentralization, centralization, territoriality, regionalization, etc., as the "re-distribution of authority." It then asks experts in a varied range of geographic areas to address the causes of this phenomenon. The results, we believe, cross both analytical and geographic boundaries in the study of governance, and give new insights on how and why authority shifts among levels within and beyond the modern nation-state.

The editors are grateful to each other for keeping the project going, even during its more difficult moments, and for the friendship that has endured through long editing sessions. They also very much appreciate the enthusiasm, hard work, and most importantly, the high level of scholarship and professionalism that each of the contributors to this volume brought to the task we put before them.

We wish to thank Dr. Edward A. Kolodziej for playing such a large role in ensuring that we have the skills necessary to pursue the type of research and analysis found in this book. Swarna also expresses her gratitude to Dr. Stephen P. Cohen for his continuing encouragement and guidance.

Jeanie Bukowski acknowledges the technical support in the preparation of the manuscript from the Institute of International Studies, and is especially grateful to Jeanne Clayton for all her expertise, patience, hard work, and friendship.

Finally, both editors are indebted, as always, to their families. Their support, encouragement, patience, understanding, and love have been an indispensable part of this project.

Chapter 1

Re-distribution of Authority: Crossing Boundaries

Jeanie J. Bukowski and Swarna Rajagopalan

THE DEBATE REFORMULATED

At the turn of the century, we are witnessing a motley collection of power shifts, at every level of human interaction and especially in the political arena: the breakup and creation of states (Lebanon, Czechoslovakia, Yugoslavia, the Soviet Union), the transfiguration of other states (Belgium, South Africa), the growing importance of substate actors within and across states (the Association of European Regions, Kashmir, the Basque separatist movement ETA, the nongovernmental development community in Senegal and Bangladesh), and the emergence of suprastate actors (the North American Free Trade Association, the European Union, the Asia-Pacific Economic Forum).

Hard-pressed to comprehend the simultaneity of these processes, scholarship in political science has taken the "Six Blind Men and the Elephant" approach, and separate bodies of literature address pieces of the puzzle, but none captures the phenomenon in its entirety. Accustomed to a snapshot perspective on politics, we are moved to ask: Why? Why does the re-distribution of authority occur–within, without, and across states? What factors explain shifts in the distribution of authority, such that authority comes to be distributed in certain ways at certain times? If the answer is not in local descriptions of the Elephant, it may well be somewhere "between and betwixt" these descriptions. This book therefore proposes to approach the question in such a way as to broaden the analysis and consider as many of these descriptions as possible, while searching for commonalities, differences, and linkages among them.

The cases presented in this volume are India, Pakistan, Sri Lanka, the United States, Russia, Spain, Portugal, Senegal, and South Africa. What is comparable across the diverse states examined is that they are dealing with similar issues of state consolidation and continuation: how to integrate different "parts" of the state (that may be drawn along ethnic, linguistic, cultural, economic, and political lines) into the whole; how to create and maintain a balance of authority between the central state and substate entities; and how to prevent conflict (political, economic, and/or military) among the state's constituent units. These cases focus primarily on the process of authority distribution within the state, but this process does not occur in isolation from developments outside the state. For example, the cases of Spain and Portugal must of necessity take into account how the European Union may affect the re-distribution of authority. Likewise, Senegal, in seeking the capital necessary for development, has had to respond to international pressures to decentralize. Each case presented here answer two questions: Which are the factors that explain the re-distribution of authority? Under what conditions are some of these factors more important than others? The answers to these questions allow a comparison of factors involved in the distribution and re-distribution of authority that spans both geographical and analytical boundaries.

RE-DISTRIBUTION OF AUTHORITY

By re-distribution of authority, we mean the process whereby and the outcome wherein who gets to decide and do what on behalf of a group of people in a polity are adjusted. We argue that this is an ongoing process and that the outcome is subject to continual renegotiation.

What, then, is authority? As authority is one of the central concepts in the consideration of politics, debates on the relationship between power, authority, and legitimacy form the subject of most political studies (for example, Boulding 1989; Axelrod 1984; Oye 1986; Raz 1990; Mann 1986; Mamdani 1996). In this work, we define authority as power which is legitimate. When any political order is first established, its legitimacy is predicated on expectations of the future. We identify four such expectations:

1. The promise of survival: If those who have power are unable to convey their intent and ability to survive as rulers, then there is no reason for their potential subjects to pay them any heed.
2. The promise of effectiveness: Each political order is founded as a historical response to certain events or issues. At the moment of founding, it is assumed that such an arrangement will be successful in addressing those issues.
3. The credibility of its enforcement capability: Even where there is debate over endurance and effectiveness, the credible threat of force can buy legitimacy for a new political order.
4. The promise of responsiveness: In our times, the assumption is also that a particular political arrangement will represent its citizens' interests. This in turn depends on those citizens' having access to the state apparatus, both to avail of services and to provide feedback.

Beyond the moment of the founding, however, the arrangement is constantly under review. Is it in fact going to survive? Have the rulers kept their promises? Are they meeting their obligations? Are they able to carry out their policies and extract obedience from the public? Do they indeed represent us and do we have access to them? Different sets of citizens may answer these questions differently. The result is a process without end and a debate without final resolution. As this process is underway, whether a political order deserves obedience and how legitimate it is can be quite contentious. What continues to lend authority to that order is simply the recognition that it is the framework of the debate. When that framework itself is challenged, as it is by secessionists, the authority of the order is seriously undermined.

The effective exercise of governmental authority requires that it be distributed. From Aristotle's typology to Montesquieu's separation of powers to the structural-functionalism of comparative politics, descriptions and discussions of government are discussions of the distribution of authority, whether territorial or otherwise. The ability to make and enforce decisions and to "allocate values" in the fulfillment of societal demands constitutes the substance and purpose of this distribution. The dialogue between those who seek empowerment and those in positions of authority is constant, and this dialogue reconfigures the terms of the distribution of authority.

Most studies analyze the distribution of authority across one or two instances of the phenomenon, treating change either as a desirable or a disastrous disruption of the status quo. In this work, change is assumed to be the status quo. The term "re-distribution" is used to capture the fluidity of each political arrangement described herein. This removes the focus from what we argue are temporary outcomes to what we regard as the more important question, that of the movement from one outcome to another. Moreover, this conceptualization allows us to consider the debates and the reasoning that lead to the creation of the next set of outcomes or the next distribution of authority, not in isolation, but in the context of a larger historical legacy. The analysis that follows is more comprehensive and dynamic than conventional approaches allow.

RE-DISTRIBUTION OF AUTHORITY: NINE CASE STUDIES

As land and natural resources are the first bases of power in society, so is the territorial restructuring of a state an early stage of the re-distribution of authority among its peoples. Rajagopalan's chapter, "Demarcating Units, Re-distributing Authority: Pakistan, India, Sri Lanka" is a comparative historical analysis of internal territorial organization in the colonial and postcolonial contexts of these states. Within this time frame, units have been created, altered, and effaced to reflect the ongoing conversation—sometimes cordial, sometimes hostile—over who is included, who is excluded, who governs, and who is governed. Two key relationships are discerned: that between identity and land, particularly linguistic identity and land, and that between territorial self-definition and the process of state formation. As a consequence, the battle between territorially concentrated identity groups (who reappear in the cases of

Russia and Spain) and those who control the state is waged over the issue of unit demarcation. Units are sought as a guarantee of access to the political system, and the nature of both the unit sought and that finally created seem partly to depend on the stage of state formation at which each exchange takes place.

India, Pakistan, and Sri Lanka are new states, and in each of these, the demarcation of units has followed the constitutional creation of the state. The United States, which is considered the classic, even perfected, federal polity, was formed by the coming together of the federating units. Bowman's chapter, "Pulling and Tugging: The Distribution of Authority in a Mature Federal System," demonstrates that haggling between the federal and state levels over the locus of authority in different spheres has never ceased. In her words, "The national government pulls one way; state governments tug the other way." Tracing the evolution of the US federal system, Bowman disabuses us of the notion that the act of founding a set of institutions precludes further debate on their nature and functions. Through a careful narration of events and ideas that mark this evolution, she reveals a more dynamic pattern of centralization and decentralization than is conventionally associated with this case. Economic conditions, changing levels of state effectiveness, and public opinion have driven the alternation between phases in which the federal government was able to expand and phases in which the states successfully reclaimed authority.

While the US federation has come to epitomize a standard in democratic practice, Dowley's essay, "Re-distributing Authority in Russia: Regional Governors' Preferences," reminds us that we should not take the consensual foundations of the federal compact for granted. The distinction between the US and Russian federations lies in the levels of stability and maturity of the two systems. While in the US system, the pulling and tugging occur within a structure that is stable and about which there is a fundamental consensus, this is not so in the Russian case. Its predecessor, the Soviet federation, was founded in a manner that resembles more closely the federations of India and Pakistan than it does the American. Where the units came together to form the American federation, in the other three instances, the federating units were created after the founding of the state as a whole. The federation inherited by this successor-state would appear to still be negotiating the terms of its basic compact. Thus, the pulling and tugging here, or the bargaining to use Dowley's term, have a very fluid, fragile context. Indeed, the future of democratic government in Russia appears to be at stake.

The Russian federation is challenged in a variety of ways by unit leaders. Dowley demonstrates that the demands made by these elites are determined by both ethno-national and economic considerations. She uses statistical analysis to evaluate the relative influence of these factors on the bargaining positions adopted by unit leaders. While her study reinforces the findings of the South Asian and Spanish cases that ethno-territorial identity is important, she does not dismiss the significance of feelings of neglect and deprivation. In fact, this study shows how vital the interaction of factors are, as well as the role of political agency in ordering that interaction. Dowley suggests that among the "missing pieces" of her puzzle may be the relationship that local leaders bear to the people(s) they claim to represent and their own political ambitions. What is a suggestion in Dowley's case study becomes abundantly clear in Bukowski's discussion of Spain and Portugal. Where the political ambitions of local leaders coincide with the aspirations of their publics, strong demands for increased autonomy are more likely.

In her essay, "Complexity Matters: Re-distribution of Authority in Spain and Portugal," Bukowski focuses on these states from the fall of their respective dictatorships to the present. Spain and Portugal have peacefully transformed themselves from centralized, dictatorial systems, re-distributing authority both across territory and across political and social institutions. However, this process has been neither uniform nor unidirectional in the two states. Spain has devolved authority to territorially based substate governments to a much greater degree than Portugal, and in both states there is a pulling and tugging between the central government and substate units, resulting in both centralizing and decentralizing trends.

Bukowski first distills the primary explanatory factors for the re-distribution of authority as set forth in the various bodies of literature utilized in the study of decentralization and regionalism in the European arena. She then seeks to discover which factors are most important in explaining the shifting of authority in Spain and Portugal and how these factors interact. She concludes that structural factors, including inefficiencies of centralization, territorially based economic differences, and ethnic nationalist cleavages, create the conditions under which political actors (political parties, central state and substate elites) make demands on the system. Whether decentralization or centralization occurs depends largely on how successful the various political actors are in using these conditions to their advantage. This chapter illustrates that it is necessary to consider the complex interaction of factors in order to fully explain the re-distribution of authority.

As Patterson's discussion, "Decentralization in Senegal: Reordering Authority or Reinventing Past Reforms?" tells us, a complicated interplay of influences provides both the impetus toward decentralization as well as the inhibiting resistance to that process in this case. The association of development and democracy with decentralization, the postcolonial rejection of French centralized state structures, pressures arising from the growth of civil society, and the advocacy of the international community have simulated favorable conditions for decentralization. This has, however, remained administrative decentralization or deconcentration, largely due to the weakness of the Senegalese state–a problem that Patterson says is mirrored in other parts of Africa. The state lacks both legitimacy and the ability to act effectively, and as such is unable to meet the growing demands of nascent civil society.

In "Re-distribution of Authority in South Africa: Centralizing the Government, Rainbowing the Nation," Pirro and Zeff explore both institutional and territorial shifting of authority. The authors of this chapter find that while post-apartheid South Africa has re-distributed authority to a certain extent institutionally, through enfranchisement of the nonwhite population and a significant restructuring of the system of opportunities, the new government has actually centralized power both territorially and administratively. Indeed, the complexity and volatility of the South African transition to a post-apartheid system may, paradoxically, require government centralization in order to achieve the goals of economic development while creating a civil society in which the majority may participate.

RE-DISTRIBUTION OF AUTHORITY: FINALLY GLIMPSING THE ELEPHANT

As different as these nine contexts might seem, certain factors emerge as common threads. These are issues of identity, economic imperatives, political agency, and administrative effectiveness. In South Asia, Russia, and Spain, the issue of autonomy is inextricably tied to that of identity politics. The overlap of regional and communal boundaries makes the demand for territorial recognition potent and well-nigh irresistible, although the range of demands for political space is not merely territorial. While many of the factors operating to cause re-distribution are internal, in several cases (e.g., Senegal, Russia, and Spain) we see external influence stemming from globalization and interdependence. Moreover, territorial economic differentials interact with these external imperatives. Arguments for both more and less centralized control of economic decision-making arise from the desire to alleviate a state's unequal economic development, but differing strategies on how to achieve that goal (as demonstrated in the cases of Senegal, Spain, Portugal, South Asia, Russia). From the political agendas of the major parties in the US to the bargaining stances developed by unit leaders in Russia, political agency emerges as a crucial factor. And as illustrated in Spain and Russia, if political ambition corresponds with a strong ethno-linguistic identity in a substate territory, demands for autonomy will be particularly strong. The argument that it would be easier to achieve a political or administrative goal through either centralization or decentralization facilitates re-distribution both ways. With unit demarcation in South Asia, developmental arguments in Russia, Portugal, and Senegal, and also, the reallocation of functions and resources in Spain and the US, this is often the coup de grâce for any prevalent arrangements. As we have pointed out in the previous section, the evidence summoned by the following chapters is that these factors neither occur nor act in isolation from each other. They affect each other and impel the continual re-distribution of authority.

Chapter 2

Demarcating Units, Re-distributing Authority: Pakistan, India, Sri Lanka

Swarna Rajagopalan

Battles over how authority within a state should be distributed take many forms. They are struggles over specific privileges (the right to levy a particular tax or to organize a particular activity), negotiations over appointments and dismissals, or demands for autonomy or separation. They are also, most fundamentally of all, battles over what shall constitute the shape and form of the unit to which authority shall or shall not be distributed. The recognition of the region occupied by a group as an identity-based political unit unto itself constitutes the first victory of the group in its quest for a place in the political arena, regardless of whether it is accompanied by an actual delegation of authority. In federal polities, where the units have ostensibly existed prior to the collective entity (the state as a whole), the demarcation of a new unit is even more significant, as it concedes the precedence of the new unit over the whole in its previous form.

Predictably, any proposed demarcation of units is bitterly contested. The acrimony arises because there is a close relationship between territorial organization and the vision of the state. The relationship between external boundaries and the continued existence of a state in a certain form is axiomatic in the study of politics. The relationship between internal boundaries and the state's identity is less articulated. The internal boundaries of a state are indicative of how the whole differentiates itself from its parts. It precedes the actual distribution of functions and powers within the state. For instance, where the state is formed through the union of its parts, the parts delegate powers to the state as a whole and predispose the power relationship to favor themselves, at least theoretically. Further re-distribution may diminish this potential. Likewise, theoretically, when the parts are creations of the whole, they may be altered at the initiative of the whole, and correspondingly, their powers also depend on the pleasure of the state as a whole. Studying the politics of unit demarcation is thus also to study the politics of how authority and power are distributed within a state.

Three bodies of academic writing address this relationship, each exploring one dimension of it, and all three ultimately treating it as a given. The writing on federalism and intergovernmental relations takes the territorial question for granted, pointing out the relationship between federalism and plural societies (Elazar 1987; Smith 1995). It is pointed out in most recent writings that the context of federalism has changed due to globalization and substate nationalism, among other things, and it is commonly held that federalism is a reasonable solution to the problem of diversity within society (Elazar 1987; Smith 1995; Agnew 1997). We are told by a leading scholar on the subject that federalism combines self-rule and shared rule (Elazar 1987). Writers on ethnic conflict accept this view as well (Horowitz 1985; Diamond and Plattner 1994; Enloe 1986; Montville 1990). However, there is also concern that in some instances, federalism and similar territorial arrangements will facilitate secession (Kymlicka 1998), and indeed some of the evidence that writers on nationalism summon substantiates this concern (Anderson 1991, 113–140). The natural conflict between the nationalism of the state and the nationalism of groups within the state is reflected in the writing on nationalism and ethnicity. It is hard to make land central to national identity at both those levels and reconcile the arguments that result. Political geographers underline the importance of territory to all of the above issues, explaining the importance of land to identity on the one hand (Hooson 1994) and identifying territory as a key organizing principle of government (Paddison 1983, 14–21). While they are more concerned with regions than scholars of federalism or nationalism, they do not dwell too explicitly on the link between state identity, regions, and substate units and structural arrangements. This chapter teases out this relationship from the three cases that are narrated herein.

India, Pakistan, and Sri Lanka retained enough elements of the colonial states that they succeeded to have in-built mechanisms for centralization. In spite of that, Pakistan and India began their postcolonial existence as federal states, while Sri Lanka continued to be unitary. Within these countries, this chapter tells the story of three regionally based communities—Tamil speakers in India and Sri Lanka, and Sindhis in Pakistan—as they have had, lost, won, or regained a unit of their own. What were the push factors for changes in unit demarcation, and what larger issues for authority re-distribution did they seek to address? What is the nexus between territoriality, identity and the re-distribution of authority? If we postulate that unit demarcation is an important early stage of any re-distribution of authority and that there is a relationship between territorial arrangements and the state's vision of itself, then we might expect the call for redefinition of units to reflect challenges to this vision of the state. What propositions do the cases yield?

A UNIT FOR SINDH, 1847–1973

From the moment of the annexation of Sindh to the British Empire in 1847, Sindhis have fought for a unit of their own. Although we divide this century-long struggle into four parts, there have essentially been two issues that have troubled the Sindhi leadership. The first is that the cultural and political integrity of Sindh should be recognized, and the second is that Karachi should remain a "Sindhi" city. Sindh's alternate disappearances and resurrections as a distinct province have reflected the whims and visions of the government of the day, be it the colonial government or the Pakistani government.

Sindh and the Bombay Presidency, 1847-1935

British colonial practice was to append newly annexed territories to an existing, adjacent province or Presidency, and in 1847, Sindh was merged with the Bombay Presidency and remained so until 1935. At the time, the British were not accountable to anybody for this decision and so we are left to assume that it was simply an act of consolidation of empire and subordination, based on its effects. Sindh was administered as a distinct, "non-regulation" province within the Presidency by a Commissioner, who enjoyed greater autonomy than other provincial commissioners, in compensation for Sindh's merger with Bombay (Khuhro 1978, 16; Majumdar and Datta 1963, 331–332).

For Sindhis, the evidence of British neglect of their province was glaring. The financial allocations for Sindh were inadequate and such returns as they yielded accrued to the Hindu mercantile class and to the immigrant traders from other parts of the Presidency, rather than to the local Muslim elite (Khuhro 1978, 52; see also, Lari 1994, 176; Khan 1993, 2). The question of whether the union of Sindh and Bombay was rational seems to have exercised British minds as well. However, in their thinking the choice was not Bombay or autonomy but Bombay or Punjab. This was in contrast to the Sindhi desire to have the province restored as a distinct and separate part of the British Indian polity. Over the years, the arguments for separating Sindh (Mateke 1982, 58–59) from Bombay included the following:

- Bombay was neglecting the development of Sindh (Khan 1993, 3).
- Sindh was the natural trade outlet for and a natural adjunct to Punjab (Khuhro 1978, 19).
- Sindh and Punjab were part of the same riparian system, had compatible legal systems, and derived their agricultural settlement systems from tribal patterns. On the other hand, the loss of Sindh would make no difference to Bombay.

- A new frontier province including Punjab and Sindh would be politically and militarily advantageous. It would unify command and integrate administration along the frontier.
- As part of Bombay Presidency, Sindh required a separate local government and that meant that the Commissioner was unusually powerful.

None of these arguments moved Lord Curzon, the Viceroy of India from 1899 to 1905, however, and he rejected the idea, saying that the people of Sindh had had sixty years to get used to being a part of Bombay, and it would be imprudent to disrupt the working relationship that had grown between the two. He also hoped that improved rail communications between Sindh and Bombay would lessen the distance between them. Further, it was pointed out that transfer to Punjab would necessarily reduce the autonomy of the province without any increase in investment from Punjab, which was not in a position to devote resources to the development of Sindh. Another reason why the separation of Sindh was opposed was that Sindh was not in a position to repay the loan that the Bombay government had undertaken in order to build the Lloyd Barrage at Sukkur (Khuhro 1982, 55).

Nevertheless, the question of the separation of Sindh from Bombay was raised in 1913 at the Karachi session of the Indian National Congress, in 1917 by the Sindh Branch of the Central National Muhammadan Association, in 1925 by the Aligarh session of the All-India Muslim League, and by the Nehru Report in 1928. Between 1928, when the Simon Commission came to India, and 1935, the movement for a separate Sindh gained momentum in both the official and political spheres, with the issue being raised successfully at the First Round Table Conference (1930) and the Second Round Table Conference (1931). Upon their recommendation, the questions of financial losses and compensation for the separation of Sindh were studied. Led by Sheikh Abdul Majid Sindhi and Shahnawaz Bhutto, the Sindh Azad Conference met twice, in April and August 1932. In spite of opposition from Hindus, their call to observe "Separation Day" all over Sindh on the 16th of September, 1932, was successful. The 1932 findings of a joint parliamentary select committee in favor of separation were duly stated in a White Paper published in April 1933. The demand for separation was finally conceded in the Government of India Act of 1935.

The divide over the separation of Sindh loosely coincided with communal lines (Tahir 1990, 179). While Hindu support for separation declined, the idea of a separate Sindh gained currency among Muslims because having one Muslim-majority province would strengthen their case against a united India. The impression one is left with on reading accounts of the arguments for separation of Sindh is that for Sindhi politicians, working with the Muslim League was a means to this end and the Pakistan movement held out to them the promise of autonomy (Khuhro 1982, 56–57). Thus, at the Karachi session of the Muslim League in 1938, Sindhi politicians did join the League hoping that it would yield the desired results for them and their province. It was mobilization around the issue of regional autonomy that facilitated mobilization around the idea of Pakistan. The first grievance of Sindhis against the Pakistani state originates herein.

Karachi as the Federal Capital, 1948

The postcolonial state of Pakistan comprised, in its western flank, East Punjab, the North-west Frontier Provinces, Baluchistan, and Sindh; and in its eastern flank, East Bengal and Sylhet in Assam. For Sindh, partition had three important consequences: First, the influx of refugees into Sindh altered the demographic equation in the region, particularly Karachi; second, Karachi became the federal capital, and was separated from Sindh; finally, the Sindhi language went into a period of decline for lack of patronage and recognition by the state.

Karachi, which was both the main commercial center as well as the capital of Pakistan in its early years as an independent state, was the main recipient of the massive immigration during the partition of the subcontinent. The refugees who settled in Karachi came from every part of the subcontinent that was to remain with India, altering permanently the demographic profile of the city. Iftikhar Malik quotes the 1951 census as showing that in that year, 49% of the population of Karachi and 71% of the population of Hyderabad were refugees (1993, 57). This demographic change was compounded first by the fact that, unlike the refugees who moved to other places in Pakistan, those who came to Sindh by and large stayed in Sindh. Secondly, in the years after independence, Karachi remained a magnet for Pakistanis from less developed parts of Pakistan, as did other parts of Sindh (Malik 1993, 59).

In May 1948, Karachi was made the federal capital, with the federal government taking over the provincial government's premises, whereupon the latter relocated to Hyderabad. Sindhis were more aggrieved, however, because there were no professional colleges outside Karachi, placing Sindhis at a disadvantage since the quotas reserved for them in Karachi's now nationalized institutions were low and ever falling (Panhwar 1990, 44). Just as central and contentious was the marginalization of the Sindhi language. With Karachi separated and Urdu the national language, Sindhi students had to learn Urdu, while Sindhi was not compulsory for non-Sindhis in Karachi. Sindhi continued to be taught in the rural areas. The relationship between these three developments is spelled out by Hyder Baksh Jatoi: "When the name 'Sind' goes from the map of Pakistan, logically, Sindhi language should also disappear. That must be the vision and the ideal of the powers that be, in our Islamic Republic of Pakistan" (Jatoi 1978, 42–43).

One Unit in Pakistan, 1955–1973

While the 1949 Objectives Resolution passed by Pakistan's Constituent Assembly acknowledged the right of units in the federation to autonomy (without defining what "autonomy" meant), history conspired against them (Jalal 1995). Ayesha Jalal argues that the politicians who were running the affairs of state had no provincial support bases and were therefore dependent on the bureaucracy that they had inherited from an authoritarian colonial ruler. The chances of the provinces being granted real autonomy were further diminished by the conflict with India over Kashmir. Finally, Jalal makes the case that resource-strapped Pakistan's defense effort was dependent on its maximizing its extractive capability in the provinces. The two most important issues here were that of autonomy and representation of units in the federal upper house and of center-state power distribution (Salamat 1992, 78). For those in the western wing of this new state, the preferred formula was "parity"—equality in autonomy and representation with the eastern wing, which was essentially East Bengal. For the east, a fair arrangement would involve a greater degree of autonomy (and majority representation) for them based on population alone. In the first Constituent Assembly, the Bengalis were in a majority, and in the second, although membership was equally apportioned, there were more people from the west serving on the committees of the legislature.

To meet the rationale of "parity," in 1955, the Establishment of Western Pakistan Act merged the provinces of Western Pakistan into one province, including the Governor and Chief Commissioner's Provinces and the princely states of West Pakistan. Central control was to continue over the frontier and tribal areas. West Pakistan was divided into ten divisions, with Lahore as capital. The status of Karachi remained as it was. The first constitution of 1956 was based on this consolidation of the provinces of East and West Pakistan into "One Unit" each. Under this arrangement, the center was the only winner, arrogating to itself similar powers to those the colonial center enjoyed. Parity was achieved by a false equation of the total population of the West with the East, rather than conceding that the East had a preponderantly larger population. This had the effect of finessing the specific needs of the Western population and dismissing the claims of the Eastern (see Jahan 1972). This development made a significant difference in West Pakistan, which comprised regions and peoples with distinct styles and traditions of governance, but more simply, who spoke different languages and who had always been separate from each other.

The campaign against One Unit marks the second high point of mobilization around a Sindhi identity, the first being the movement to separate Sindh from Bombay (Malik 1993). In Sindh, non-Sindhis had benefited most from One Unit. Now that Sindhis were in a minority in the provincial legislature, they could do nothing to prevent the flow of jobs and land away from their community. Sindhis and the non-Sindhi bureaucracy were unable to communicate with each other. In 1953, G. M. Syed founded the Sindh Awami Mahaz, a four-party nativist coalition based in Sindh. This was the precursor to many other Sindhi political parties and organizations across the ideological continuum. In 1957, an Anti-One Unit Resolution was passed in the West Pakistan Assembly (Shah 1983, 10).

The 1956 constitution established a federation, still based on One Unit, where the residuary powers rested with the provinces. However, the federal government retained all of the emergency provisions of the Act of 1935. The brief period that this constitution was in force was marked by continued political mobilization around the issue of One Unit and by federal intervention in the functioning of the provincial governments, using the emergency instruments at their disposal. The situation deteriorated steadily (see Salamat 1992; Jalal 1995; Jahan 1972). In 1958, Prime Minister Iskander Mirza abrogated the constitution—in force for only over a year—and enforced martial law. General Ayub Khan was the Chief Martial Law Administrator. Economic growth in the Ayub period was growth with great regional imbalances, resulting in an increased migration into Sindh, particularly Karachi, sowing the seeds there of future conflict. The 1962 constitution created yet another centralized federation (with East and West Pakistan as its two constituent units) where the provincial government was subordinate to the federal, and the president's powers were extensive. Existing emergency powers were retained and the provincial governor continued to function as an agent of the federal executive.

In 1971, East Pakistan successfully seceded to form Bangladesh. In 1972, the Jeeye Sindh Mahaz demanded provincial autonomy, adoption of Sindhi as a national and official language, one-fourth share in civil and military services, and repatriation of all lost land to Sindhis. Even as Sindhi nationalism was regaining momentum, Pakistan's first Sindhi Prime Minister, Zulfikar Ali Bhutto, was ushering in important changes. One Unit was rescinded and provinces were restored in 1972, making it possible for Sindhi to be adopted once more as the official language of the province, for Sindhi and Urdu to be made compulsory subjects for study in high school, and Sindhi to be taught at an early age in school. It also made possible state patronage of the language through educational and cultural agencies as well as through the progressive use of Sindhi in administration. This restoration of Sindhi's place gave rise to protests on the part of the Muhajirs—the Urdu word for "refugees" now having become the name for the community into which the Partition refugees had coalesced in Pakistan. The 1973 constitution restored a federal structure where residual powers rested with the units. The constitution specified a Federal List and a Concurrent List. While residuary powers lay with the units, there was no Provincial List. The federal government continued to retain the power to topple provincial governments and impose central rule—a power that was certainly exercised. As one writer puts it, from 1935 to 1973 the powers of the provinces had been steadily reduced and now, in 1973, provinces had no powers exclusively their own (Panhwar 1990, 61).

Karachi, Now Battleground

Sindh raises an important question in the consideration of unit demarcation. When the state decides to demarcate units on the basis of culture, what is it to regard as a yardstick—historical occupancy or contemporary demographics? Even as Sindhis claim their eponymous province for themselves, the post-colonial reality of Sindh is that members of many other ethnic groups live there too. In the case of Karachi, they outnumber native Sindhis. So whom should the state recognize as natives? In the context of the larger discussion on re-distribution of authority, to whom should authority be delegated? Regardless of the state's willingness to delegate authority, the Muhajir-Sindhi struggle over Karachi highlights the difficulty of settling this issue.

Shared status as refugees welded the ethnically diverse Muhajirs into one community, who adopted Urdu as their lingua franca. In this early period, Pakistan itself was the province of the Muhajirs, and therefore, there was no need for the community to find itself a territorial home. The early rulers of Pakistan were largely from this community, and they were the ones who detached Karachi from Sindh to make it a federal capital and later favored the One Unit arrangement. With the creation of Bangladesh and the restoration of the old provinces in a federal structure, this situation changed. Suddenly, everyone had a home, except the Muhajirs. Mohammed Waseem describes the Muhajir Qaumi Mahaz as a unique nativist movement of migrants (1997). The first generation of Muhajirs dominated the state of Pakistan, the second was witness to the decline of the community, and the third has been instrumental in its politicization.

The Muhajirs responded to the Sindhi reclamation of Sindh by identifying Islamization with the idea of Pakistan. Relations between the Muhajirs and other communities in Karachi deteriorated as immigration into Karachi continued. Waseem identifies three waves of migration into Karachi after the Muhajirs settled there in the late 1940s—up-country Punjabis and Pathans in the late 1960s, Sindhis from the rural areas in the 1970s when Karachi reverted to being the capital of Sindh, and finally, Afghans in the late 1970s. Although they had originally settled in a Sindhi city, now the Muhajirs were the natives and their position was threatened every day. In 1983, the Movement for the Restoration of Democracy saw the unprecedented mobilization of rural and urban Sindh. The Pakistani government responded with the use of the army (which unfortunately was dominated by Punjabis and Muhajirs) to suppress the movement in a process that took several years. Muhajirs had not participated in the MRD but were witness to the strength of Sindhi nationalist sentiment.

In 1984, the Muhajir Qaumi Mahaz (MQM) was founded by educated youth from the Muhajir middle class, for whom employment was becoming a problem in Karachi. They recast the Muhajir position vis-à-vis other communities thus: No longer would Muhajirs identify with an Urdu-speaking, Islamic Pakistan, which was an abstract ideal at best, but now they would call themselves Pakistan's fifth nationality and demand recognition and quotas as such. This permitted them to enter into alliances with other ethnic communities, because this vision permitted four other such communities to exist. With the Sindhis in particular, Muhajirs can make a more palatable case for reservations (quotas or affirmative action in the language of other political systems) within Sindh for educational admissions and for employment. This still stops short of the Sindhi hope that Muhajirs would assimilate but it is better than conflict. The MQM followed the Muhajir *Suba* (province) or Karachi *Suba* movements, but its separatism took the form of demands for quotas and for recognition as a distinct ethnic group. As violence in Karachi has escalated, the army has been deployed there, giving the federal government an opportunity to intervene once more in the affairs of Sindh.

Summary Conclusions from the Sindh Case

The push-pull factors that we saw in the case of Sindh may be summarized as follows. The dissolution or submergence of Sindh's distinct identity as a province was a consequence of the following factors:

1. British colonial policy in a period of expansion, in which consolidation and control imperative rather than thoughtful policies of unit demarcation governed the outcome of merger;
2. "One Unit" was prompted by the need felt by the Pakistani government to "balance" the two wings of Pakistan, which at bottom was an interethnic elite competition between the Muhajir and Punjabi-dominated west wing on the one hand, and the Bengali-speaking east wing on the other;
3. While the establishment of the federal capital at Karachi may be explicable in geostrategic terms, the unilateral manner in which the decision was taken suggests the ruling elite's disregard for the place and opinions of the people of the province, relative to the needs of the center.

Territorial reorganization that effaced units seems to have occurred in Pakistan as a part of the process of establishing the colonial state, as a consequence of elite competition, and as a matter of right for the center. On the other hand, the demand that Sindh as a province be reinstated has stemmed from a mixture of factors:

1. The power of the traditional elite eroded as the British annexation opened the flood-gates to immigrants from other parts of India, and the new rulers appeared to choose another segment as their allies. This pattern is repeated somewhat in postcolonial Pakistan, with Sindhis resenting first the flood of refugees after Partition and their growing preponderance in Karachi and then the other refugees who came in from other Pakistani provinces.
2. Perceived neglect on the part of Bombay, and subsequently, Pakistan.
3. The distinctive culture of Sindhis and anxieties about the decline of the language.
4. The restoration of the four provinces after the secession of East Pakistan may be attributed to the lessons of that secession on the one hand and the election of a non-Punjabi, non-Muhajir to the prime ministership on the other.

Thus, the arguments for a separate unit included nativism, relative deprivation (see Dowley, this volume), cultural nationalism, and the threat of secession.

INDIA'S DEMARCATION DIALECTIC, 1905–1998

In what is now India, the debates over what constitute the proper bases for the demarcation of units date back to the 1905 partition of what had been the (combined) province of Bengal, Bihar, and Orissa and continue to date. Over the decades, arguments have been heard for administrative efficiency, for cultural integrity, for linguistic nationalism, for regional development and full circle, administrative efficiency! We will recount four phases of this story: (1) the phase of administrative reorganization that led to the rise of linguistic demands (the partition of Bengal); (2) the full flowering of linguistic nationalism (the Dravidanadu movement) parallel to the demarcation of linguistically defined units (from 1956 to the early 1960s); (3) the testing and spelling out of limits to linguistic nationalism (the demand for a separate Dravidanadu and the antisecession movement); and (4) the return to demands based on administrative and developmental needs.

Demarcation for Administrative Convenience: The Partition of Bengal, 1905

When Lord Curzon, the Viceroy, partitioned Bengal in 1905, the rationale proffered was administrative convenience. What made it convenient to partition Bengal? The initial motivation is said to have been the development of Assam, a frontier province (Misra 1990, 158–167). In order for Assam to develop, it would need to be separated from Bengal and to be made independent of the Bengal government's largesse, with the additional advantage of streamlining administration in Bengal. As it happened, the Partition of Bengal created a new province of Eastern Bengal and Assam. This met British political and economic needs and gave the province a natural boundary, but as far as the development of Assam went, it was simply appended to a culturally distinct and relatively prosperous province, Eastern Bengal. Moreover, when the partition was revoked, Assam was neglected because it still did not have its own provincial administrative unit.

Indian nationalists countered this rationale for reorganization with another—linguistic or cultural unity within a region. The protests against the partition of Bengal on the grounds of administrative convenience centered around the common language spoken by all Bengalis. Also, the reunification of Bengal gave rise to complaints from the Oriyas and Biharis, who had little in common with each other or the Bengalis. In a period of mass mobilization, linguistic politics was a handy way to organize and it was all the more useful for the fact that the British view on this subject differed so starkly from the Indian. Pronounced impracticable by the Montague-Chelmsford Report (1918), language was considered an inadequate approach to the question of unit demarcation, which must take into account the resource base, ethnic and religious factors, geopolitical and economic interests (Misra 1990, 181–182).

In the period of the freedom movement, the Congress regarded linguistic provinces as the local expression of the self-determination impulse. At the Nagpur session of the Indian National Congress, language was accepted as the basis for demarcating units within India. In 1917, the linguistic areas of Andhra (Telugu-speaking) and Sindh (Sindhi-speaking) had been designated "Congress Priorities." In 1920, the Congress was itself reorganized into 21 pradeshiya or provincial committees, each of which was linguistic. Partition changed this view somewhat, and afraid to set any precedents that might further fracture the nation-state, the Constituent Assembly set up a highly centralized state, not very different from the British colonial state.

Linguistic Reorganization of Indian States, 1956

The 1950 Constitution of India begins by describing India as a "Union of States" (Article 1) (see Rajagopalan 1997). While this suggests that the whole is equal to the sum of its parts, in fact, the very next two articles qualify this, giving the Central Legislature the power to admit or establish new States (Article 2), and also, to form new States from old ones, to alter the area and composition of any State or rename a State (Article 3), with no more than a simple majority vote of those present and voting. There is some mention of consulting the Legislature of the State in question, but it is not a prerequisite (Article 3 proviso): "the affected State or States may express their views but cannot resist the will of Parliament" (Basu 1982, 67). Therefore, it is a "Union" where the very existence of the units depends to some extent on the Union.

Independent India was a Union, and as the argument in the Constituent Assembly went, the units had no existence prior to the formation of the Union. They came into existence as a feature of the Union. Therefore, as India commenced, apparently without history, on the basis of the social contract of its peoples, so did the units into which it was divided. When you do not recognize the historicity of units, the question of other historically rooted or shared characteristics becomes irrelevant. Therefore, in the India of modernizing leaders like Nehru, the past and its legacies are not relevant. They must be disregarded as obstructions and it is India's "unity in diversity" that must be celebrated. In such a vision of India, administrative efficiency can be the only basis for unit demarcation.

The first set of units in independent India followed largely *administrative* lines. They varied in size, in composition, and in the terms of their relationship with the center. The Dar Commission, which was appointed in 1948, rejected the notion of linguistic provinces on the grounds that they would result in a loss of administrative efficiency, that each such province would also be home to other linguistic communities—minorities within that province—and that they would threaten national unity. "Administrative convenience" was the principle favored by the commission, especially in the case of Madras, Bombay, and the Central Provinces, although just twenty years before, the Congress Party had endorsed linguistic units. In December 1948, the party appointed the Linguistic Provinces Committee to look at the question politically rather than administratively. Concurring that the idea of linguistic provinces was not a good one, this committee nevertheless acknowledged that the demand for them might escalate to a point that it would harm national unity more not to concede them. The Andhra claim to separation from Madras was implicitly endorsed, and the first linguistic state, Andhra Pradesh, was created in October 1953. This opened the floodgates, and following deliberations and recommendations of the States Reorganization Commission and the proliferation of demands for separation, between 1953 and 1963, sixteen linguistic states were formed, several of which had minorities that spoke other languages.

The Limits of Linguistic Nationalism: The Demand for a Separate Dravidanadu

Where linguistic nationalism and its separatist demands challenged the outer form of the nation-state, it was harder for the state to accommodate them with unit demarcation and re-distribution of authority. The evolving demand for Dravidanadu, its polemic, and the response it received from the central government show that while the land-language assault on any prevailing distribution of authority is hard to resist, there is nothing inevitable about the march to complete self-determination and secession.

Under British rule, Madras Presidency included Malayalam-, Telugu- and Kannada-speaking areas, and in the Telugu-speaking areas particularly the demand for a separate linguistic province grew with the encouragement of Congress in the 1920s. Even as the Congress began to espouse linguistic self-determination in the 1920s, E. V. Ramasami's (later called Periyar by his followers) leadership[1] of the anti-Hindi agitation in 1939 established him now as the leader, not just of the Self-Respect Movement, but in a sense, of all Tamils. The steadfast refusal of the Congress government to yield on this point and on the point of separate communal electorates for untouchables (also referred to as Dalits or Harijans), as well as the increasingly sharp identification of the Congress with its Brahmin leadership in the Madras Presidency areas, established the equation of Aryan-Brahmin-Hindi on the one hand and Dravidian-Non-Brahmin-Tamil on the other in the popular imagination.

Beyond the initial phase, there were no non-Tamil leaders in the Dravida movement. Nevertheless, in the hope that a shared linguistic origin and relative historical insularity would continue to be salient, the movement demanded a "Dravida Nadu for Dravidians." The Congress was seen as being dominated by Hindi speakers and Marwaris. It was believed that independence would result in the transfer of power from the British to this Hindi-speaking, caste Hindu elite. An independent Dravidanadu was preferable to changing masters. Between 1940 and 1947, the idea of secession gained currency in the Dravida movement. By C. N. Annadurai's[2] account, the Dravidanadu demand follows the Pakistan demand only by a couple of months and the resolution seeking a separate Dravidanadu was passed in 1940 at Tiruvarur (Annadurai 1985, 9–10). In 1944, the Justice Party was renamed Dravidar Kazhagam or the Dravidian Movement.

One of the earliest debates was whether it should be called Dravida Kazhagam or Dravidar Kazhagam. The moment it is Dravida Kazhagam, Dravida is the region: you make it region-specific. Dravidar means people. Periyar feels we can't be geography specific. We can't reduce ourselves to a nation-state imagination which has been determined by a territory. Not a territorial imagination, it's a people-centric imagination. So he shifts to Dravidar Kazhagam and he defines Dravidar as people who do not respect Sanatana Dharma.[3] People who have the ability to overcome the divisions imposed by the Sanatana Dharma imagination which divides people as Brahmin and Sudra, are all Dravidas. And therefore it becomes Dravidar Kazhagam. (Interview response, I1)

In 1947, India became independent. Periyar declared August 15, 1947, a day of mourning while Annadurai welcomed independence. This was the point of divergence between the two streams within the party. In 1949, the party split. Annadurai and his followers formed the Dravida Munnetra Kazhagam and Periyar continued to lead the Dravidar Kazhagam.

In the early years, there was little popular discontent in Madras state with the rule of Delhi, because of the popular leadership of Prime Minister

Jawaharlal Nehru, because of the promise of development that the Five Year Plans held out, and because the influence that Tamilian leaders in the Congress Party, K. Kamaraj and C. Subramaniam, wielded in Delhi ensured the steady flow of resources and projects into Madras. Further, in the Nehru period, regional leaders acquired great influence and were able to cultivate independent power bases—Kamaraj himself was one of these. Between 1964 and 1969, these leaders played a decisive role in the formation of the Shastri and Gandhi governments. Nevertheless, the DMK's slogan, "*Vadakku vaazhgiradu, therkku theiygiradu*" (The north flourishes, the south languishes), found favor outside party ranks with Madras-based capitalists and also with the local Congress leadership (Interview response, I57). The latter were able to use the slogan to negotiate more central projects and investments in the state. During his parliamentary tenure in the early 1960s, Annadurai had made the case repeatedly that the secessionist platform should be seen in light of the relatively low investment in Madras state (Interview response, I75; see also Annadurai 1975b, 38).

In 1956, the linguistic reorganization of states reduced Madras to its Tamil-speaking areas, and the question of renaming Madras Tamil Nadu became an important one. The first agitation for linguistic provinces had come from the Andhra region of this state, ultimately forcing the center to review the demarcation of its units. The DMK's base was in the Tamil-speaking regions that made up Madras, and they led the demand to rename the state "Tamil Nadu." The party constitution identified Dravidanadu as a central objective and its cadres still mobilized support around the anti-Hindi plank. The Justice Party leadership had envisaged an India that would be a Commonwealth or Confederation of two Federations in North and South India. Each of these would be made up of autonomous linguistic or culturally based states (The Laputan Flapper 1959, 7).

The National Integration Conference met in 1961 for the first time and in 1962, a National Integration Council was established (Singh 1989, 26–28). The Council in turn established a Committee on National Integration and Regionalism, chaired by C.P. Ramaswami Aiyar. The Committee abandoned its inquiry in the face of the unity shown when conflict with China broke out in December 1962 (Singh 1989, 26). The Committee nevertheless recommended an amendment to the Indian Constitution that would ban secessionist propaganda and activity. This was duly adopted in 1963 and it fell to Annadurai's lot to fight the introduction and passage of this bill in Parliament. At the passage of the bill in the Lok Sabha (the lower house of the Indian Parliament), the law minister, A. K. Sen, is reported to have said: "The object of the bill was that [the] demand for separation should never be made an election issue" (Anti-Secession Bill Passed 1963). The next day, a Private Member's Bill was introduced by West Bengal Communist leader Bhupesh Gupta in the Rajya Sabha (the upper house), seeking to rename Madras state as Tamil Nadu. This was defeated. Within a week the Anti-Secession Bill was passed in the Rajya Sabha.

The bill came up in the Madras Assembly for ratification in August 1963 and received presidential assent in October 1963.

During the debates on these bills, Annadurai exhorted the members of the Rajya Sabha to consider why one part of the country would want to secede. Why did they feel like a colony? By way of explanations, he offered regional economic disparity, psychological alienation, and the conflict over language. In the circumstances, he said, these people felt that they would be at a disadvantage by remaining within the Indian Union. He asked for better reasons to stay than the indissoluble nature of the Union (Annadurai 1975a, 46–48). Remaining in the Indian Union meant accepting linguistic domination, economic backwardness, and "psychologically we would not have so much of solace as we would have if we were to be separate" (Annadurai 1975a, 46–48). The lone naysayer in the vote that followed, Annadurai begged the government to appoint a committee to consider the reasons for the alienation of Tamilians.

On November 3, 1963, the Executive Committee of the DMK amended the party constitution, giving up the demand of Dravidanadu. It now stated: "The objective of the DMK is to strive for the formation of a closer Dravidanad Union, comprising the four linguistic States of Tamil Nad, Andhra, Kerala, and Karnataka with as large powers as possible within the framework of the sovereignty and integrity of India and of the Constitution" (DMK to Strive for New Union in South 1963).

In the 1967 general elections, several Congress-led state governments fell and were replaced by regional parties. The Congress lost Tamil Nadu to the Dravidian parties, a situation that remains unchanged. Almost immediately in 1968 Madras was renamed Tamil Nadu. In the intervening decades, center-local disputes have revolved largely around the center's emergency powers to intervene in the affairs of the states. In the late 1990s, while the state guards its political independence jealously, the integration of Tamil Nadu into the Indian mainstream appears complete, as its representatives have come to play a key role in the formation and survival of national governments.

The Dravidanadu demand is, by the admission of the Dravida movement's leadership, an example of how the demand for and the resistance to units being demarcated in any particular way are, in fact, debates over the way in which power should be shared (or authority should be distributed) between the central government and the units of the state. Whether these demands are met seems to depend on whether they are couched in terms of challenges to the form and composition of the state (secession, for instance) or challenges to the details of this composition (the demand for a separate province or name changes). On the other hand, we also see that there is a moment, of greater or lesser length in this process, in which it is possible to read the grievances behind the demand. If these are redressed effectively, then there is no escalation of tension—authority is re-distributed peacefully and almost routinely.

The New Politics of State Demarcation

Since 1996, the idea of linguistic states has been undermined as the Center is looking favorably at demands for statehood made by regions within existing states. Uttarakhand (Uttaranchal), Jharkhand (Vananchal), and Chhatis-garh are to be carved out of India's three largest states. In each of their cases, negligence by the state government and both geographical and cultural distinct-iveness have been the most important reasons for the demand. While as yet only in principle, the demand has come to be conceded for three reasons: first, the coalitions that have ruled at India's center in recent years have been dominated by regional actors; second, at different points, these parties have espoused one or the other of these causes; and finally, it has become clear that very large states are not able to bring development and welfare to peripheral regions under their jurisdiction. Having conceded this demand, there is some debate as to the names of the new states, underlining the close relationship between identity, territory, and what are ultimately re-distribution of authority issues.

Summary Conclusions from the Indian Case

In the colonial period, historical regions and frontiers were disregarded and in the drive for paramountcy, each territory was appended to an adjacent region as the empire expanded. After independence, the power to create and efface units rests with the Union government, but units have been effaced pri-marily to carve out more units. Centralization has taken other paths, such as financial dependence and the abuse of emergency powers.

Thus, if we can attribute the centralizing drive of the colonial period to consolidation, then we are left accounting for the demands for the creation of new units, as and when they occurred.

(a) While the Partition of Bengal involved the subdivision of a unit, it was protested because it partitioned a unit with cultural integrity.

(b) From the 1920s onward, there was support in all quarters of the nationalist move-ment for the separation of Sindh, Andhra, and Orissa from the Presidencies to which they were attached on grounds both of cultural distinctiveness and neglect.

(c) There was also support for the principle of linguistic provinces, underlining the notion that the nationality-state equation might well pertain to units within the state as well.

(d) For the Dravidian movement, the demand for a separate state unit seemed to follow naturally with its evolution from a social reform movement to one with a linguistic base and platform. The demand for a separate Dravida Nadu encapsulated the pro-test against multiple categories of oppression—Aryan, North Indian, Hindi, Brah-minical.

(e) The demand for a separate Andhra state that precipitated the linguistic reorganiza-
     tion of the Indian Union had its roots in the pre-independence period, and the argu-
     ment was again twofold: cultural distinctiveness and relative neglect.
(f) Finally, in the newest wave of changes in state borders, the argument is both re-
     gional neglect and administrative efficiency; i.e., smaller units are easier to admin-
     ister.

The two factors most frequently pushing for the creation of new units in the Indian experience have been perceptions of neglect within the existing arrangement and the consciousness of being culturally distinct.

SRI LANKA: SECESSION, UNIT DEMARCATION, AND A UNITARY STATE, 1948–1998

The history of Sri Lanka includes alternating periods of regional, trans-regional and extraterritorial sovereignties. Over the centuries, historians have identified several sovereign centers on the island—the kingdom(s) of Anurad-hapura and Polonnaruwa, those of the southwest quadrant of the island, of Kandy and of Jaffna (de Silva 1987, 23–24). With the advent of Buddhism, Anuradhapura acquired some importance. Differing visions of the Sri Lankan political community and the concomitantly varying claims to autonomy or juris-diction are played out in the struggle over the northeastern part of the island.

The advent of the colonial age brought two brief encounters with the Portuguese (1619–1663) and the Dutch (1658–1796) before the long period of British rule. In 1802, the Crown took over the administration of Ceylon. In the 1820s the British introduced infrastructural and administrative change to bring the island under one rule. Roads were built giving access to every part of the island, and an administrative structure was set up that led to a unitary form of government. In the context of the present conflict, it is asserted that Sri Lanka has been a unitary state all along and the British colonial structure was not the first instance of the unification of the island. One scholar dates the idea back to Buddha's time (Interview response, S84). The Chakravartin was the universal emperor, bringing under his (of course his) "ekatchhatra" or one umbrella, the entire universe. In the Sri Lankan context, that was taken to mean that the entire island came under the sway, more or less, of one political identity. This is, of course, contested by the Tamils, who hold that the existence of a separate Tamil kingdom is proof to the contrary.

When Tamils make the claim that there has always been a separate kingdom in Jaffna, they seem to be referring to a succession of arrangements in which Tamils played a dominant role. To start with, there was the reign of the south Indian dynasty, the Cholas, in Polonnaruwa during the tenth to the thir-teenth centuries. Then, in the period after the fall of the invader from Kalinga in southeast India, increasing numbers of Tamils settled the northern part of the island. As the Tamils who had ruled Polonnaruwa were forced further north by the Sinhalese rulers of the south, it became possible for a Tamil kingdom to come into existence in the Jaffna area in the thirteenth and early fourteenth centuries. Quite powerful in its time, it faced an alliance between the Sinhalese and Pandyas throughout its existence. The ruler in Jaffna—called the Arya Chakravarti—was originally a feudatory of the Pandyas but gained independence when the Pandyas were in decline thanks to the southward expansion of Allauddin Khilji's empire in India. At the same time, in the forests of the Vanni, the Vanniyar chieftains seized autonomy as central authority declined. Then, after a brief period in which northern rule extended almost up to the Colombo area in the mid-thirteenth century, the locus of power shifted gradually to the southwestern part of the island. The Vijayanagara armies from India invaded the island around 1432 and forced the north into submission. This continued until Parakramabahu IV vanquished first the Vanni and then Jaffna. The Jaffna kingdom revived in the late fifteenth century. But this v s for a brief period before the Portuguese conquered Jaffna in 1619.

Units in the Colonial Period

The Colebrooke-Cameron reforms introduced in 1829 were prompted by the need to increase the profitability of the Ceylonese colony. The most important change they wrought was in the reorganization of the colonial territory into a nascent unitary structure. The number of provinces was reduced and each province was divided into districts, and the districts into chief headmen's divisions. Colebrooke recommended this reorganization for a number of reasons. First, it would end the special status of the Kandyan Province. It would reduce the powers of the Governor of Ceylon, encourage mixing and homogenization of the population of the island, and diminish what he saw as an obstacle to the integration of the colony—the separate identity of Kandy Sinhalese. While initially five provinces were created (Colombo, Galle, Jaffna, Trincomalee, and Kandy), between 1845 and 1889, the North-Western, North-Central, Uva, and Sabaragamuva provinces were added, and in 1889, Sri Lanka was divided into nine provinces.

Martin Wight wrote that the creation of an electorate and the creation of a nation were parallel processes (1952, 25).[4] Indeed, the historical record in Sri Lanka shows that center-local relations, especially the definition of local units, are closely related to the structure of the electoral system. Electoral organization and the demarcation of administrative units both perform the same function of dividing up a space and hence, its occupants, into several groups. The link between communal electorates (introduced in 1912) and representation on the one hand, and center-local relations on the other, is to be found in the location of the groups in that society. When the communities so represented live largely in different regions, as is the case in Sri Lanka, communal representation reinforces the difference between the regions. Thus, the Tamil electorate, broadly speaking, comes from parts of Colombo, the Northern and Eastern provinces, and its separateness in electoral matters reinforces its other separateness.

In 1927 the Donoughmore Commissioners "proposed an expansion and democratization of the island's local government institutions as a remedy for over-centralization" (K. M. de Silva 1993, 101). To this end, electoral constituencies were to be reorganized so that the population of each constituency was around 70,000 to 90,000. The chief consequence of this was that the populous southwestern quadrant of the island gained a larger number of constituencies and therefore, seats. This meant that the economic and political influence of this region was reinforced by these reforms, and in order to diminish this influence, the Donoughmore Commissioners suggested what A. J. Wilson has called some "federalizing" features (1988, 15). They recommended the delegation of selected administrative functions to Provincial Councils, subject to Central laws and ordinances. Further, they encouraged legislators to acquaint themselves with the views of various ethnic groups. To this end, sessions of the legislature might be held in Kandy and Jaffna. Neither the Provincial Councils nor the relocation of legislative sessions ever came into being.

It is at this point that the issue of Provincial Councils was adopted by some Sri Lankan politicians. Notable among these was S. W. R. D. Bandaranaike. Bandaranaike was Minister for Local Government Affairs between 1936 and 1947, Cabinet Minister between 1947 and 1951 and later, Prime Minister of Sri Lanka. In 1926, he advocated a form of federalism with nine provinces. He remained an indefatigable advocate for the institution of Provincial Councils but was unable to transform his ideas into reality. K. M. de Silva cites two political reasons for this (1993, 101). First, in the 1940s, while the Provincial Councils would reduce the powers of other ministries (and hence, ministers), they would reinforce Bandaranaike's own support base in local institutions. Second, in 1949, the Federal Party was established, and its objective was the establishment of federalism in Sri Lanka. Unfortunately, the Federal Party's Tamil name (*Ilankai Thamizh Arasu Katchi*, Tamil Government/State Party) lent itself to multiple interpretations, so that federalism came to be associated with separatism.

Independence came in 1948. Even though the political "debate" on solutions in the present day is largely centered on administrative solutions, the emphases in the postcolonial narrative are almost entirely on the cultural and educational policies of the state. Tamils identify three policies as particularly perfidious: the citizenship laws passed in 1948–1949, the Official Language policy adopted in 1955-6, and the "standardization" of examination results for university admissions in the early 1970s. According to the new citizenship laws, the immigrant Indian Tamils who worked on the tea estates were no longer to be considered Sri

Lankans citizens. The Tamil Congress split on the issue and the Federal Party was formed. Next, replacing the earlier commitment to education in one's native language, Sinhala was made the official language of Sri Lanka, leading the non-Sinhalese minority to feel excluded from government jobs.[5] Finally, in the early 1970s, the "Standardization" policy was introduced, whereby the university entrance requirements for students from some districts in Sri Lanka were lowered, ostensibly to redress the overrepresentation of students from other districts. Tamils saw this as part of a design to marginalize them further.

In the years after independence, the lowest tier of the administration was strengthened, whereas there was no consensus about the intermediate level—neither about what (districts or provinces) constituted this level nor about the powers it should enjoy. Decentralization and delegation took the form of dumping more and more functions on this bottom layer, which got instructions and funds (usually inadequate) from Colombo. In 1955, a Commission of Inquiry recommended that the provincial secretariats be restructured. Regional committees should be formed with a majority of elected members, as a first step toward the formation of regional councils.

The 1956 election brought a coalition government of left-central parties, led by S. W. R. D. Bandaranaike, to office. The Federal Party, which emerged as the most important Tamil political party, was an advocate of devolution of power to regional units. The fortuitous conjunction of Bandaranaike's premiership with the Federal Party's new preeminence made possible negotiations on the Provincial Councils question that led to the signing of the Bandaranaike-Chelvanayakam Pact in 1957. This agreement endorsed the idea of administrative decentralization and political devolution to the Tamil areas. The North would constitute a single administrative unit. The East, which is more diverse, would be divided into two or more regions, which would retain the right to merge. The authority of the region would cover infrastructure, development, social services, and "colonization."[6] However, it was not clear what constituted a region. "The concept of a 'region' lacked clarity because it was at once larger than a province, and smaller than a province" (K. M. de Silva 1993, 105). The regional administration was also given access to financial resources. As a further concession to Tamils, it was agreed that the Tamil language would be used in all administrative work in these provinces. This caused a sharp reaction from the Sinhala Buddhist clergy, and the public outcry in the Sinhalese regions forced Bandaranaike to retract his support for the Pact. Thus, the devolution that the Pact envisaged did not come about.

Between 1965 and 1970, a White Paper was presented on District Councils in the House of Representatives, but it was abandoned because of its adverse reception. The 1968 elections returned a United National–Party Federal Party coalition to power, and the Senanayake-Chelvanayakam Pact established District Councils (rather than Provincial Councils) that would function under the overall supervision of the Central Government. This Pact was a compromise on two counts. The UNP gave up its opposition to devolution in return for Federal Party support in the legislature and the Federal Party compromised on the unit of devolution. Interestingly, Bandaranaike's Sri Lanka Freedom Party now began to oppose any form of devolution. When the largest unit of local government below the state is the district, the degree of devolution is still very limited. Provinces have a larger resource base, and if a province might be demarcated on the basis of the shared identity of its denizens, districts divide those denizens. Therefore, from the perspective of the people in the "would-be province," districts are a form of "divide-and-rule."

In addition to the compromise the Federal Party had to make, the Senanayake-Chelvanayakam Pact faced opposition from the Sinhalese, who associated devolution with federalism and federalism with separatism. The Muslims of Eastern Sri Lanka also feared that under the arrangement outlined in the Pact, they would be completely swamped by the Tamils. The result was a broad-based coalition of forces against the District Councils, comprising the SLFP, Sinhalese Buddhists, the Marxist left, and Muslims. The scheme was withdrawn in the middle of 1969.

At the time of independence, the constitution adopted by the Soulbury Commissioners was retained as that of the new state of Ceylon. The Soulbury Constitution survived for almost twenty-five years because it was flexible and because minority groups saw in Article 29(2) their only safeguard against the infringement of their cultural and religious rights by a majority. The Privy Council of Britain continued to be the highest court of appeal, ensuring some impartiality in the evolving political environment. These constraints were resented by enough sections of the political system that a new republican constitution was adopted in 1972. This constitution, making no major institutional changes, established a unitary Sri Lanka, where Buddhism had the "foremost" place and the state was charged with its protection. It contained a chapter on Fundamental Rights, which Soulbury did not have. It lasted only six years.

The United National Party's manifesto for the 1977 election, and the Statement of Policy (August 1977) issued after the election, encapsulated the UNP's policy toward the Tamils. This policy had two general foci; the first was a constitutional proviso on minority rights and the second was the decentralization of administration. The administrative apparatus was now to include a District Development Council headed by a District Minister, and having as its other members, district Members of Parliament, elected heads of local bodies, and government officials. The implementation of this plan was delayed by the outbreak of communal violence in August 1977. In August 1979, a Presidential Commission was appointed to report on administrative decentralization through the District Development Councils. Plagued by ethnic divisions among its members, the Commission came up with one core proposal—Development Councils. That too essentially endorsed the 1977 UNP policy.

The North-East Question in Sri Lanka, 1990s

In 1978, the second Sri Lankan Republic was constituted. It was a combination of the Soulbury and 1972 constitutions, with the introduction of the executive presidency and the addition of Tamil as a national language. It retained the Sinhalese Buddhist cast of the 1972 constitution but with stronger guarantees of minority rights. However, for the Tamils, it was too little and it was certainly too late. In 1974, the Federal Party, sections of the Tamil Congress, and the Ceylon Workers Congress combined to form the Tamil United Front. With the adoption of the Vaddukodai Resolution in 1976, they renamed themselves the Tamil United Liberation Front (TULF). The Tamils, they resolved,

by virtue of their great language, their religion, their separate culture and heritage, their history of independent existence as a separate state over a distinct territory for several centuries till they were conquered by the armed might of the European invaders, and above all by their will to exist as a separate entity ruling themselves in their own territory, are a nation distinct and apart from the Sinhalese....
Whereas throughout the centuries from the dawn of history, the Sinhalese and Tamil nations have divided between them the possession of Ceylon, the Sinhalese inhabiting the interior parts of the country in its southern and western parts from the river Walawe to that of Chilaw and the Tamils possessing the northern and eastern districts....Tamil Eelam shall consist of the Northern and Eastern Provinces. (Loganathan 1996, 58–59)

Up to this point, the TULF youth wing had engaged, without reprimand, in some violent activities, and they reorganized themselves in 1975 as the Liberation Tigers of Tamil Eelam (LTTE). Walking a fine line between banditry and political militancy, the Tigers targeted centers of economic and political importance in the Jaffna area. Hostility between the communities grew. Since 1977, escalating violence has set the stage for the negotiations over unit demarcation. There were communal riots in 1977 and 1983. Funding from expatriate Tamils and support and training by the governments of India and of Tamil Nadu contributed first to the proliferation of Tamil militant groups and then to the internecine violence that resulted in the virtual elimination of every group other than the Tigers. Their activities further antagonized the Sinhalese and the spiral of mutual hostilities has polarized Sri Lankan society.

In 1980, the Development Councils Act was passed, based on the minority recommendation of a Committee chaired by former Chief Justice Victor Tennekoon. It exceeded the limited recommendations of the Presidential Commission and accommodated the TULF's dissenting arguments to the Commission's report. Councils thereby elected in 1981 were very effective in the Tamil areas. However, the complaints about the lack of finances and decision-making power continued. A 1983 committee to examine the working of the Development Councils attributed the financial, political, and personnel constraints to the fact that district-level officers did not have a clear mandate with regard to these councils, that there had been legal and constitutional difficulties, that money earmarked for the councils had not reached them, and that there was no thought to recruit people to run the councils or work for them. The 1983 riots put paid to the Development Councils scheme. The TULF withdrew its support, arguing that the councils did not constitute genuine devolution.

The politics of decentralization became more charged as the TULF's demands escalated, as the influence of militant groups like the Liberation Tigers of Tamil Eelam grew within the Tamil community and the pressure from India mounted in favor of a thoroughgoing decentralization. The TULF once more spoke of a "traditional Tamil homeland" in the North and East, and they now demanded provincial councils as suggested in the Bandaranaike-Chelvanayakam Pact (1957), which would be linked by regional councils. Thus, the Northern and Eastern provinces would be linked to form a unit where the Tamils would be the dominant majority.

Between 1983 and 1986, the years of the All-Party Congress on the issue, it is safe to say that by and large, the TULF's intransigence over these demands was matched only by that of its opponents. In 1986, the Provincial Councils scheme was revived. In this cast, it resembled the Indian "quasifederal" state but within the framework of the Sri Lankan unitary system. However, the TULF's demand for recognition of the Tamil "homeland" was staunchly opposed by other parties, and the LTTE's demand for a separate state only served to stiffen their stance. According to K. M. de Silva, the Indians suggested that the Eastern province might be divided into three parts, and the Tamil parts linked by a corridor. They further suggested "the excision of the Sinhalese parliamentary electorate (Amparai) of the Batticaloa district of the Eastern province so that the Tamil component of the latter would reach a level of parity with other ethnic groups there" (1993, 118).

The Indo-Sri Lankan Agreement of July 1987 included an undertaking that the Sri Lankan government would reinstate the Provincial Councils. The Northern and the Eastern provinces were to be merged, subject to a referendum held in the Eastern province within a year. The Provincial Councils Bill and the Thirteenth Amendment to the Constitution were passed in 1987 and in spite of the inevitable protests, the North-eastern province was created in 1988. The Provincial Councils Act detailed the procedure to be followed in the councils, the Provincial Public Service, sources of finance for the councils, and interim provisions for uniting more than one province into an administrative unit. The Thirteenth Amendment located the Province within the power structure of the state.

The other provision of the 1987 Accord was the stationing of the Indian Peace-Keeping Force (IPKF) in Sri Lanka. The IPKF went in to disarm the militants and every group other than the LTTE surrendered arms. The LTTE, which had been close to the Indian government, held out and as it turned out, went to war with the IPKF. The peculiar political alignments that followed isolated the Indians, who pulled out in 1989. In August 1994, the People's Alliance coalition, led by Chandrika Bandaranaike Kumaratunga, won the elections, and several initiatives for constitutional reform toward greater devolution have emerged. However, the devolution debate became a "dialogue of the deaf" with the hard-liners in either community refusing to hear the other side out.

Muslims and the Battle over the Sri Lankan State

The Sri Lankan case raises the question of infinite regress in the demarcation of units by culture. The Sri Lankan Tamil subsumes the Muslim into the Tamil community, but the Muslims of Sri Lanka have always resisted that. A subnational administrative unit that follows the territorial claims of the Tamils would reinforce the minority position of the Muslims.

The Muslims of Sri Lanka make up about 7 percent of the Sri Lankan population as a whole; they are 17 percent of the population of the North-east and 32.5 percent in the Eastern Province alone (Sivathamby 1987, 200–201). If Muslim grievances may be recapitulated on the basis of Sivathamby's 1987 essay, they are rooted in the Tamil inclusion of Muslims among their number, without consulting them; in a 1915 decision by Ponnambalam Ramanathan to support the Sinhalese leadership in the wake of anti-Muslim riots; and finally, in their anxieties over the consequences of a Tamil province or state dominated by non-Muslim Tamils in the East. Finally, in the years since 1982, with the rise of militant Tamil youth groups, Muslims in the Eastern province have occasionally been the targets of their violence. The Muslim-Sinhalese relationship is also fraught with anxiety, caused first by the relocation of Sinhalese in large numbers to the newly irrigated areas of Amparai, changing the demographic balance in their favor. This is particularly ominous, as the Sinhalese draw on myth and legend to reclaim the north-eastern part of the island as their cultural center. Secondly, in the conflict between themselves and the Tamils, the Sinhalese have used the Muslims as a buffer. By so doing, it has become possible for some Sri Lankan leaders to treat the ethnic crisis as a local Northern province problem and to overlook the Muslim concern over the Sinhalese settlers in Amparai. The Sri Lankan government has also used the plight of the Muslims in the East for diplomatic leverage with the Arab states on the issue of support to the Tamil position.

After the experience of 1915, when the class affinities of the Tamil and Sinhalese prevailed over the shared ethno-linguistic context, Muslims have chosen to support the group that dominated the government of the island—be it British or Sinhalese. Their skillful negotiation of a distinct position between the two major groups on the island is reflected in their attitude to language. Although Muslim writers in Tamil have contributed equally to the literature of Sri

Lankan Tamil, Muslims supported the "Sinhala Only" policy. Tamil was their "home language," not their mother tongue. Sivathamby believes this policy reflects the interests of Colombo Muslims and not the Muslims of the North and East (1987, 192–225). The Muslim community seeks to protect its interests through several organizations, the most significant of which is the Sri Lanka Muslim Congress (SLMC), which currently supports the People's Alliance government's devolution initiatives.

Of all the provisions in the devolution package, the Muslim community is most concerned with the unit of devolution. They would like a referendum on whether the people of Batticaloa and Trincomalee wish to join either Northern or Eastern province, or even, remain outside both. The question of merger is unthinkable, and their primary objection to the changes introduced after the signing of the Indo-Sri Lanka Accord in 1987 is that Muslims were not part of the negotiation of an arrangement that drastically disenfranchised them. One of the provisions being discussed as a safeguard for Muslims (and Sinhalese) in the North and East is the establishment of a council to represent them, but with safeguards for Muslims outside Amparai or any other region to which it is attached (Kalansooriya 1998).

Summary Conclusions from the Sri Lankan Case

Colonialism in Sri Lanka replaced a loose system of autonomous but interacting political centers with the unitary state. Where the old system had tolerated, perhaps thrived, on the survival of a number of alternative centers, the new one was predicated on the elimination of all but one. As it happened, the last of the old political capitals to fall was Kandy, and it was in order to diminish the influence of the Kandyan aristocracy that the British established their capital in Colombo. So in the first instance, and again here, centralization may be read as an act of consolidation.

In the postcolonial period, the unitary Sri Lankan state has sought its moorings in an idealized version of this Kandyan past, where the majority community is able to claim the island and the state as its historical legacy. The pulling away and the demand for a separate unit—first as a province and then as a state—by the Tamils are a response to this vision, and to the language and education policies that implement it. The demand is couched in terms of self-determination.

For the Muslims, the terms of this demand constitute a loss of space. They will be swamped in the political arrangement that follows and so for them, the argument against this new, consolidated Tamil region or province is a fear of internal colonialism.

DEMARCATING UNITS, RE-DISTRIBUTING AUTHORITY

In all three cases, why units are effaced, demanded, or created affirms the argument that this is indeed the first step in the process of re-distribution of authority. The effacement of units eliminates them from the arena of political authority. There is no need to devolve authority to them because they do not exist in the same manner as those units that are not effaced. This re-distributes authority toward the center. Conversely, the creation of units is a precursor to the creation of "competencies." Once created, a unit must have some purpose for its existence, some function that it performs. This is not to argue that the mere creation of a unit is any substitute for the delegation of authority to its offices, merely that it can be the first step to such delegation. The effacement and creation of units amount respectively to the de-recognition and the recognition of sections of the citizenry as political entities. This is particularly salient to the national integration process when the boundaries of these entities are coterminous with the area in which an ethnic population is concentrated. Then, acts of effacement and creation are acts of inclusion and exclusion. The degree and terms of that inclusion and exclusion determine in turn the way in which authority is distributed.

The mode of state formation also relates both to the demarcation of units and ultimately to the distribution of authority. Here, one needs to differentiate between the historical mode of state formation and the mode of state formation as it is officially described (hence, the official mode). For instance, the Indian constitution postulates the constitution of the Indian state by an undifferentiated Indian people (Rajagopalan 1997). However, the Indian Union came into existence partly through the transfer of power in the British provinces and partly through acts of accession by individual rulers of principalities in the subcontinent. Likewise, the very name, Pakistan, drew on the provinces that would constitute the proposed state. However, while Pakistan defines itself as a federation, it has effaced and recreated these constitutive provinces from time to time. Finally, the Sri Lankan state succeeds the British colonial state in Ceylon, and it retains the unitary structure of that state. In the debate over devolution in the 1990s, the present-day Sri Lankan state is sometimes endowed with an antiquity in which its structure and form were the same. In this form, any space it concedes to sections of its citizenry is conceded in an act of magnanimity and must be recognized as such. If one looks at the provisions on unit creation in the other two constitutions, they are essentially the same. In all three countries, notwithstanding historical circumstance, the state—the central government—makes decisions on the creation, reshaping and effacement of units within. The assumption by the state of this power presages the relationship between the state as a whole and the units within. In fact, the key question in the relationship between the whole and its parts may well be whether according to the laws of the state the parts are constitutive of the state or constituted by it. If the state (central government) can create and efface units at its own initiative, then the balance of power is tilted unmistakably in its favor.

Another question to consider is the relationship between the stage of state formation and the likelihood that a state would create or efface the distinct identity of units. (Of course, there is considerable overlap between the phases, as society changes unevenly in response to the process of consolidation.) The colonial experience in all three countries suggests that in the establishment and consolidation phase, it is to be expected that units would be effaced and merged into larger collectives. The institutionalization phase opens the space and the terms for the dialogue between people in the units and those who would rule the state as a whole. In this phase, the structure, functioning, limits, and privileges of government and citizenry are laid out, making apparent each citizen's or group's place in the larger scheme. To reiterate, for groups that place is nowhere more apparent than in their recognition, or lack thereof, as territorial entities. This opens the dialogue between them and the state (central government) on the subject. Thus, it might be hypothesized that as the state moves from the consolidation to the institutionalization phase, it is likely to look more favorably on demands for unit creation. Finally, in the phase of decline or disintegration, the state's ability to resist the demand for new units declines, even as its will to do so increases once more. The proliferation of new units can be one symptom of disintegration if it is accompanied by a weakening of the center and alienation from that center. On the other hand, the disintegration of the state can be delayed by an early accommodation of the demand for a separate unit.

The pattern being traced here is cyclical, and it is easier to illustrate with the historical examples of pre-state polities. How does it follow from our three cases?

1. In all three cases, we see the relationship between consolidation of the new colonial polity and the effacement of preexisting units. In any case, this represented a corrective to the earlier British practice of simply creating large units by adding new acquisitions to adjacent units, suggesting that perhaps there is to administrative organization a pattern of large, centralized units until the center is sure of its paramountcy, followed by a confident downsizing and decentralization.
2. With the inauguration of the postcolonial polity and arguably, a new drive toward institutionalization, there was internal territorial restructuring in India and Pakistan. This restructuring took the form of both creating and effacing units. In India, following the constitution of the Indian Union, several categories of units were recognized by that Union. The bases and boundaries of these were reshaped in response to regional demand. In Pakistan, the new federation de-recognized its original units and consolidated them into two wings. In Sri Lanka, there was some restructuring of district-level units as a response primarily to developmental needs, but the unitary form of the colonial state has continued.
3. In subsequent years, in India, the creation of new units has been a common response to subnational demands and complaints. The 1956 reorganization has been followed

by several smaller acts of reorganization and recognition. In Pakistan, "One Unit" was an important cause of the secession of Bangladesh, and following that secession, the western wing reverted to its original provincial structure. In both of these instances, unit demarcation has been an important concession from the state to the regional group and has usually been successful in diffusing tension. If such demarcation does not disadvantage another group within the unit, then it facilitates institutionalization in the unit in tandem with that of the whole state. If however, it does disadvantage another group—the Muhajirs in Sindh and the Muslims in the Northeastern part of Sri Lanka—then institutionalization may be delayed further in the area.

4.   In all three cases, notwithstanding the severity of the conflicts faced by the states, it seems premature to discuss their demise. However, protracted disputes over the nature and shape of units, related as they tend to be to nativist arguments, diminish the prospects for state survival. While states regard internal boundaries as less important to their survival than external boundaries, prolongation of disputes over such issues can threaten such survival. In both the cases of Karachi and the Sri Lankan northeast, there is no doubt that the state has paid a very high price as a consequence of the conflicts there.

The re-distribution of authority follows as a corollary from all of these acts of internal restructuring. Effacing a unit requires that someone else perform its functions, resulting in the re-distribution of authority. New units are in essence new agencies and offices of government, and hence a re-distribution of authority follows from their creation.

Are there intermediate positions between and beyond the creation of new substate units and the creation of new states? Indeed there are, and these intermediate positions are determined by the extent of authority and autonomy they enjoy. That is, these intermediate units resemble the "provincial" units that are largely the subject of our inquiry, but they differ in their level of autonomy. We may divide these into two categories, those that enjoy less autonomy than other units within a political system, and those that enjoy more autonomy.

In the first category fall the Union Territories of India and the Tribal Areas in Pakistan. Union Territories in India are administered directly by the President of India through a special administrator that s/he appoints. There is a great deal of variation in the structure of government within this category. Some Union Territories, which are now States, like Delhi, Goa, and Arunachal Pradesh, had structures quite similar to the States. The Tribal Areas in Pakistan fall into two categories, those administered by the federal government and those administered by the provincial Governments (Pakistan Constitution, Article 247 clauses 1–7). While legislation at both these levels does not automatically apply to the Tribal Areas, provision may be made (by the President or the Governor) to extend the scope of the legislation to these areas. Further, the President may intervene in the provincial administration of Tribal Areas designated as their charge. Finally, although charged to consult the tribal *jirga* in question, the

President has the power to rescind the "Tribal Area" status of such an area. In the second category fall units for which special provisions have been made. In India, this includes Kashmir and other States to which Article 370 and the Article 371 cluster apply (Elazar calls such an arrangement a "federacy" [1987, 44]). In Sri Lanka, this includes the North-eastern province created by the Thirteenth Amendment following the Indo-Sri Lanka Agreement of 1987. Azad Kashmir's status vis-à-vis Pakistan spells out a third possibility. It is described by the *Encyclopaedia Britannica* as a "quasi-state," not being a part of Pakistan although there is some dependence on the government of Pakistan.

Therefore, in addition to creation and effacement, one might speak of upgrading and downgrading territorial units. In India, an upgrade can mean movement from Union Territory status to Statehood, or from either to "Special Status" under the constitution. It is more possible politically to upgrade units than to downgrade them. The downgrading effect is achieved through emergency measures that in all three countries centralize power and decision-making authority.

The gray area thus spelled out underscores the relationship between unit demarcation and (re)distribution of authority. In the negotiation on collective identity and the "place" of specific groups within that identity, these intermediate actions provide compromise options. It may be argued as a concomitant, that the more open a political system is to the proliferation of these intermediate positions, the less likely it is that these negotiations will result in militant secessionism or ruthless state repression.

At this point, let us sum up the propositions that have been put forth on the relationship between unit demarcation and the distribution of authority.

1. The existence or nonexistence of units are prior conditions to the (re)distribution of competencies, functions, or powers.
2. The creation and effacement of units are prima facie acts of recognition and de-recognition of sections of the population.
3. There is a relationship between the mode of state formation and the future of units within that state.
4. There is also a relationship between the stage of state formation and the fate of units within.
5. There are intermediate positions between creation and effacement of units and they are more transparently (re)distributions of authority.
6. Intermediate positions mark the possibility of averting conflict over the issue of demarcating units and distributing authority.

It is this relationship between the demarcation of units, re-distribution of authority, and the presence or absence of internal conflict that has made federalism and devolution popular institutional solutions among writers on ethnic conflict. The argument is made in terms of the re-distribution of authority, but assumptions about the importance of territory and territorial organization are tucked into that argument.

Why is it important to elucidate this? Drawing out the relationship between identity, unit demarcation, and the re-distribution of authority brings together concerns of scholars on nationalism, intergovernmental structure, and political geography. It expands the scope of any study of the re-distribution of authority to include unit demarcation as a prior stage of that re-distribution. It permits us to spell out intermediate positions in the reconciliation of self-determination demands and sovereignty claims. In other words, it forges a continuum between separation and centralization, first in physical terms and then in terms of the distribution of authority. Any consideration of re-distribution in terms of functions and resources that disregards physical reorganization of territory is therefore an incomplete consideration of the re-distribution of authority.

NOTES

This chapter is based on legal and constitutional sources, print materials, and interviews. Where interviews are cited, names and withheld as a matter of courtesy.

1. E. V. Ramasami began his career with the Indian National Congress, left to found the Self-Respect Movement, and then became leader of the Justice Party. The Justice Party had its origins in the 1920s movement to expand representation for non-Brahmins in the government of the Madras Presidency. Opposition to the Congress, which was depicted as a coalition of North Indian, upper-caste speakers of Hindi and Sanskrit, was one facet of Justice Party politics.

2. Along with E. V. Ramasami, C.N. Annadurai was one of the most politically significant leaders of the Dravida movement. He was a member of the Indian Parliament in the early 1960s and then became Chief Minister of Tamil Nadu.

3. *Sanatana Dharma* is one of the phrases Hindus use to describe their faith. It means "old" or "traditional" faith and in this context, a *Sanatana Dharmi* (follower) would be a person who accepted the existence and continuance of caste.

4. "The existence of an electorate presupposes political unity in the broad sense—a feeling of community, a common consciousness. Every dependency is by definition an administrative unity; but these administrative units are in varying degrees arbitrary frameworks, fastened by alien power upon territories containing wide diversities of culture, tradition and race. The Ceylonese nation is the direct creation of British rule, and so are the Nigerian and Malayan nations insofar as they have already come into existence. *The task of forming an electorate is simply one aspect of the task of converting an administrative into a political unity*" (Italics added) (Wight 1952, 25). Horowitz's two institutional solutions—federalism and proportional representation—to ethnic conflict are likewise related (1985).

5. While this was not necessarily the case, it became a self-fulfilling prophecy as promotions began to be predicated on learning Sinhala and the number of political appointments rose. I owe this clarification and the information that follows to a personal communication from Chandra R. de Silva, dated 5–12–98.

6. Control over the last is particularly germane to the question of state integration. The movement of peoples, on any scale, upsets not just the ecological, but also the demographic, balance. Mass population movements seem to take two forms: (1) movement into an area where others groups have lived for generations, and (2) movement into settler colonies. Of course, "settler colonies" in recent history have been founded in areas where others did live, and it is through their elimination, subjugation, or marginalization that these colonies placed their own stamp on the area. This is what "natives" fear the most.

Chapter 3

Pulling and Tugging: The Distribution of Authority in a Mature Federal System

Ann O'M. Bowman

The United States of America (US) has had more than 200 years of experience with a multi-nucleated governmental structure. The Constitution of the US, adopted in 1789, established a system of government in which the power and functions of government are divided between a central government and a specified number of geographically defined regional jurisdictions, called "states."[1] In the US, the national government possesses both constitutionally enumerated and related implied powers; the states draw their authority from the powers listed in the Constitution as well as the guarantee of the Tenth Amendment. In addition, the national and state governments share a set of concurrent powers.

Federalism disperses power between the central government and regional governments but this dispersal is seldom fixed or immutable. Consequently, federal systems tend to be dynamic. Shifts in authority have characterized the US federal system since its founding. The national government pulls one way; state governments tug the other way. This chapter traces the evolution of American federalism, focusing special attention on the pulling and tugging in the center-periphery dynamic. Woven into the evolution are explanations for the occasionally dramatic, frequently subtle re-distribution of authority.

FEDERALISM IN THEORY

The meaning of federalism is a bit imprecise; varying definitions and alternative conceptions exist. Smith (1995, 4) offers a general orientation: "Federalism can be considered as an ideology which holds that the ideal organization of human affairs is best reflected in the celebration of diversity through unity." In an operational sense, federalism offers a balance between centralization (unity) and decentralization (diversity). Typically, federalism is considered a midpoint between, at one end, a unitary governmental structure in which a central government possesses all power and authority, and at the other end, a system of independent, separate states. As James Buchanan (1995, 24) puts it, "An effective federal structure may be located somewhere near the middle of the spectrum, between the regime of fully autonomous localized units on the one hand and the regime of fully centralized authority on the other." Definitions of federalism posit two polities—one national, the other regional. According to Riker (1964, 11), a federal structure exists "if (1) two levels of government rule the same land and people, (2) each level has at least one area in which it is autonomous, and (3) there is some guarantee (even though merely a statement in a constitution) of the autonomy of each government in its own sphere." Similarly, to Carl Friedrich (1968, 17), what distinguishes a federal system is "the notion that in a federal system of government, each citizen belongs to two communities, that of his state and that of the nation; that these two levels of community should be clearly distinguished and effectively provided each with their own government; and that in the structuring of the government of the larger community the component states as states must play a distinctive role."

As applied to the operation of the US federal system, the distinctive characteristic is its organizing principle: the division of powers between general and regional governments that are coordinate entities, with neither being subordinate to the other in its own sphere (Wheare 1946). Borrowing from the US model, Watts (1993, 11) identified ten components of a federal structure:

- two orders (not levels) of government,[2]
- a national government that deals directly with individual citizens,
- a formal distribution of legislative and executive authority,
- revenue resources allocated between the two orders of government,
- some autonomy for each order,
- provision for the representation of regional views within the national policy-making institutions,
- a written constitution,
- a constitution not unilaterally amendable and requiring the consent of all or a majority of the constituent units,
- an umpire (courts or referenda) to rule on disputes between governments,
- processes to facilitate intergovernmental relations.

Other scholars of federalism focus less on the structure and functioning of government and more on its covenantal basis. As Elazar (1987) and Ostrom (1991) have pointed out, the word "federal" comes from the Latin word *foedus*, meaning covenant. The word "covenant" itself has religious roots, identifying as it does the partnership between humans and God. Consequently, one might view federalism as a partnership. In a political sense, "federalism has to do with the constitutional diffusion of power so that the constituting elements in a federal arrangement share in the processes of common policy making and administration by right, while the activities of the common government are conducted in such a way as to maintain their respective integrities" (Elazar 1987, 6).

Ultimately, federalism is all about power. "The theoretical argument for federalism revolves around the potential of political power for evil. Federalism is seen as one of the devices to curb the evil use of power by dividing power among a number of competing power-units" (Neumann 1955, 45). And although the size of the slices of the power "pie" may change over time, the concern over all-too-powerful government never gets lost in the mix.

WHY THE US ADOPTED A FEDERAL SYSTEM

Overall, a belief in limited government and individual liberty set the context for constitution writing in late eighteenth-century America. Federalism was seen as an end in itself, not simply a convenient means of distributing power (Verney 1995). Most analysts agree that the framers of the US Constitution subscribed to the belief of English political philosopher Thomas Hobbes that human beings are contentious and selfish.[3] James Madison formulated the problem in terms of factions, groups that pursue their own interests without concern for the interests of society as a whole. Political differences and self-interest, Madison believed, generated factions, and the framers' duty was to identify "constitutional devices that would force various interests to check and control one another" (Hofstadter 1948, 9).

The US Constitution reflects the concern with factions. Included in the document were three practical devices intended to control them. The first was representative government. Citizens would elect officials who would filter and refine the views of the masses. The second was the separation of powers into three branches—legislative, executive, and judicial. Checks and balances were built into the system, requiring interaction among the branches. (The legislature was further divided into two houses, each with a check on the actions of the other.) Third, the government was designed as a federal system in which the most dangerous faction of all—a majority—would be controlled by the sovereign states. The conflicts and cleavages that have structured political discourse in the ensuing years were evident in the Constitutional Convention. One statistical analysis of Convention debate showed that two federalism-related issues, state integrity and the scope and power of the national government, were among the dominant themes of the Convention (Jillson 1981).

Yet although the Constitution established a federal system, nowhere in the document does the word "federal" or "federation" appear. "Confederation" is mentioned in Article 1, Section X, but only to prohibit states from entering into "any treaty, alliance or confederation." The federal nature of the US governmental structure is set in the manner in which the Constitution assigns responsibilities to the two spheres.

It is in *The Federalist* where one finds the quintessential statements of US federalism.[4] The theoretical defense of the federal system that had been crafted at the Convention rested on two foundations. First, a federal union would protect its citizens from external attack and internal tyranny. Second, the federal government needed to be sufficiently strong to carry out its functions (Friedrich 1968). Despite the embrace of these foundations by the framers, there remained great concern by some that the newly created national government might become too powerful and tyrannical. A minority of delegates to the Convention refused to endorse the new Constitution. Alexander Hamilton and James Madison, both of whom had actively opposed some of the federalizing features of the document, wrote a series of essays in support of the Constitution.[5] The goal of the essays that appeared in the New York press was to convince opponents of ratification that the new national government would not lead to the obliteration of the states (Wills 1981). Hamilton attempts to provide some reassurance in *Federalist* Number 9 when he contends that "the proposed Constitution. . . makes (States) constituent parts of the national sovereignty, by allowing them a direct representation in the Senate, and leaves in their possession certain exclusive and very important portions of sovereign power." In *Federalist* Number 32, he argues that "the plan of the Convention aims only at a partial union or consolidation, the State governments would clearly retain all the rights of sovereignty which they before had, and which were not, by that act, exclusively delegated to the United States." Further, in the opening paragraph of *Federalist* Number 34 he claims that states have "co-equal authority with the Union" with regard to taxation.

At the end of *Federalist* Number 39, Madison acknowledges the centralizing and noncentralizing elements of the Constitution. Using the word "federal" in a sense that in contemporary times we would be more likely to label "confederal" (Diamond 1974), he sums up the document in this manner:

The proposed Constitution, therefore, is, in strictness, neither a national nor a federal Constitution, but a composition of both. In its foundation it is federal, not national; in the sources from which the ordinary powers of the government are drawn, it is partly federal and partly national; in the operation of these powers, it is national, not federal; in the extent of them, again, it is federal, not national; and finally, in the authoritative mode of introducing amendments, it is neither wholly federal nor wholly national.

The structure becomes more comprehensible when it is compared to the Articles of Confederation, the first constitution adopted by the former colonies. Adopted in 1777, the Articles effectively subordinated the central government to the states, by establishing what has been called a "loose league of friendship." A one-house legislature governed the national government. The powers held by the national government were few: to wage war, make peace, enter into treaties and alliances, appoint and receive ambassadors, regulate Indian affairs, and create a postal system. The states held all powers not expressly granted to the Congress.

Problems quickly emerged, problems directly related to the insufficient authority of the national government (Bowman and Kearney 1999). For example, because the central government depended on the good will of the states for all of its revenues, it often was unable to honor its financial obligations to individuals, firms, and foreign governments. In addition, the national government lacked the power to regulate domestic and international commerce. Thus when states engaged in discriminatory trade practices and imposed protective tariffs, the central government was powerless to take corrective action. But the event that brought the national-state power imbalance to the forefront was Shays' Rebellion. The national government had difficulty in quelling the armed revolt of New England farmers angry about debt and taxes. Fear that Shays-like insurrections would spread caused leading politicians to seek an alternative to the confederacy. The ineffectiveness of the Articles of Confederation led to the Constitutional Convention of 1787.

One of the basic disputes at the Constitutional Convention involved the structure of the central government, especially the legislative branch. The Virginia Plan, supported by large states, proposed a strong central government led by a powerful bicameral Congress. Representation in both houses of the Congress was to be based on population, thereby benefiting larger states. The New Jersey Plan, favored by small states, called for a unicameral legislature composed of an equal number of representatives from each state. The plans varied on other dimensions, e.g., the Virginia Plan had a single chief executive while the New Jersey Plan had a multimember executive, but the issue of state representation was the key. Resolution of the dispute came in the form of a compromise: representation in the lower house would be based on the population of each state while in the upper house each state would have equal representation.

Two other compromises paved the way for approval of the new constitution: the specification of powers of the central government and the designation of the Supreme Court as the final arbiter of nation-state conflict. Seventeen powers—including taxation, regulation of commerce, operation of post offices, creation of a national court system, declaration of war, conduct of foreign affairs, and administration of military forces—were to be exercised through Congress. And by selecting the Supreme Court as the arena for the resolution of national-state disputes, the framers rejected the notion that Congress or state courts play that role.

Compared to the Articles of Confederation, the US Constitution enhanced substantially the power of the national government. Still, the states were to remain sufficiently endowed. In *The Federalist* Number 45, James Madison underscored that point. "The powers delegated by the proposed Constitution to the federal government are few and defined. Those which are to remain in the

State governments are numerous and infinite." Yet it is precisely on that point that 200 years of debate and discussion have ensued.

Even at the outset, disagreement over the distribution of power and authority raged. Proponents of national supremacy, or nation-centered federalism, clashed with advocates of state-centered federalism. Clarification was not forthcoming, even after ratification of the Tenth Amendment in 1791.[6] State-centered federalists relied on a compact theory of federalism. To them, the US Constitution was a compact—an agreement—among the sovereign states that maintained their right to self-governance. As a consequence, the powers that the Constitution accorded the national government were to be interpreted narrowly. Further, the states were obliged to resist any unconstitutional efforts by the national government to extend its authority (Walker 1981).

The compact theory of federalism retained its appeal over time. The states' rights movement that emerged in the 1820s took the compact theory as its foundation. The precipitating event was congressional enactment of a national tariff on imported manufactured goods from Europe. The slave-based agricultural economy of the South was already in decline; Northern states were prospering. Southern states, which relied heavily on European goods, blamed what they called the "tariff of abominations" for many of their economic woes. John C. Calhoun, vice president of the United States and a Southerner, resurrected the compact theory in his attack on the tariff.

According to Calhoun, the national government's authority was based on powers entrusted it by the states. At any time, however, states possessed the power to reinterpret or even reject the compact. Calhoun argued that if an individual state found an act of Congress to be in violation of the Constitution, the state had the right to nullify or veto the law, thus making it invalid within that state's borders. In 1832, Calhoun's home state of South Carolina convened a state convention, declared the federal tariffs of 1828 and 1832 unconstitutional, and forbade the federal collection of customs duties in the state (Beer 1993). This action led to extensive congressional debate over national-state authority, even as the president threatened military action to force the state to comply. The immediate issue was resolved by a lowering of the tariffs; however, the matter of states' rights never receded. Calhoun declared that even if the majority of states agreed with a federal law, a nullifying state had the right, if it so chose, to secede from the union. Debate raged, debate that ultimately resulted in the secession of eleven southern states and the ferocious conflict of the Civil War.

Calhoun's defense of the compact theory directly contradicts the arguments of Madison in *Federalist* Number 46. In that paper, Madison refers to "the great body of citizens of the United States," and "the people. . . as individuals composing one entire nation." Calhoun, on the other hand, posits the states as the primary behavioral units in the politics of the nation as a whole (Beer

1993). According to Calhoun, "the very idea of an *American People*, as constituting a single community, is a mere chimera" (Meriwether 1959).[7]

THE FEDERAL CONTEXT: THE NATION AND THE STATES

Federalism has traditionally been associated with democracy and modern democratic federalism with market economies (Saunders 1995). As such, federal structures are characterized by a number of features. One of those characteristics is flexibility, that is, government policies can be customized to fit regional desires or problems. In the US case, a state with a more conservative political culture may design a set of public policies quite different from a state dominated by a more liberal ideology. State laws on abortion, for example, reflect the prevailing ideology. Related to that, federalism is said to stimulate innovation. US Supreme Court Justice Louis D. Brandeis (1932) said it best in *New York Ice v. Liebmann*: In a federal republic, "a single courageous state may, if its citizens choose, serve as a laboratory, and try social and economic experiments without risk to the rest of the country." For example, over the past decade, many states have tried out a range of measures intended to reform their welfare systems. Innovations diffuse horizontally—a new solution in one state may be adopted in another state. Certain states serve as regional leaders in particular policy areas. Furthermore, there is vertical diffusion of policy. Successful state-based solutions often are appropriated by the federal government. Recent federal laws on gun control, assistance for the homeless, and motor-voter registration had their genesis in the states. And the well-known federal welfare reform statute—the Personal Responsibility and Work Opportunity Act of 1996—capitalizes on many of the policy initiatives that had been developed by the states.

In addition, a federal structure provides its citizens with multiple points of access to public power. A claim or demand that is not responded to at one level may be taken to another government. In the abortion example cited above, conservative antiabortion activists who are dissatisfied with their state's abortion policy can take their case to the federal government. Environmentalists who consider federal regulations on urban air pollution too lax seek tighter restrictions from their state governments. As Kincaid notes (1995, 32), "multiple governments can also check and balance each other in various ways, including competition and cooperation, thereby curbing centrifugal tendencies toward anarchy and centripetal tendencies toward monopoly." The existence of different levels of government provides citizens with options, as does the existence of multiple governments at the same level. Citizens dissatisfied with the policies of their jurisdiction have the option of exit, or "voting with their feet." As many analysts since Tiebout (1956) have argued, government jurisdictions offer different packages of taxes, public services, and civic values. Interjurisdictional mobility allows citizens to seek out the package most in line with their preferences.

Multiple points of access means that social and political conflict can be dispersed. Further, political participation in government is maximized. But not all of the features of federalism can be cast in a positive light. For instance, the dispersal of power over many units of government and the multiplicity of decision centers creates an enormous capacity for delay and obstruction (Nice and Fredericksen 1995). Thus it may be that the workings of a federal system frustrate the will of an activist majority. At the same time, a federal structure creates an array of coordination problems. The same characteristics that encourage customized governments complicate standardization. Complexity, duplication of effort, and inefficiency are interrelated in a federal structure. As Nice and Fredericksen have commented, "the task of getting all the participants pulling in the same direction at the same time is often staggering and sometimes impossible" (1995, 21). These conditions raise questions about public accountability, or more precisely, its loss. The diversity that federalism celebrates leads to concern over asymmetries in the size and wealth of constituent jurisdictions. Inequality is an inevitable concomitant. States and their local governments offer unequal bundles of public services and in some cases, unequal protection of basic rights. The consequences of a federal structure, or more precisely, of the way in which federalism works in the US, have led analysts such as Paul Peterson (1995) to consider "the price of federalism." He argues that regional inequalities and administrative inefficiencies are two of the costs of federalism. However, Peterson (1995, 14) contends that when state and local governments have economic development as their main objective and when the national government assumes the major responsibility for redistributive policy, "then the price of federalism can be kept to an acceptable level."

THE NONFEDERAL COMPONENT: THE STATES AND THEIR LOCAL GOVERNMENTS

The federal system in the US is officially one of a national government and numerous (since 1959, fifty) state governments. Each state contains a series of local governments, known in statutory language as political subdivisions of the state. All told, by 1998, there were 87,453 units of local government (counties, municipalities, towns and townships, special districts, and school districts) in the US. The number of local governments varies from state to state. In Kansas, for example, there are 3,917 units of local government: 105 counties, 627 cities, 1,355 townships, 1,506 special districts, and 324 school districts. Nevada, on the other hand, has a grand total of 211 local governments.

The relationship between the state and its local governments is unitary. Local governments possess the powers granted explicitly to them by the state, those clearly implied by these explicit powers, and those absolutely essential to the declared objectives and responsibilities of the local government. This doctrine, known as Dillon's Rule, means that when doubt arises regarding the legality of any specific local government power, the courts will resolve it in favor of the state.[8] The result of Dillon's Rule is that local governments have relatively little discretionary power. When local officials want to take on a new responsibility or provide a new service, they must first be granted the appropriate authority by the state legislature, or in some cases, the governor. Thus in theory and in constitutional law, local governments are cloistered within the walls built by the state.

However, almost all state constitutions have partially opened the doors for at least some types of local governments through a grant of home rule. Home rule is a legal arrangement by which the state issues local governments a charter that allows discretion and flexibility in carrying out their activities. In effect, it recognizes a kind of dual federalism within states by constitutionally delegating certain powers to local governments. And although home rule expands and clarifies a local government's sphere of authority, it does not eliminate legal wrangling over specific actions. Currently, municipal home rule is authorized in forty-eight states; county home rule is provided in thirty-seven states (US ACIR 1993).

But state capitals continue to cast a long shadow over their local governments. For instance, states may regulate local finances (by, among other things, establishing debt limits and requiring balanced budgets), personnel (by setting qualifications for certain positions, prescribing employee pension plans), government structure (by establishing forms of government, outlawing particular electoral systems), processes (by requiring public hearings and open meetings), functions (by ordering the provision of public safety functions, proscribing the pursuit of enterprise activities), and service standards (by adopting solid waste guidelines, setting acceptable water quality levels). These examples make the point: The distribution of authority between the state and its local governments can be as expansive or circumscribed as the state desires.

Local governments are not mentioned in the US Constitution. The national government's constitutional relationship to local governments is indirect, via the state government. However, in practice, the federal government has extensive direct links to local units of government, dating as far back as the eighteenth century's Northwest Ordinance, which provided land grants for public education. These links, both programmatic and fiscal, have expanded greatly since the Great Depression.

OTHER FEDERATED LINKS

In addition to the standard national-state relationship, the US has other federated connections. Both Puerto Rico and the Northern Marianas are linked to the US in a federacy arrangement. The status of Puerto Rico has been the subject of much discussion and debate. In 1967, the issue of statehood went before the electorate. Sixty percent of the voters favored retaining the island's commonwealth status. In 1993, Puerto Ricans reconsidered their link to the US and although commonwealth status won, it was by a far narrower margin (Bowman and Pagano 1994). Half of those voting preferred a change in status: 46.2 percent voted for statehood, 4.4 percent favored independence. Continuation of the commonwealth arrangement was the choice of 48.4 percent of the electorate. As a result of the election, Puerto Ricans have called for an "enhancement" of their relationship with the US. Their delegate to the US Congress began lobbying for a set of special provisions for the island, including the restoration of the federal tax benefits once given to Puerto Rican subsidiaries of mainland firms, extension of Supplemental Social Security benefits to island residents, and special protection for Puerto Rico's main agricultural products.

Within its borders, the US recognizes several hundred Native American tribes as "domestic dependent nations" that possess certain residual rights of sovereignty (Elazar 1995). Early federal court rulings held that state governments had no jurisdiction in Indian country. Over time, tribal-state relationships have grown more complicated and conflictual as states tested the reach of tribal sovereignty. One analysis of formal policy statements of governors and legislators regarding land and resources found that the statements were much more likely to be in opposition to Native American interests than aligned with them (Jones 1997). That same study found that the level of Indian-state conflict was correlated with the number of contiguous reservations, state administrative capacity, and reservation population size. The national government, the tribes, and the states are bound in a legal/political quagmire. Simmering national-tribal-state issues in the late 1990s included Indian gaming, federal funding formulas, and tribal sovereign immunity (Mason 1999).

The Constitution established a decidedly nonfederated relationship with the District of Columbia—the seat of the federal government. The territory of the District was created by the ceding of land from the states of Virginia and Maryland. The District, frequently included in listings of the fifty states,[9] is quite unlike a state government. It possesses limited powers of self-government and its residents elect nonvoting delegates to the House of Representatives. Other federal systems have created a capital district; however, in no instances do the jurisdictions experience the limited representation and restricted autonomy of the District of Columbia. Improvement of the District's enfeebled status is unlikely in the near future. Like Puerto Rico, the District is often the subject of discussions of the possibility of statehood. But the most recent attempts to gain sufficient congressional support for the admission of the state of "New Columbia" into the Union in 1993 were unsuccessful. Other options exist for the District, including retrocession to the state of Maryland; semi-retrocession, in which District residents would vote for federal legislators in Maryland; and full representation and self-determination rights for D.C. as a kind of faux statehood. Failure to empower the District can be attributed to many factors; such as the inherent conflict between national interests and local concerns. However, factors such as ideology, partisanship, parochialism, and race stoke the conflict (Harris 1995).

EVOLVING US FEDERALISM: CENTRALIZATION PULLS, DECENTRALIZATION TUGS

Early federalism in the US was built on the principle of dual sovereignty. The period from 1789 to 1860 was one that reflected the presence of two sovereign entities—each one supreme in its area of authority, with minimal but conflictual overlap. The rulings of the Marshall and the Taney Courts underscored the principles of dual federalism even as they were carving out the role of the federal judiciary. Despite their affirmation of dual federalism, the two courts differed in their sympathies. The Marshall Court was more apt to find state acts unconstitutional, while the Taney Court was more wary of the national government's encroachment into the state sphere. In practice, the few national functions were handled by a small federal bureaucracy; the many state functions by a growing number of public administrators. The national government was financed in large measure by customs and receipts from the sale of Western lands; the states relied on excise taxes. Occasional efforts of the national government to enter the states' sphere, e.g., legislative proposals to allocate federal funds to states for internal improvements or other specific purposes, met with defeat during this period. The politics of the time, more specifically the party system, further reinforced dual federalism. Political parties performed an integrative function during this period of nation-building, but they remained decentralized organizations, oriented toward the state (Walker 1995).

The period from the 1860s to 1933 is typically considered a second phase in the dual federalism era, one that produced increased centralization of power and authority. The conclusion of the Civil War effectively nullified state-centered conceptions of federalism. The US Supreme Court ruling in *Texas v. White* (1869), on whether the secession of Texas in 1861 meant that the state had actually left the Union, diminishes the compact theory.

When, therefore, Texas became one of the United States, she entered into an indissoluble relation. . . The act which consummated her admission into the Union was something more than a compact; it was the incorporation of a new member into the political body. And it was final. The union between Texas and the other States was as complete, as perpetual, and an indissoluble as the union between the original States. The Constitution, in all its provisions, looks to an indestructible Union, composed of indestructible States.

The words of Chief Justice Salmon P. Chase in the *Texas* decision did not signify the obliteration of state authority. Even as constitutional amendments (the Thirteenth, Fourteenth, and Fifteenth) and Reconstruction expanded the national government's domain, states retained substantial independent spheres of authority. Still, there can be little dispute that the national government enhanced its role during this seventy-year period. Walker's (1995, 78) comment is apropos: "It is certain that the federal portion of the dual-federalism layer cake in 1930 was much greater than its 1860 counterpart." The national government took on a new important functional responsibility in the early twentieth century: regulator of various aspects of the economic system. The assumption of this role came about through anti-trust and fair trade practices legislation, a series of interstate commerce prohibitions, and direct regulation of railroads and radio communications. In most instances, the national government's expansion did not represent a diminution of the states' role.[10] One can make the case that the national government moved into activities that were either interstate or national in scope, and thus beyond the effective control of the states' police power. And even as the federal bureaucracy increased, its growth was outpaced by public employment at the state and local levels. This was an era of fiscal change as well. The national government came to rely less on tariffs and land sales to finance its operations and more on federal income tax receipts. And by the end of the period, there was a hint of the intergovernmental fiscal transfers that would characterize the subsequent era (Walker 1995).

Dual federalism gave way to a different form of national-state relations during the period 1933 to 1960. The label of the period, "cooperative federalism," reflects the clear break with the earlier orientation. The language of separate spheres was replaced by discussions of shared powers and collaborative efforts. The Great Depression—and the states' inability to respond effectively to it while the Roosevelt administration's New Deal program did—closed the door on the old era. But dual federalism did not go quietly. Roosevelt's New Deal program initially encountered rough sledding in a federal judiciary still attuned to the two spheres of the past. Through the mid-1930s, the Supreme Court ruled that certain aspects of the New Deal went beyond the authority of Congress to regulate commerce. But in the face of an extremely popular president (who was floating proposals to restructure the Court in order to secure favorable rulings) and persistent economic stagnation, the Court reversed its series of anti-New Deal decisions in 1937. American federalism was off on a new course, one that would shift even more power and authority to the national government. Congress moved in many directions: the sale of securities, public-utility operations, agricultural production and marketing, labor-management relations, flood control, and regional development. Federal expenditures increased from 2.5 percent of the gross national product in 1929 to 18.7 percent thirty years later, far sur-passing the growth in state and local government spending during the same pe-riod. The number of federal grants in aid rose from 12 in 1932, with a value of $193 million, to 26 in 1937, with a value of $2.66 billion. A substantial amount of the federal aid was sent directly to local governments, particularly counties and school districts. The variety of grant programs exploded. As early as 1939, there were federal grants for maternal and child health, old-age assistance, aid to the blind, fire control, treatment of venereal disease, public housing, road and bridge construction, and wildlife conservation (Walker 1995). By 1960, there were 132 separate grant programs. The politics of the period, as evidenced in public opinion, the interest group system, and congressional coalitions, sup-ported centralization. Political party organizations, however, became more fragmented.

Amid the centralizing fervor, there were few countertrends. Minor events can be identified, items that provided a seedbed for the devolutionary period some three decades later. One event was the release in 1955 of the report of the Commission on Intergovernmental Relations. Its comprehensive exami-nation of the workings of the federal system led to questions about the appropri-ate allocation of governmental functions between the national government and the states. In response, the House Committee on Government Operations initi-ated a series of hearings and studies on intergovernmental relations, thus ele-vating the centralization-decentralization issue to a new level. In 1957, President Eisenhower, in an address to the National Governors' Conference, proposed the shift of some functions and tax sources to the states. Although his proposal failed to gain support, his vice president, Richard Nixon, must have been lis-tening. It was the creation of the US Advisory Commission on Intergovern-mental Relations (ACIR) in 1959 that provided a forum for the systematic study of federalism, writ large. Given that the ACIR's mission was to monitor the op-eration of the American federal system and to recommend improvements, it was inevitable that the issue of center-periphery relations would emerge.

The emphasis on intergovernmental sharing of the cooperative feder-alism period gave way in 1960 to a brief period of "creative federalism" (1960–1968). These were the days of the War on Poverty and the Great Society, and the role of state government was effectively minimized. Public support for an activist national government was high. The Johnson administration and its allies in Congress launched a massive attack on the most serious problems facing the nation: poverty, crime, poor health care, and inadequate education, among oth-ers. The vehicle for the attack was the federal grant in aid. More than 200 new grants were put into place during the five years of Johnson's presidency. The "creative" aspect of the approach was that much of the vast government spend-ing bypassed the states. Federal disbursements went directly to cities and other local governments, and in some instances, to citizen action groups. The pur-poses of the grants reflected less the needs of the recipient government and more the priorities of the national government. Federal spending rose rapidly, nearly doubling from 1964 to 1968.

The centripetal forces of creative federalism waned somewhat with the election of Republican Richard Nixon to the presidency. The Nixon administration arrived in the nation's capital in 1969 with a label for its preferred brand of intergovernmental relations: New Federalism. This kind of federalism had several components: decentralization of federal activities, devolution of spending decisions to state and local governments, and streamlining of the grant delivery system. The Nixon administration was successful in several endeavors. Federal administrative regions were established, a General Revenue Sharing program that provided federal funds without strings was adopted, and the grants application and management procedures were standardized and simplified. But the New Federalism of the Nixon administration had to work with a Congress controlled by the Democratic Party. Thus, despite the distinctive features of New Federalism, most of the programmatic agenda and spending patterns of the creative federalism period continued.

Federal grants in aid as a percentage of state and local government spending peaked during the last year of Carter's presidency. The arrival of the Reagan administration and its version of New Federalism shook national-state power relations. Ostensibly similar in emphasis to Nixon's federalism of the same name, the Reagan brand of decentralization and devolution reflected a different primary goal: shrinking the size of the national government. State and local governments were given more freedom to spend a declining amount of federal funds. Reagan enjoyed some early success: eliminating sixty categorical grants, converting fifty-seven others into nine block grants, and reducing funding levels. However, proposals for more eliminations and conversions and deeper cuts were mostly rejected by Congress. The Congress balked at the "turnback" proposal in which states would assume financial and administrative responsibility of two massive programs, Aid to Families with Dependent Children (AFDC) and the food stamp program, and forty smaller programs in exchange for a national takeover of the Medicaid program. But although the Reagan administration fell short of its ambitious efforts to restructure the national-state relationship, it did place the twin issues of decentralization and devolution firmly on the national agenda. Subsequent presidents have offered their own versions of New Federalism, and the 104th Congress, in one of its first actions, passed the Unfunded Mandates Reform Act of 1995 (P.L. 104-4) making it more difficult for Congress to require states and localities to pay the costs of national directives.

Public support for a restructured national-state relationship remains strong. A recent NBC—Wall Street Journal poll gauged the public mood on this question:[11] "Congress is considering eliminating certain federal spending programs and instead giving funds to state and local governments for them to provide services in those areas. Do you generally favor or oppose this change?"

Two-thirds of those surveyed favored the change; only twenty-three percent opposed it. Thus, after six decades in which centralizing actions trumped decentralizing actions, the public wanted change. This does not suggest, however, a return to the days of dual federalism. Far from it. Instead, contemporary attitudes signify a desire to push the intergovernmental system of shared functions in the direction of the states and their localities. Increased public confidence in non-national governments is largely a result of the phenomenon that has been called the "resurgence of the states."

THE RESURGENCE OF THE STATES

For much of the twentieth century, American state governments were havens of traditionalism and inactivity. Their policy-making institutions were unrepresentative and dominated by elites. They were considered the "weak links" and the "fallen arches" of the federal system. However, during the 1980s, amid a rapidly globalizing economy, state governments blossomed to become viable and progressive political entities (Bowman and Kearney 1986). This resurgence of the states was precipitated by a number of factors. Foremost among them is the reform of state governments. Throughout the country, states modernized their constitutions and restructured their institutions. The constitutions, once called "the drag anchors of state programs" and "the protectors of special interests" (Sanford 1967), have been streamlined and made more workable. Modernized constitutions have led to a variety of internal adjustments intended to improve the operations of state government. Gubernatorial powers have been strengthened by increasing their appointment and removal powers and by allowing longer terms, consecutive succession, larger staffs, enhanced budget authority, and the power to reorganize the executive branch. State agencies are staffed by more professional administrators and the bureaucracy is more demographically representative of the public. Annual rather than biennial sessions, more efficient rules and procedures, additional staff, and higher salaries have played a part in making reapportioned state legislatures more professional, capable, and effective. State judicial systems have been the targets of reform as well; examples include the establishment of unified court systems, the hiring of court administrators, and the creation of additional layers of courts.

These revitalized state governments have generated a series of positive outcomes. Improved revenue systems is one of the most notable. To position themselves for the positive and negative consequences of a global economy, states have diversified their revenue structures. In a related vein, states have created "rainy day funds" to cushion periods of economic recession. Additionally, they have made their revenue systems more equitable. The gap between tax capacity and tax effort has been narrowed in many states. Another of the positive outcomes is the expanding scope of state operations. In some instances, the states are filling in the gap left by the national government's de-emphasis of an activity, e.g., the provision of state-sponsored low-income housing. In other cases, states have taken the initiative in ongoing intergovernmental programs by creatively utilizing programmatic authority and resources. States were at the forefront of health care reform long before the issue reached the national stage. Other examples represent the initiative of state governments in identifying new activities, such as the gubernatorial forays into export promotion. Related to the expanded scope of state operations is the faster diffusion of innovations. As states develop new programs and undertake new initiatives, they look to other states for advice, information, and models. As a result, the learning curve is reduced as successful solutions spread from one jurisdiction to another.

The resurgence of the states was a necessary condition for the development of New Federalism. No longer were the states automatically dismissed as backward and incapable. Less frequently was the "Alabama syndrome" invoked in Washington—the inference that the conservative, racist administration of Alabama Governor George Wallace in the 1960s was the norm for states. The transformation of the states made New Federalism a legitimate option.

POWER SHIFT: THE ISSUE OF DEVOLUTION

One of the consequences of reinvigorated state governments is the reinstatement of the tension that characterized national-state relations in the days of dual federalism. James Madison in *Federalist* Number 46 wrote that

ambitious encroachments of the federal government on the authority of the State governments would not excite the opposition of a single State, or a few States only. They would be signals of general alarm. Every [state] government would espouse the common cause. A correspondence would be opened. Plans of resistance would be concerted. One spirit would animate and conduct the whole.

Perhaps Republican Governor Tommy Thompson of Wisconsin was thinking of James Madison when he addressed the National Conference of State Legislatures meeting in the summer of 1995. He declared that it was time for the federal government to step aside, time for the states to trumpet the death of Washington sense and the rebirth of common sense, time for them to take control over a variety of befuddled and bloated federal programs. In the governor's view, states can more than meet the challenge. As Thompson (1995, 27) said to the assembled legislators, "There is more brain power in this room than there is in the US Congress."

Governor Thompson's oratory aside, his argument strikes a responsive chord in contemporary America. The states were never intended to serve merely as delivery mechanisms for federal programs. They are not simply another special interest group, despite Supreme Court rulings in cases such as

South Carolina v. Baker[12] that instruct states to forego Tenth Amendment challenges and instead use the political process to press their claims against actions of the national government. Most states are not content to take a subsidiary role in governance. Increasingly, they are reasserting their place as partners in the intergovernmental system. Their argument has a special currency, as the analogy offered by the Republican Governor of Utah, Michael Leavitt (1995), suggests.

The Industrial Age of centralized authority and top-down management is over. We are entering a new era, the Information Age, in which small, flexible, autonomous units will out-compete and out-perform their bureaucratic counterparts. If this country is to compete in the emerging global marketplace, its government needs to be structured like small but flexible and powerful PCs networked together, rather than a monolithic, rigid federal government mainframe.

Leavitt's comment reflects the objectives of devolution. These include (1) more efficient provision and production of public services, (2) better alignment of the costs and benefits of government for a diverse citizenry, (3) better fits between public goods and their spatial characteristics, (4) increased competition, experimentation, and innovation in the public sector, (5) greater responsiveness to citizen preferences, and (6) more transparent accountability in policymaking (Kincaid 1998, 13).

Actually, insofar as devolution signifies the "transfer of specific powers or functions from a superior government to a subordinate government," it is a constitutional impossibility in the US federal system (Kincaid 1998, 14). Given the constitutional provisions for dual sovereignty, the national government does not possess the authority to devolve powers. Instead, it can "delegate" by authorizing another level of government to act on its behalf. It is increasingly common, for example, for the national government to charge the states with the implementation of federal legislation. Recently, the responsibility to implement has brought with it an opportunity for increased flexibility for design and financing. Executive Order 12875 issued by President Clinton, entitled "Enhancing the Intergovernmental Partnership," provided greater discretion to states. The order required federal agencies to streamline the waiver application processes for state and local governments. Yet even within this more permissive climate, the government that implements remains accountable to the government that delegates.

As the gubernatorial pronouncements of Thompson and Leavitt indicate, the states are more than willing to assume a leadership role in addressing the public policy challenges of the era. One policy area in which this has occurred is welfare. As one member of the Clinton administration acknowledged, "any recent innovation in welfare has been at the state level" (Ellwood 1998, 45). Over time, states became quite adept at using the waiver provisions to increase state discretion in implementation. For example, states sought exemptions that would increase the amount of money a recipient could earn before welfare benefits were reduced and that removed restrictions on two-parent families. These waivers increase costs up front but generate long-term savings.

The twin pressures of gubernatorial persistence and a Republican-controlled Congress led to the enactment of a welfare reform bill in 1996 that contains many devolutionary features. The Temporary Assistance for Needy Families (TANF) block grant eliminated Aid to Families with Dependent Children. Approximately $16.4 billion will be provided to states annually during fiscal years 1997 to 2003 through TANF. These funds will provide cash assistance to needy families, but with time limits and work requirements for most recipients. Section 404(a) of the act frees states to use their federal funds in any way "reasonably calculated to accomplish the purposes of TANF." The discretion of states extends to the determination of eligibility, the design of methods of assistance, and the establishment of benefit levels (Kincaid 1998). For instance, states can decide whether to operate new food stamp and employment and training programs or whether to shift some welfare functions to local governments. Although certain portions of TANF have met with legal challenges (e.g., the provision that gives states the option to set different benefit levels for newly arrived welfare claimants from another state), implementation has proceeded apace. Initial reports confirmed the wisdom of devolution—states reported a substantial paring of their welfare rolls. Whether this will translate into long-term success is uncertain. One thing is certain: The states' own fiscal and administrative capacities will play a crucial role in their ability to take advantage of whatever opportunities they are offered.[13] Another certainty: State capabilities vary as do their levels of fiscal comfort (Tannenwald and Cowan 1997).

Most Republican governors enthusiastically supported the reforms and remain publicly optimistic about the possibilities; Democratic governors are more cautious. The different perspectives were symbolized by the Republican governor of Iowa's comment that devolution of welfare is "a golden opportunity" to unleash high-quality reforms that have eluded the bureaucracy-laden national government. However, in the assessment of the Democratic governor of Indiana, Congress is simply off-loading the budget deficit to the states and localities.[14] The memory of the Reagan administration is fresh. When nine block grants were pushed through Congress in 1981, the budget for those programs was cut by twelve percent in fiscal year 1982. The states raised taxes and replaced the money. The larger trend makes the same point: States are increasingly funding a greater share of the costs of governance. From 1980 to 1996, the federal government reduced its domestic spending as a percentage of Gross Domestic Product while states and localities increased their own-source spending (Tannenwald 1998). As long as state economies boom, the assumption of greater fiscal burdens is cushioned. However, an economic downturn might dampen the enthusiasm for devolution.

Currently, states are enjoying budget surpluses due to a rising economy and fiscal prudence. They are in the best financial shape they have been in since 1989. And although the TANF block grant provides ample funding, the welfare reform act contained other decidedly non-devolutionary elements that limit flexibility (e.g., states must spend at least four percent of the TANF funds for child care), impose mandates (states must record Social Security numbers on official documents such as drivers' licenses), and reduce funding (states can lose a portion of their TANF allocation if they fail to meet work-participation requirements). Eventually, however, the bill for devolution could cause those budget surpluses to vanish. In a time of economic reversals, states will be hard-pressed. A further problem for states is the relentless pressure for other spending. Spending for prisons consumes about 9 percent of a state's budget, public education expenditures account for an estimated thirty-five percent. The recent "three strikes, you're out" laws and the baby boomlet will raise those proportions to fourteen percent and forty-seven percent, according to one projection (Stanfield 1995).

Ultimately, welfare may not provide an apt test of devolution, regardless of its provisions. Peterson (1995) has argued that states should focus on economic development, e.g., activities such as education, training, and infrastructure, and the federal government should redistribute income through welfare programs and health care. Thus he favors the job-training block grant but predicts that welfare or Medicaid block grants will pit the states against one another in a competition to cut benefits to the poor. His research on AFDC (a program in which states could set eligibility and benefit levels) suggests that when one state cuts benefits, neighboring states often follow suit. As one analyst noted, "We are seeing a period of real innovation, because states do not have money crunch problems. But when the welfare caseload comes back up again during a recession, the danger is very real that the states will start cutting benefits" (Ellwood 1998, 47).

Devolution, then, is likely to be a double-edged sword for resurgent state governments. The administrative side of devolved social programs will mean less paperwork and fewer bureaucrat hours taken up writing reports for federal agencies. Also the flexibility will mean that states can use the dollars for programs high on their priority list, to integrate services and provide streamlined, one-stop shopping for beneficiaries. Devolving welfare and other programs to the states shifts the locus of politics to state capitals. States can expect mega-lobbying once the block grant funds reach their jurisdiction. Different groups possessing varying levels of clout will likely create a new set of winners and losers. In the old days, some states engaged in a duplicitous game of "blame the feds."[15] In the coming days, that game can no longer be played.

RESTRUCTURING INTERGOVERNMENTAL RELATIONS: THE ISSUE OF REGIONALISM

The multiplaned structure of the US federal system accommodates and promotes regionalism. As Elazar (1984) has written, sectionalism—the expression of social, economic, and political differences along geographic lines—is characteristic of American political life. Clusters of contiguous states are tied together by particular historical events and cultural similarities, as well as shared interests of long standing. Thus the six states of the New England section remain bound together despite the differences between the lower portion (Massachusetts, Rhode Island, and Connecticut) and upper New England (Maine, New Hampshire, and Vermont). Regionalism develops within and through these sectional clusters. In effect, US states are regional governments. Thus most regional problems are shaped into matters of state concern. Yet there are many other regional configurations that supersede, subdivide, or in some instances, ignore the states. The creation of federal reserve district boundaries in 1912 and 1913 was one of the nation's first excursions into regionalism. "The nation's leading cities competed for designation as federal reserve district headquarters, and those that won had districts drawn to reflect their spheres of influence, regardless of state lines" (Elazar 1994, 11). The federal reserve district example underscores an important reality: The US is a network of economic regions. However, in defining these regions, political boundaries seldom jibe with economic boundaries (Barnes and Ledebur 1998). Local economic regions radiate out from an urban center, irrespective of jurisdictional boundaries.

More fanciful suprastate ventures into regionalism are based on image and "feel." Garreau (1981) identified nine distinctive regions (or "nations," as he calls them) in North America. Using evocative phrasing, he labeled them Ecotopia, the Empty Quarter, the Breadbasket, the Foundry, Dixie, Mex-America, the Islands, New England, and Quebec. According to Garreau (1981, 1–2):

Each has its capital and its distinctive web of power and influence. . . Each has a peculiar economy; each commands a certain emotional allegiance from its citizens. These nations look different, feel different, and sound different from one another, and few of their boundaries match the political lines drawn on current maps. Some are clearly divided topographically by mountains, deserts, and rivers. Others are separated by architecture, music, language, and ways of making a living. Each nation has its own list of desires. . . Each has a different future. . . Most important, each nation has a distinct prism through which it views the world.

Garreau dismissed state boundaries as irrelevant. "Colorado," for example, is a misleading idea—Eastern Colorado and Western Colorado are fundamentally unalike. The eastern part of the state is oriented toward the

Breadbasket, the western part toward the Empty Quarter. State boundaries, he claimed, are the result of "historical accidents and surveyors' mistakes."[16]

Unlike Garreau's regional "nations," most treatments of the topic move beyond territory and culture to governance. One means of categorizing these regions is by their genesis, that is, whether they are top-down creations of the national government or bottom-up creations of states or localities.

Top-Down Regionalism

The Constitution created several mechanisms to facilitate interstate co-operation, such as the full faith and credit clause and the privileges and immunities clause. In addition, Article I, Section 10 of the Constitution sowed the seeds of regionalism in the interstate compact clause, a provision that authorizes the creation of legally binding, multistate agreements. Early interstate compacts were used to settle boundary disputes between pairs of states. During the twentieth century, the focus of compacts broadened and their use increased. Beyond dispute resolution, interstate compacts are now used to study problems, coordinate regulatory policies, and to provide public services (Zimmerman 1992). More than 120 are in effect in a variety of areas, including shared water resources, riverboat gambling, law enforcement, and education. Interstate compacts begin with the negotiation of a draft document by delegates representing interested states. The draft must be ratified by the legislatures of the potential member states, and the compact must receive congressional consent. Once affirmed by Congress, it is ready for implementation. In a typical case, a compact commission composed of representatives of member states serves as the implementing agency.

The case of interstate compacting is illustrated in the federal Low-Level Radioactive Waste Policy Act of 1980. The Act made each state responsible for the disposal of certain types of nuclear waste generated within its borders. States have the option of managing low-level waste within their own jurisdictions (that is, developing their own disposal sites) or entering into an interstate compact for out-of-state disposal. As expected, a few states (such as New York) have chosen an independent course of action, but most have joined with neighboring states to forge a regional answer to the disposal question. By 1994, nine interstate low-level radioactive waste disposal compacts had been formed. With two exceptions (the unlikely Southwestern compact joins two pairs of states, Arizona and California, with North Dakota and South Dakota, and a proposed compact would link Maine and Vermont to Texas), the compacts are geographically based.[17]

Another instance of large-scale regionalism can be found in the division of the US into federal administrative regions. Although federal agencies had operated field offices for many years, President Nixon's New Federalism provided a systematic regionalization. The reorganization of the field structure of federal departments in 1969 led to the creation of ten standardized regions, each with a single headquarters city. This process was part of a larger effort to decentralize the administration of federal grant programs. By the early 1970s, nine federal agencies were operating in these regional offices. As part of the structure, federal regional councils were created to facilitate interdepartmental coordination and intergovernmental liaison (Walker 1995). These federal administrative regions have survived various attempts at reorganization.

Yet within the federal government, agreement on what constitutes a region has been absent. The boundaries of the twelve federal reserve districts do not correspond to the ten federal administrative regions. Neither of them reflect the regional breakdown used by the Census Bureau or the still different designations that were used by another federal unit, the ACIR. Within the national government, the notion of region has been neither automatic nor uniform.

The federal government, through statute and executive order, has stimulated the creation of specific regional institutions. One of the most prominent is the Tennessee Valley Authority (TVA), a public corporation established during the 1930s to bring water and electricity (and therefore, economic development) to the rural areas in the south central US. The promotion of economic growth and development was the impetus for other targeted regional efforts. The Appalachian Regional Commission (ARC), established in 1965, was intended to bring prosperity to one of the poorest regions in the mid-eastern part of the country. Over time, the TVA and the ARC have acquired a special status among regional organizations. For one, despite their single-region focus, they have maintained widespread political support. For another, they have been somewhat successful in accomplishing their stated objectives (the TVA more so than the ARC). As a result, they are the examples that are regularly offered in discussions of the promise of multistate regionalism.

The TVA and the ARC are noteworthy because federally created multistate organizations typically experience a different fate. Illustrative are the Title V Commissions established by federal statute in 1965. These organizations, also intended to spur economic development in their respective regions, numbered eight by the early 1980s. They never gained the necessary legitimacy to be much of a force in regional development, primarily because little federal funding was channeled through them (Nice and Fredericksen 1995). As a consequence, neither federal nor state officials paid them much heed.

The fundamental issue with top-down multistate regional organizations is their empowerment. A powerful regional institution is perceived as a threat by both the national government and by the states. Federal officials resist the loss of control; state officials resent the intrusion. As a consequence, regional institutions contain within them the element of their own destruction: insufficient authority. Their ineffectiveness is more than predictable; it is intentional.

Bottom-Up Regionalism

Despite the prevalence of interjurisdictional competition in the US federal system, there are occasions in which jurisdictions work together. Recognition of shared problems and the benefits of joint action has led to the formation of an assortment of multistate groups. They vary in their level of institutionalization, their focus, and their permanence. For example, the National Governors' Association, a government interest group, has formed regional subsets to facilitate collaboration. Because the groups are composed of a state's highest ranking elected official, they are especially effective at attracting media attention to their endeavors. Membership in a regional grouping can be problematic for border states, however. In 1990, the governor of South Dakota, arguing that his state felt more of a kinship with Western states than with Midwestern jurisdictions, changed his membership accordingly. It is not only the governors who have established such groups. Other state officials such as attorneys general and budget chiefs have created their own national organizations and regionally focused subgroups.

Economic development, an activity that unleashes fierce interstate competition, is frequently the catalyst for interstate cooperation. The coexistence of two opposing behaviors is not unusual. The Great Lakes region, plagued by intraregional pirating of industry, was unsuccessful in forging a pact among its governors to forego such raids. Yet at the same time, the governors agreed to a Great Lakes protection fund and launched a million-dollar international marketing campaign to promote "North America's Fresh Coast." Similarly, a loose confederation of six states in the south central part of the country created the Mid-South Trade Council to promote the region's exports and to encourage foreign investment in the region. On a rotating basis, each state leads an overseas visit for the other states. The calculus for cooperation seems to have been the low cost of involvement compared to the potential return.

A slightly different calculus drove the formation of the joint Monongahela River Valley economic summit (Bowman and Kearney 1999). This 7,400-square-mile section of southwestern Pennsylvania, northern West Virginia, and western Maryland found that the markets for its products and traditional sources of investments had dried up. The economic problems extended jurisdictional borders, symptomatic of a regionwide malaise. Despite initial reluctance, community leaders journeyed across county and state lines to develop a coordinated agenda for economic revival. As a report by the Monongahela River Valley Steering Group (1986, 3) put it: "Our theme is [regional] unity. We have no other choice."

Other examples, such as Portland, Oregon's development of a regionwide plan for the future (the 2040 Plan), suggest that, on their own, some local jurisdictions are adopting a "big picture" orientation to the situations they face. Whether motivated by notions of economies of scale or a sense of shared destiny, the "go it alone" approach appears to be losing ground to a more collaborative style. As one commentator said, "The whole idea of regionalism has had so many false starts in American local government that anybody who doesn't treat it with a large measure of skepticism is a fool. Nevertheless, it is hard to miss noticing that in the mid-1990s, the conversation has suddenly started to pick up again" (Ehrenhalt 1995).

The trend toward locally inspired regionalism remains problematic. Research in two regions of California makes that point. A recent study of the San Jose area suggested that public concern about serious urban problems had generated new support for regional governance (Gerston and Haas 1993). But in Southern California, surveys of the public report persistent negative attitudes toward regionalism (Baldassare 1994). A long-time advocate of regionalism is not optimistic: "I used to think that distress would create the climate for regionalization. Now I don't think that anything creates it."[18] Others contend that if there is to be a new era of regionalism, it will not be initiated by government alone. That is, only through a coalition of public and private interests will enough momentum be generated to overcome the centrifugal forces. One student of regionalism has commented, "What binds such coalitions is a sense of identification with the region: as a place, as history, as people and communities."[19]

Thus far, bottom-up regionalism has been conceptualized primarily as the politics (and occasionally, economics) of place. But interest in regionalism is coming also from an altogether different sector: ecology. Many ecologists advocate redefining contemporary society (and politics and economics) around regions that are delineated by nature (Thomas 1995). "Bioregions are geographic areas having common characteristics of soil, watersheds, climate, and native plants and animals" (Berg 1983, 19, as quoted in Merchant 1992, 218). Bioregionalists would redraw the global map in terms of these naturally occurring areas. Each bioregion would be self-governing, connected to others through an informal confederation. Their economies would be self-sufficient and sustainable.

CONCLUSION

US federalism established a multiplaned, regionally based structure for governance. The end of dual federalism ushered in a period of nationalization, slowed recently by the New Federalism of various presidential administrations. The pull of centralization has been far stronger than the intermittent tugs of decentralization. Many factors have contributed to the expansion of the authority of the national government, among them economic change, underperforming state governments, and public opinion. But despite the centralizing trend, states have maintained their significance as political systems and civil societies. In the current era, eminent federalism scholar Daniel Elazar (1994, 272) has gone so far as to claim that "the states have once again become the leading innovators and sources of energy in American government." That sentiment has legitimized the push for devolution, an effort that otherwise might be dismissed as ideologically motivated. Perhaps related to the current decentralizing mood, support for top-down regionalism has faded. Only one recent piece of federal legislation included a regional requirement: the Intermodal Surface Transportation Efficiency Act of 1991, which reinvigorates metropolitan planning organizations. The impetus for regionalism remains strong, but from a bottom-up direction.

As time has passed, federalism has evolved. Like Rivlin's (1992) call to revive the American dream, David Walker (1995, xiii) has developed a series of proposals that he contends will produce "an authentic rebirth of federalism." Why is a rebirth necessary? According to Walker, the federal system has become dangerously overloaded. It exhibits simultaneously centralizing and decentralizing trends, cooperative and competitive behaviors, co-optive and discretionary actions, as well as activist and retrenching tendencies. Only by empowering the states and reducing the national government's authority can effective governance be achieved.

It is unlikely that the US federal system will experience the revival and rebirth advocated by Rivlin and Walker. Instead, we are likely to see more of the pulling and tugging that has characterized the past forty years. Currently, the direction is one that favors decentralization of authority. Kincaid (1998, 16) calls it "a process involving restoration, deaccession, and rebalancing, that is, restorations of powers to the states and their local governments as well as deaccessions of unwanted functions, which, together, could produce a rebalancing of power between the federal government and the states."[20]   State leaders continue to demand a more powerful role in the national-state partnership. In 1997, four major state organizations—the National Governors' Association, the Council of State Governments, the National Conference of State Legislatures, and the American Legislative Exchange Council—convened a summit on federalism (Weissert and Schram 1998). Summit participants crafted an eleven-point plan aimed at rebalancing the national-state relationship. Among the points was a demand that Congress justify its constitutional authority to enact a given bill; another called for limitation and clarification of federal preemption of state law. Thus even as the language of federalism has shifted from "nullification" and "interposition" to "underfunded mandates," "regulatory flexibility," and "intergovernmental partnerships" (Nugent 1999), the tugs of decentralization keep the US federal system vibrant.

NOTES

1. In this chapter, the word "state" refers not to nation-states but to the constituent units of the United States of America.

2. The word "level" implies a hierarchy, thereby suggesting superior-subordinate relationships. The word "order" does not necessarily convey such an arrangement.

3. There is some debate on this point. Garry Wills (1981) argues that the framers' world view was far from Hobbesian. Instead, leading framers were much more positive about human nature and the possibilities of governance.

4. Quintessential yes, clear no. The *Federalist* reflects some of the "on the one hand, on the other hand" compromises of the Convention. Parts of some essays suggest the nationalizing aspects of the document, others emphasize the federalizing features. The papers were designed as part of a campaign to secure ratification of the Constitution, thus there is an effort to appeal to a broad cross-section of the public.

5. It is ironic that the defenders of the Constitution, a document that, compared with the Articles of Confederation, significantly empowered the national government, called themselves "Federalists." Their opponents, dubbed the "Anti-Federalists," disliked the Constitution because it did not contain a sufficient number of federalist features. In short, the Anti-Federalists wanted more federalism while the Federalists supported less.

6. The Tenth Amendment reads: "The powers not delegated to the United States by the Constitution, nor prohibited by it to the States, are reserved to the States respectively, or to the people."

7. It should be noted that Madison was not entirely consistent in his argument. As pointed out by Beer (1993), in *Federalist Number* 39, Madison speaks of "the people of the several states. . . are united as parties to a constitutional compact, to which the people of each state acceded as a separate sovereign community." However, Madison's nationalist sentiments were made more clear in the 1830s when he attacked nullification, arguing that no single state had the power of nullification or secession. Only by the vote of the people of all of the states could the union be dissolved.

8. *Merriam v. Moody's Executors,* 25 Iowa 163, 170 (1868). Dillon's Rule was first written in the case of *City of Clinton v. Cedar Rapids and Missouri Railroad Co.* (1868).

9. See, for example, the list of tables in Van Son 1993.

10. Concern that congressional action might usurp traditional police powers of the states led some officials to advocate uniform state lawmaking. They contended that concurrent state adoption of similar or uniform laws might obviate the need for federal legislation. Their actions led to the establishment of the National Conference of Commissioners on Uniform State Laws, an organization that exists to this day. See the discussion in Nugent 1999.

11. As quoted in Pagano and Bowman 1995, 2.

12. 108 S.Ct. 1355 (1988).

13. The March 1999 issue of *Governing* assessed and compared the governing capacities of the states. Five performance categories were analyzed: financial management, capital management, human resources, managing for results, and information technology. States were found to vary widely in their capacity.

14. As quoted in Power to the States 1995.

15. See, for example, Shanahan 1996.

16. There are aberrations in Garreau's new configurations, places that simply do not fit their regions. These include New York City and Washington, D.C. (both located in the Foundry but apart from it), Alaska (a small strip is in Ecotopia, most of the state is located in the Empty Quarter but neither is a successful classification), and Hawaii, which is not part of North America at all.

17. Unlike most compacts, the interstate low-level radioactive waste disposal compacts do not distribute costs and benefits across a unified area. Instead, the compacts concentrate public bads (the location of the disposal site) in one or two states, while the benefits (the ability to use the site) are enjoyed by all member states.

18. William Dodge, as quoted in Ehrenhalt 1995, 32.

19. Allen Wallis, as quoted in Ehrenhalt 1995, 32.

20. As rebalancing occurs, other pressures test the US federal system. One of the most intriguing comes from the state of Hawaii and involves identity issues. In 1893, a group of businessmen intent on the lifting of sugar tariffs, bolstered by US Marines, ousted the Hawaiian queen, Lili`uokalani, from her throne, seized crown lands and ended Hawaii's independence. A year later, the group organized the Republic of Hawaii and within four years, the islands were annexed as a US territory. A ballot measure in 1959 gave Hawaiians the choice of remaining a territory or becoming a state. Voters overwhelmingly approved statehood. Since the overthrow of the Queen, the issues of self-determination for native Hawaiians and the return of their lands have bubbled under the surface. In 1993 when Governor John Waihee, the first governor of Hawaiian ancestry, raised the Hawaiian flag over the state capitol to mark the 100th anniversary of the takeover, the issues boiled over. A formal apology from President Clinton for the century-old action was not effective in silencing the voices calling for sovereignty for native Hawaiians. That same year, the legislature adopted a bill authorizing the creation of the Hawaiian Sovereignty Advisory Commission (Nakashima 1996). In 1996, 73 percent of eligible Hawaiians voted in favor of a plan to elect delegates to propose a native Hawaiian government. Underlying the vote was a pervasive sense that native Hawaiians had been wronged in their native land. Accommodating their demands for self-determination and territory leads to interesting questions of asymmetrical federalism.

Chapter 4

Re-distribution of Authority in Russia: Regional Governors' Preferences

Kathleen M. Dowley

October 1991—General Dzhokar Dudayev wins controversial election to the new Chechen Republic Presidency. His first decree proclaims the sovereignty of the Chechen state. His first press release expresses his readiness to engage in a conflict with Russia, since he does not intend to betray the freedom and sovereignty of the new state entity (CDSP, Vol. XLIII, No. 43).

March 1992—President Shaimiyev of Tatarstan holds popular referendum on sovereignty, which 61 percent of the voters supported. Shaimiyev announces he cannot sign Federal Treaty with Russia, and demands a separate treaty as befits relations between two independent states (CDSP, Vol. XLIV, No. 16).

July 1993—"Carrying out the will of the multinational people of Sverdlovsk Province, striving to create an effective federal structure for Russia based on equal rights for its members, and defending the rights of citizens of all nationalities, the Sverdlovsk Province Soviet of People's Deputies declares the elevation of the status of Sverdlovsk Province to the level of a republic within the Russian Federation (Urals Republic)" (CDSP, Vol. XLV, No. 27).

February 1994—Russia and Tatarstan sign a separate bilateral treaty, in which Tatarstan agrees to drop the clause "sovereign state subject to international law," in exchange for very generous tax terms (CDSP, Vol. XLVI, No. 10).

December 1994—More than 10,000 Russian Interior Ministry troops enter Chechnya to halt armed resistance to its membership in the federation.

The events detailed above illustrate the challenge of building federal institutions in multinational Russia after Soviet disintegration in 1991 along ethno-republic lines. Soviet Premier Mikhail Gorbachev's *perestroika* (restructuring) beginning in 1986 unleashed separatist forces not only in the fifteen union republics, such as the Ukraine, Latvia, and Estonia, but within the Russian state as well, as the bloody war of independence in Chechnya tragically demonstrates. While some amount of "pulling and tugging" (Bowman 1999, this volume) between a federal center and its constituent parts is normal in dynamic federal regimes, it is possible that these centrifugal tendencies in Russia will result in further ethnic fragmentation. It is also possible that the mere threat of such a future will endanger existing democratic progress and bring about a return to authoritarian rule.

Indeed, making the transition to a federal democracy from a formally federal authoritarian state—such as existed in the USSR, Yugoslavia, and Czechoslovakia—complicates an already difficult process. New leaders are faced with the additional challenge to the territorial integrity of the state undergoing such a transition. As Przeworski, argues, "institutional failure at the center provides a context in which regionally based nationalists can effectively mobilize to promote an autonomy movement" (Przeworski 1996, 22). The collapse of the Communist Party of the Soviet Union, the main centralizing organization of the state, provided just such a context for nationalists (most of whom were former Communists) in the fifteen Union Republics, and each of them successfully took advantage of it and achieved independence at the end of 1991. The rebels in Chechnya were not deemed equally deserving in their claim to independent status from the new Russian Federation and thus resorted to war in December of 1994.

Yet secession from the federation with Russia remains only one alternative for the various ethnic and regional formations in Russia. In fact, the majority of the administrative units within this former empire have not sought to secede even in the face of the disintegration of the Soviet center. Przeworski may be right to suggest that while institutional collapse at the center is necessary to the rise of separatist movements, it is not sufficient. As Charles Tilly explains, institutional collapse at the state's political center may provide "opportunity" but not necessarily "mobilization," which depends on group "resources" and "organization" (Tilly 1978, 7). Thus, most of the members of the former Russian Soviet Federated Socialist Republic (RSFSR) have chosen to negotiate a federal bargain, primarily in terms of political and economic autonomy from the new federal center. Secessionist wars for independence, then, are only one form of conflict among groups competing for power in a transitioning federal state, and they are not the most common form we observe in Russia. The Russian case then provides us with a unique opportunity to analyze the process of re-distributing authority within existing state boundaries in a state undergoing a democratic transition, and the factors that ultimately shape the debate over that re-distribution process and consolidation.

The central concern of this chapter is to identify the factors related to a state's preferred "federal bargain" with the national center. In one assessment of emerging center-periphery relations in Russia, Lapidus and Walker assert that "no single indicator is available for assessing the seriousness of the challenge to the center from a particular area" (Lapidus and Walker 1995, 104). Nonetheless, when one explores which state leaders are actively engaged in struggles for greater local control and which are consistently opposed to such devolutions of power and responsibility to the federal unit, some patterns do emerge. Identifying and explaining such patterns in the preferences of regional elites in Russia are important to, indeed prior to, any predictions about the future devolution of power and authority in Russia. Indeed, elite preferences are an oft overlooked factor in explaining the pressures for the re-distribution of authority in a transitioning state. With the former center collapsed and the new center attempting to consolidate its power, the terms of the bargain are up for debate. But who wants what and why?

FEDERALISTS, ANTIFEDERALISTS, AND NATIONALISTS

Bargaining between the center and the periphery refers to bargaining between the central executive authority under Boris Yeltsin and the regional governments of each of the constitutionally defined eighty-nine members of the federation over the distribution of power and authority between the center and the regions. During state-building constitutional assemblies or conventions, some representatives have historically argued for a strong union, while others have argued for the primacy of local power over central authority. In exploring the origins of American federalism, Riker (1964) suggested that the state actors who supported federal arrangements did not do so out of a yearning to guarantee social freedom, control tyranny, or protect democracy against abuses of power, as the early American theorists argued in *The Federalist Papers*, and as Bowman, in this volume, also asserts. Instead, Riker suggests that the proponents of federalism advocated this kind of institutional arrangement as a strategy to protect the territory from an external military threat, or as a means of territorial expansion.[1] Thus, elites interested in strengthening the power of the federal center while maintaining lower level checks on that power were not "ideologically" concerned with liberty and freedom per se, but with practical issues of national security or economic well-being. Riker's fundamental assumption is that those who negotiate a federal bargain do so out of a conviction that their interests are better served by some kinds of institutional arrangements over others. Expanding on Riker, Burgess (Burgess and Gagnon 1993, 104) argues that elite advocacy of federalism over confederalism or unitary government represents the pursuit of self-interest and reflects the self-interest of those representatives making the case. Advocates of particular distributions of power between a national center and its peripheral parts posture, lobby, cajole, threaten, and move to establish a certain type of constitutional division of power because they see it as the preferred political order.

Following the collapse of the old Soviet regime and the unifying presence of the old Communist Party, the question in Russia becomes: Who benefits from a particular division of power? What interests are being defended or promoted? Conversely, which state leaders benefit from the re-centralization of political and economic power? And which local elites benefit from complete independence from the new Russian Federation?

One could still make the case, as Publius did over two centuries ago, that federalism remains a means by which the rights and liberties of individuals and minorities (religious or ethnic) are best protected from the violence of majority factions. In its ethno-territorial form, such as the one adopted by the USSR in 1922 and the former Yugoslavia after World War I, ethno-federalism remains a potential institutional solution to the problems of governing a large, diverse multinational state, such as India and today, Russia. In many ways, the renewed debate over the benefits of federal, confederal, ethno-federal, and unitary state institutions parallels that which the Bolsheviks confronted from 1917 to 1922. Though Marxism taught that national identity would disappear in the socialist state, or at least become secondary to one's socialist identity, Lenin initially supported the right to self-determination for the non-Russian nationalities of the Empire, and he codified this in the Soviet Constitution. He similarly came to accept the necessity of ethno-federalism in the new Soviet state ("National in form, socialist in content"), and he did so because he believed it would serve to, as Goldhagen suggests, "nip the desire for independence in the bud" (Goldhagen 1968, x). National republics and federal forms of political organization could persist, as long as they helped to fulfill socialist goals conceived in Moscow. With the disintegration of the Soviet state along the ethnic republic lines drawn by the Soviet state, this logic has been called into question.

Which regions and republics in Russia are "federalists" and which are "anti-federalists," and why? In which states is ethno-nationalism a force to be reckoned with, and in which others is it virtually absent? And perhaps more importantly for democratic theory and constitutional engineers in transitioning societies: What are the implications of various types of federal arrangements for the stability of the regime? To what extent are past institutional arrangements a prologue to current and future secession crises?

SOVIET AND RUSSIAN FEDERALISM

Because Russia was at least nominally federal prior to 1991 within the Soviet Union, most actors expected it to remain federal after 1991. But as in the former British colonies separately administered under the Crown prior to 1776, there remained a lot of room for negotiating the terms of the federal bargain after the collapse of the previous governing center.

The national-territorial structure of the Soviet Union evolved over a number of years, but had not, with the exception of the forcible annexation of the Baltic states in 1940 and Tuva in 1944, been territorially altered since the 1936 Stalinist Constitution, though changes in the status of particular territories did occur.[2] In 1989, the country was vertically divided between the fifteen national union republics, twenty autonomous ethnic republics, eight autonomous *oblasts* (provinces), and ten autonomous *okrugs* (districts), in descending order of status and privilege under the Constitution. The Russian Soviet Federated Socialist Republic (RSFSR) contained sixteen of the autonomous republics, five of the autonomous *oblasts*, and all ten of the autonomous *okrugs*, in addition to forty-nine non-ethnically defined *oblasts* and six *krais* (regions). Table 4.1 lists the thirty-one "autonomies" (*avtonomii*) within the RSFSR and the date each was formally created.

Table 4.1
Autonomous Republics, *Oblasts*, and *Okrugs* in the RSFSR

ASSRs

      Bashkir ASSR
            Created in March 1919.
            21.9% Bashkir
      Buryat ASSR
            Created in May 1923 as Buryat-Mongol ASSR. Renamed in July 1958.
            24.0% Buryat
      *Chechen-Ingush ASSR
            Chechen Autonomous *Oblast* created in 1922. Ingush Autonomous *Oblast* created in 1924. Merged in 1936, then abolished during the 1944 deportations. Recreated again in 1957.
            57.8% Chechen/12.9% Ingush
      Chuvash ASSR
            Created as an Autonomous *Oblast* in June 1920. Became an ASSR in 1925.
            67.7% Chuvash
      Dagestani ASSR
            Created in January 1921.
            80.1% Dagestani

Kabardino-Balkar ASSR

> Kabardinian Autonomous *Oblast* created in 1921. Kabardino-Balkar Autonomous *Oblast* created 1922. Became an ASSR in 1936, but when Balkars were deported in 1944, renamed Kabardinian ASSR. In 1957, it was again renamed Kabardino-Balkar ASSR.
> 48.2% Kabardinian/9.4% Balkar

Kalmyk ASSR

> Created as an Autonomous *Oblast* in 1920. Became an ASSR in 1935. It was abolished during deportations of 1943. Recreated in 1957.
> 45.3% Kalmyk

Karelian ASSR

> Created as Karelian Labour Commune in 1920. Became an ASSR in 1935. It was renamed the Karelo-Finnish SSR from 1940-56, but demoted to Karelian ASSR in 1957.
> 10.0% Karelian

Komi ASSR

> Created as Komi-Zyryan Autonomous *Oblast* in 1920. It became Komi ASSR in 1936.
> 23.3% Komi

Mari ASSR

> Created as an Autonomous *Oblast* in 1920. Became an ASSR in 1936.
> 43.2% Mari

Mordvin ASSR

> Created as an Autonomous *Oblast* in 1930. Became an ASSR in 1934.
> 32.5% Mordva

North Ossetian ASSR

> Created as an Autonomous *Oblast* in 1924. Became an ASSR in 1936.
> 52.9% Ossetian

Tatar ASSR

> Created in May 1920.
> 48.5% Tatar

Tuvin ASSR

> Independent until 1944. Made an Autonomous *Oblast* in 1944, and became an ASSR in 1961.
> 64.3% Tuvin

Udmurt ASSR

> Created as an Autonomous *Oblast* in 1920. Became an ASSR in 1934.
> 30.9% Udmurt

Yakut ASSR

> Created in April 1922.
> 33.4% Yakutian

*The Chechen-Ingush ASSR split in late 1991–early 1992 into two separate republics.

Autonomous *Oblasts*

Adegeia AO

Created in July 1922. Known as Adegeia-Cherkess AO until 1928.
22.1% Adegei

Gorno Altai AO

Created in June 1922. Known as Oirot AO until 1948.
31.0% Altai

Jewish AO

Created in May 1934.
4.2% Jewish

Karachai-Cherkess AO

Created in 1922. In 1926, it was divided in two. The Karachai AO was abolished in 1943, and a joint AO was reestablished in 1957.
31% Karachai/9.7% Cherkess

Khakhass AO

Created in October 1930.
11.1% Khakhass

Autonomous *Okrugs*

Agin-Buryat AOk

Created in 1937 from the split of the Buryat-Mongol ASSR. 54.9% Buryat

Chukchi AOk

Created in December 1930. 7.3% Chukchi

Evenki AOk

Created in December 1930. 13.9% Evenki

Khanty-Mansi AOk

Created in December 1930. .9% Khanty/.5% Mansi

Komi-Permyak AOk

Created in February 1935. 60.1% Komi-Permyaks

Koryak AOk

Created in December 1930. 16.5% Koryaks

Nenets AOk

Created in July 1929. 11.9% Nenets

Taimyr AOk

Created in December 1930. 8.9% Dolgan/4.4% Nenets

Ust'-Orda Buryat AOk

Created in 1936 when Buryat-Mongol ASSR split. 36.1% Buryat

Yamalo-Nenets AOk

Created in December 1930. 4.2% Nenets

Altogether some fifty-eight of the over 100 nationalities that were contained within the former USSR had some form of administratively recognized autonomy under the old system. The major nationalities were granted formal autonomy in the shape of constituent republics to the Union of Soviet Socialist Republics. While the criteria for receiving this recognition seem somewhat arbitrary when examined today, one should not underestimate the symbolic and real importance such a status had on the lives of those in the national republics.

During the 1920s, the regime encouraged the use of native languages in local administration and schools, and deciphered written alphabets for unlettered peoples. While the early regime limited political autonomy, within the confines of the Union national identity was given considerable freedom to develop (Goldhagen 1968, ix). This was all to change dramatically during the Stalin years, but the memory proved impossible to banish.

Defining which were major nationalities—those deserving of national republic status—presented the regime with a new challenge, and the new Soviet leaders were not always consistent in their response. In some instances, a divide and rule policy seemed to prevail. In Central Asia in particular, union republics were set up for groups that had not yet developed into self-proclaimed "nations." But rather than create one large "Muslim" or "Turkic" state, several entities were created with separate identities. The nationally conscious peoples of Armenia, Azerbaidjan, and Georgia were given what they had once already possessed, sovereignty in an existing federation.

Moreover, while status in the four-tiered hierarchy was largely based on population, sometimes this, too, was overlooked, as the Tatars were granted only autonomous republic status though they outnumber Georgians, Tajiks, and Turkmeni peoples, all of which were granted union republic status. According to Tatar nationalists, the only reason they were denied major nationality status was because they shared no external borders with a foreign state (Sheehy 1991, 67). This was the official line as well, which said, quite simply, that a region had to be able to secede "in principle" from the Union in order to be granted union republic status in the administrative hierarchy. In other cases, special recognition was provided to very small, seemingly insignificant groups, such as the Abkhazi in Georgia, who number fewer than 100,000 and who make up less than twenty percent of the population of the Abkhaz Autonomous Region. The grounds were purely political, as the Bolsheviks attempted to dampen the very strong sense of national identity that existed among Georgians, Armenians, and Azeris by carving out autonomous formations for small groups within these existing nations (Lapidus and Walker 1995, 94).

Only the union republics were granted the nominal right to secede from the Union, though the mechanism for taking such an action was never specified in any of the Soviet Constitutions. Autonomous ethnic republics had markedly fewer rights than union republics. For example, in most autonomous republics, education in the native language above the level of primary school has been available much less frequently, and they were allotted a smaller number of deputies in the federal parliament than the union republics (Anderson and Silver

1984). But they were granted more autonomy than provinces, and special political opportunities were created for ethnic elites in the autonomous republics, opportunities not created for elites representing the nonethnic provinces (*oblasts*) and territories (*krais*) of the RSFSR.

This asymmetry in the treatment accorded the ethnic states versus the purely territorial formations has become an issue in Russia's transition and the current negotiations over the terms of the federal bargain. Despite the special status granted the ethnic autonomous republics, however, seventy percent of Russia's territory and eighty percent of her population are contained within territorial formations (6 territories, 49 provinces, 2 federal cities), much in remote parts of Siberia, all of which have traditionally received even fewer political and economic rights than the ethnic republics and autonomous formations.

In his attempt to build an independent base of support from which to challenge the authority of Mikhail Gorbachev, Yeltsin played the ethnic card as far back as 1990 in campaigns for the Russian parliament, for the chairmanship of that parliament, and even in his bid to become the first popularly elected president of the RSFSR. When the Russian parliament followed the lead of the Baltic republics in adopting a declaration of state sovereignty, it confirmed the need to broaden substantially the rights of the autonomous republics, autonomous *oblasts*, and autonomous *okrugs*, along with RSFSR *krais* and *oblasts* (Lapidus and Walker 1995, 82). And in 1990, while on a tour through Tatarstan, Bashkiria, and the Komi Autonomous Republic, Yeltsin told local elites to "take all the sovereignty you can swallow" (Keller 1990, 2). But less than a year later, he opposed Tatarstan's appeal to be a signatory to the new Union Treaty as an equal to the other fifteen Union Republics.

Relations between the center (now identified with Boris Yeltsin and his administration of the Russian government) and the regions deteriorated after the attempted coup against Gorbachev in August of 1991, when Yeltsin moved to dissolve the local elites that had supported the State Committee for the State of Emergency (SCSE) in their attempt to overthrow Gorbachev. He even heard debates among his central advisors, such as Minister for Nationality Affairs Valery Tishkov, about thoroughly reconstituting the administrative boundaries of the existing states along territorial, not ethnic, lines. This discussion parallels Rajagopalan's chapter in this volume on reconstituting the internal boundaries of federal states in Pakistan and Sri Lanka.

But by March of 1992, resistance at the local level proved too strong, and the center offered its first of several federal bargains in the form of three hastily conceived treaties known collectively as the Federal Treaty. All representatives of the member states within Russia's borders signed the treaty except Tatarstan and Chechnya. It "confirmed and consolidated" the ethnic republics' special status, in granting them a number of political and economic rights not accorded the nonethnic territories, such as the right to conduct a limited foreign policy and foreign trade independent of Moscow (Sharlet 1994, 119). It also stated that the land and natural resources of the ethnic republics belonged to the people living there and that issues regarding disposal of these resources would be regulated by both the Russian and republican governments. That the other territorial units were not granted as much autonomy in foreign policy, trade or, most importantly, natural resources, signaled that the asymmetry in the federal structure would continue. While the treaty granted that the republics were sovereign, there was no right to secession, and the treaty stipulated that republican constitutions could not conflict with the federal constitution.

Other issues, such as taxation policies, remained unresolved. Regions and republics are expected to pass on taxes to the federal budget, which then distributes subsidies to the members of the federation. This process, as it evolved under the communist system, was intended to help equalize development across the regions and republics; however, it degenerated into a means of political patronage. These issues were allowed to fester after the signing of the Treaty, given Yeltsin's preoccupation with the parliamentary challenge to his authority in Moscow.

Indeed, most of the Constitutional debates from April 1992 through July 1993 focused on the division of powers between the executive and the parliament, and not on the unresolved question of the federal division of powers between the center and its member states. Ethnic conflict in Ingushetia and North Ossetia over a disputed border territory, the Prigorodny *raion*, and the increasingly militant rhetoric pouring out of Chechnya exacerbated tensions and signaled trouble ahead, but the debate did not receive national attention until the summer of 1993, when Yeltsin unveiled his draft Constitution for the Russian Federation at the June Constitutional Convention. Republics and territories continued to pressure the center for more autonomy, by issuing declarations of sovereignty, holding referenda on upgrading their administrative status, and withholding taxes from the federal center. All of these the Yeltsin administration seemed willing to tolerate in return for support from the regional elite, as the administration continued its struggle for control with an uncooperative national parliament. Only four of the forty appointed regional administrators audited by the Chief State Inspector were "fired" through March of 1993, and these were instances of official corruption, not defiance (Slider 1996).

When the executive-legislative struggle culminated in the bloody, forcible ouster of the national parliament by Yeltsin-loyal forces in October 1993, Yeltsin then turned quickly to new elections for the parliament and a referendum on its new Constitution. Unfortunately, the manner in which the referendum and draft were designed did not resolve many of these same issues. The new Russian Constitution was adopted by a slim majority of the voters in a referendum held on December 12, 1993, though the results were far from a sweeping mandate for its provisions. This version of the Constitution, unlike the draft proposed by the Constitutional Assembly in July of 1993, fails once again to establish clearly the powers of the member states of the Federation vis-à-vis the center, and did not include any of the text of the Federation Treaty signed the year before.

Article 5 of the latest Constitution does seem, however, to resolve the structural asymmetry of the former Russian Federation by acknowledging that "the Russian Federation consists of republics, territories, provinces, federal cities, an autonomous province, and autonomous regions, all of which are equal members of the Russian Federation." Each member of the federation is to have equal representation in the Upper House of the federal legislature, the Council of the Federation. But Section 2 stipulates that each republic is to have its own constitution and legislation while every territory, province, federal city, and autonomous region is to have its own charter and legislation, which already implies a juridical difference in the status of each.

The equality provision was designed to alleviate the problems associated with the asymmetries under the old system of power, asymmetries which led some *oblasts* and *krais* to try to legislatively "upgrade" their position to republic status in order to share in the benefits promised to those holding republic status under the terms of the 1992 Federal Treaty. But while the powers of the federal government are detailed quite clearly in Article 71, Article 73 states merely that anything not covered by the federal government, or by the "joint-jurisdiction" areas detailed in Article 72, falls under the authority of the federation members.

Leaders of several vocal ethnic autonomous republics (Tatarstan, Bashkortostan, Karelia, and Komi) refused to endorse the December Constitution because they argued that it did not guarantee them enough autonomy, and that it represented a loss of autonomy granted them under the Federal Treaty, all references to which were obliterated in the new Constitution. The 490,000 eligible voters from the republic of Chechnya boycotted the referendum in April 1993 as well as the final December vote, while only 14 percent of the eligible voters participated in Tatarstan, rendering the election null and void there (Tolz 1993). And the current republic constitutions of Sakha (formerly Yakutia), Tatarstan, Tuva, and Bashkortostan clearly contradict passages of the new Russian Constitution.

Among the most important areas of contention remain the rights to dispose of republic and regional natural resources, taxation policies, and the right to secede from the federation by virtue of a vote by only the individual state's population. With the Russian attack on renegade Chechnya in late 1994, the debate was renewed, not resolved. The carnage there generated among some member states the desire to see central power more constrained and among others, the desire to see it expanded and strengthened. The cease fire negotiated by former presidential National Security Chief Alexander Lebed promises the Chechens a referendum on independence after five years.

The economic crisis of the summer of 1998 and the 1996-1997 direct election of all state leaders has reinvigorated the debate in interesting and not predictable ways. Governors have been forced, in many cases, to adopt more "autonomy" than they may have earlier demonstrated a preference for, if only because the vacuum at the center has left some parts of the Federation, i.e., remote Siberian territories and peoples, struggling to survive. In other parts of the country, the absence of a strong capable center has led to struggles between regional "governors" and the mayors of the largest (and wealthiest) cities over the budget process in particular.

THEORETICAL FRAMEWORKS FOR UNDERSTANDING ELITE STRATEGIES

To explain the variation in the expressed positions of the eighty-nine state leaders, I examine propositions derived from several competing theoretical traditions. Many scholars of the USSR and its successor states were initially stunned by the important role ethnicity has played in mobilizing individuals in the political sphere to bring about the collapse of the Marxist-Leninist state.[3] They had argued that Soviet success in achieving increased social development and greater equality between republics would bring about assimilation and the weakening of ethnic appeals. Among those scholars long interested in the national question in the USSR, however, there were those who identified nationalism as the greatest potential threat to the stability of the Soviet state (Rakowska-Harmstone 1974), and Richard Pipes went so far as to suggest that "sooner or later the empire will disintegrate roughly along the lines of the existing republics" (quoted in Linden and Simes 1977, 10). Since the collapse of the Soviet state and the independence of the former union republics, the most visible and aggressive autonomy seekers within Russia have, in fact, been the former ethnic autonomous republics of Tatarstan, Chechnya, Tuva, and Bashkortostan.

Many theories have been advanced in political science to explain away the phenomenon of ethnopolitics as a "primitive" hangover from societies that would dissipate with modernization, or as itself a product of disruptive modernizing tendencies. On the left, Marxists have suggested that the construction of ethnic or national identities is one of the strategies used by capitalist elites to distract individuals from their class identity and interests. In this understanding, "ethnic" entrepreneurs are suffering from "false consciousness," imposed on them, most likely, by a colonizing or precapitalist elite. Lenin and Stalin both believed that nations and nationalism were products of the economic stage of capitalism, and once this stage was surpassed, these, too, would disappear (Stalin 1950, 16).

Modernization theorists, however, suggest that nationalism (the ideological manifestation of politicized ethnicity), was an artifact of traditional societies which had not yet been introduced to the ideals and practices of Western, liberal politics. As these states and their societies became more modern, politicized ethnicity would disappear, especially with increased access to education and more social mobility (Geertz 1963). Cross-cutting cleavages and a convergence of new values would gradually weaken ethnic attachments.

Collapse of the USSR and Yugoslavia along ethnic lines, and the apparent resurgence of ethnopolitics in the developed and less developed world, suggest that all of these understandings are partial in their ability to explain the power of ethnicity as a force for political mobilization in the world. Nationalism seems to have survived Marxism in the USSR, and was just as evident in the most modern and Western Soviet republics of Estonia, Latvia, and Lithuania, in contrast to what early modernization theorists would have predicted. Gurr (1993) describes the two competing views of the resurgence of ethnonationalism in the literature today as "primordialist" (or essentialist) and instrumentalist. The former regards ethnic nationalism as a manifestation of a persisting cultural tradition based on a primordial sense of ethnic identity (Gurr 1993, 124) where ethnic and cultural cleavages are more objective than those of interest or class (Przeworski 1996, 20). Primordialists posit that the Soviet empire or "prison of nations" was destined to disintegrate as the nations awoke to reclaim their true identities and sovereignty. Beissinger (1995) notes that the general consensus now appears to be that Soviet Union was an empire and for this reason, it broke up. The civil war in Yugoslavia and that within Russia in Chechnya seem to be promoting a tragic renaissance for primordialist scholars discredited during the late 1970s and 1980s.

Instrumentalists view ethnicity as one of a variety of identities that can be created and subsequently recreated in response to conditions that favor its emergence (Bates 1983). With collapse at the center in 1991, it was neither inevitable nor "natural" for the many suppressed ethnic groups and previous territorial units to demand autonomy. Beissinger (1995) once again notes that many self-avowed empires eventually evolved into states. This implies that there is an inherent contradiction in suggesting that the Soviet Union broke up because it was an empire, and then defining it as an empire because it broke up. Crude primordialist explanations of the collapse of the USSR fail to explain why only some of the more than 100 groups have mobilized for greater national autonomy, while others have not. In interpreting the instrumentalist response, Gurr (1993, 124) notes that separatist movements are instead seen as an instrumental response to differential treatment. The Soviet Union failed as a state because it failed at the goal of national integration of various ethno-linguistic groups. This failure was not, in the instrumental view, predestined to occur because it was multinational.

While it is clear to even the casual observer that the most strident separatists are the leaders of overtly or formally ethnic republics in Russia, their demands have not been as obviously ethnic or cultural as those of the former union republics, say of Estonia. That is, the issues at stake are generally not citizenship or language rights, but rather, taxation rates and procedures, judicial appointments, and local control over natural resources and foreign investment. Issues one might associate with the normal tugging and pulling of nonethnic, territorially based federations are exacerbated by the possibility of elites playing an ethnic trump card.

Since most of the demands made by regional governors are economic, this lends credibility to those who view the differential responses of the governors as interpretable within the context of the local political economy of their respective regions. In Levi's (1988) analysis of the predatory state she suggests that we should expect leaders to "design institutions that they believe will be efficient in promoting their interests. More specifically, within the limits and constraints upon them, they will design revenue production policies that maximize revenues to the state" (Levi 1988, 16-17). Governors of states with resources tradable on a world market will desire the autonomy to capture the rents from these ventures. While those in regions with few local resources to capture rent will continue to press for redistributive policies from a strong center, as this would be their best chance at maximizing rents. Stoner-Weiss's (1997) case study of the political economy of three Russian regions supports this interpretation of regional demands.

In contrast, the relative deprivation school of conflict analysis suggests that the primary motivation for political action by ethnic groups is their frustration about perceived deprivation relative to comparable groups around them. This approach would then argue that those states most likely to opt out of a federal bargain with the center are those that have not benefited from such a bargain in the past. Leaders of those states that are considerably worse off than their neighbors, but with the expectation of doing better, are more likely to resist re-centralization of power because they fared so poorly under such an arrangement in the recent past. In relative deprivation theory, the "perceived discrepancy between men's value expectations and their value capabilities" is more important than any real world measures of such discrepancies (Gurr 1971, 13). Governors of states suffering such deprivation would be responding, then, to pressures from below, rather than to any interests they might have independent of their now elective constituencies.

A final theoretical approach to explaining the variation in regional elite preferences is Tilly's (1978) "resource mobilization" approach. He argues that we need to look at the different political and organizational resources of the individual governors to understand why some bargain for autonomy while others do not. This is compatible with the political institutional approach of Roeder (1991) and others. Roeder argues that the ethno-federal institutional arrangements of the USSR contributed to the potency and rationality of ethnicity as a mobilizing identity by local elites during the center's collapse. Within the mobilization school of political conflict, Roeder's political institutional explanation suggests why only some of the elites in the eighty-nine states, those privileged under the old regime, were able to mobilize group resources in response to the changing political and economic environment. Elites in the ethnic autonomous republics and national level republics were appointed to represent the ethnic group interests in the larger state, and thus, their natural political base of support was supposed to be the ethnic group. Other political appointments in these regions were made on the basis of ethnicity, a Soviet form of affirmative action for the formally and institutionally recognized ethnic groups referred to in the early years of the Soviet Union as *korenizatsiia* or nativization. As a result, assimilation rates for ethnic groups in the USSR were highest among the groups that had not received institutional recognition and lowest among the Union republic status groups (Anderson and Silver 1990).

Political structural theorists like Roeder (1991) posit that these ethnofederal institutional arrangements and the policies that accompanied them may have led not to any kind of ethnic fusion or merging, but to the maintenance of strong, separate political identities. Such arrangements also provided an administrative advantage to local ethnic elites privileged under the old regime that might not have been there had the Bolshevik government of 1917 adopted a unitary structure and contributed to the later rise of nationalist movements along lines already drawn into the Soviet federal-constitutional arrangements.

Together, these arguments represent four separate classes of explanation surrounding the behavior of regional politicians in the new Russian federated state. *Essentialism* emphasizes the importance of primordial attachments to a separate national identity, independent of the Russian center, hypothesizing that collapse at the center will allow these repressed identities to reassert themselves once more. *Instrumentalism* emphasizes the importance of the rational calculations of individual leaders to changes in their opportunity structure to capture greater rents by bargaining instrumentally for greater local control over resources. *Relative deprivation* focuses on the perception by groups of individuals that they are suffering relative to comparable groups due to some policy action or inaction by the center. *Resource mobilization* argues that the different resources and organizational capacity of governors will influence their bargaining strategy vis-à-vis the center. The four approaches fall into two broader approaches to the study of political behavior. While instrumentalism and resource mobilization offer political approaches to the question, relative deprivation and essentialism emphasize more sociological explanations.

CLASSIFYING FEDERAL PREFERENCES OF STATE ELITES

The first step to explaining variation in state leaders' and the public's preferences for one constitutional arrangement over any other is to correctly describe or measure the range of possible positions.[4] To conceptualize the potential positions that a governor could take, I developed a political autonomy scale (from 1-5) that tries to capture the range of possible constitutional arrangements, from complete independence (coded as a 5), to an ethnic confederation (which implies an asymmetrical relationship between the center and ethnic and nonethnic states), to a loose confederation (in which the relationship between the center and all states is symmetrical), to a strong federation (also symmetrical), and finally, to a highly centralized, unitary, and indivisible Russia.

To classify the positions of each state, I recorded events occurring within the regions or between regional political actors and the center that articulated or were related to a state leader's preferred position along this five-item political autonomy dimension. Events data are not used here to record exact detail about events or activities occurring in the regions, but instead to provide a systematic record of regional differentiation. Many scholars limit their focus to counts of events by type (strikes, political protests, etc.). The data I have gathered is not a count of all events, however, but a systematic collection using a defined set of criteria from all of Russia to depict each state's preferred position regarding the federal bargain.

"Events" include responses to central decrees relating to the division of powers between the center and the regions, boycotts of federal referendums or elections, withholding of federal taxes, petitions to the federal government, communiqués to the federal government, and strikes and demonstrations in favor of or opposed to a proffered arrangement. Events recorded derive from two sources, the weekly *Current Digest of the Soviet Press* and the *Open Media Research Institute's* (OMRI) *Daily Digest* from 1991 to 1995. For the period under review, which is deemed the formative years of evolving federalism in Russia, a total of 966 events by regional elites are recorded, with the mean number of events per state at 15.5. To capture the central tendency of state elites, I use their mean and median scores on the autonomy index for all events recorded during this period to classify their overall preferred position. The states range in rank from Chechnya, with a mean of 4.62, to Kursk, with a mean of 1.6. The overall mean for all eighty-nine states is 3.14, or the territorial confederative position.[5] To analyze the explanatory power of the various theoretical perspectives already identified, I used the mean score of each state on the autonomy index as the dependent variable, that is, the preference to be explained.

Essentialism

According to Gurr (1993), essentialists would largely expect groups with a strong sense of identity, cultural distance from the center, and a past historical grievance to be the most demanding of autonomy. Therefore a summated scale of potential for developing a separate national identity with separatist ambitions seems appropriate. If the population of the state is recognized as non-Russian, nonorthodox, previously punished by Stalin, and with a high reported use of its native tongue (75%+), it receives a score of 4. Any combination of three of the above is a 3, two of the above a 2, and one of the above a 1. Russian states receive a score of 0. I consider those states with all four factors to have a high potential for the development of a strong, separate national identity, while those with none to have a low potential for doing so.

Correlating this Essentialism Index with the Mean Autonomy Score Index yields the results shown in Table 4.2. The Kendall's tau-b coefficient (.575) is statistically significant (p=.000), suggesting that the essentialist propositions are important when explaining the behavior of the state elite. A closer examination of the relationship among the ethnic state elite is provided in the cross-tabulation presented in Table 4.2. While the only state (Chechnya) to pursue a course of independence is also one with the highest potential for the development of a separate national identity, five other states with similarly high levels of national identity have not opted for independence. So while presence of these four factors might be considered necessary to the leadership before embarking on a path to independence, they are not sufficient conditions for doing so.

Likewise, the only two ethnic states to adopt positions asking for less autonomy than is represented by the overall median of 3.0 are states lacking any of the essentialism factors present (the Koriak and Evenki AO). So while the presence of a strong sense of national identity is not sufficient for predicting a desire for greater autonomy, it does seem less likely that states with some potential for the development of a separate national identity will call for the return of a strong, central government at the expense of the regional government.
But the indicators cannot tell us much more about the likely behavior of these state elites beyond the most extreme positions. For example, the leader of the state of Karelia, with only one of the factors present, and that of Tuva, with all of them present, score the same on the autonomy index, in asking for the maximum amount of autonomy possible within a single state, position four We need more than what the essentialism school offers to explain the behavior of both ethnic and nonethnic elite in bargaining with the center over the distribution of political power.

Instrumentalism

In contrast to the arguments of essentialist school, the instrumentalist approach suggests that elites in states with credible economic leverage to use against the center will be most likely to demand increasing levels of autonomy from the center to capture greater rents from those same resources. In the more prosperous regions, elites may be aware of the fact that continued membership in this federation would signal a continuation of their status as donor regions,

Table 4.2
Potential for the Development of a Separate National Identity by Elite's Autonomy Score

		Essentialism Index Score			
		Low Potential (1 factor)	(2 factors)	High Potential (3 factors)	(4 factors)
Median Autonomy Position					
2.0	Strong Federation	Koriak AO	0	0	0
2.5		Evenki AO	0	0	0
3.0	Loose Federation	Evreyski AO	Komi-Permyak Gorno-Altai Ust-Orda Agin-Buryat	Dagestan N.Ossetia	Kabardino-Balkaria Karachai-Cherkessia
3.5		Khanty-Mansi Taimyr	Yamal-Nenets	0	0
4.0	Ethnic Confederation	Karelia Komi Nenets AO Chukota	Chuvashia Mordovia Mari-El Buryatia Khakhasia Sakha Udmurtia	Tatarstan Adeygeya Bashkortostan	Ingushetia Kalmykia Tuva
5.0	Independence	0	0	0	Chechnya

Kendall's tau-b: .575 ($p < .000$)

supporting poorer regions at the expense of the development of their own constituencies. Increasing levels of political autonomy then would mean that regional elites gain more control over tax revenues collected in their regions, and over wealth accumulated from the sale of natural resources in the region, and so on. This case has been made with regard to the Baltic states and their desire for independence from the Soviet Union. That they had a consistently higher standard of living than most of the other republics and felt they could be doing even better if they did not have to subsidize the development of poorer regions like those in Central Asia, are among the primary reasons for the emergence of strong independence movements in these regions.

To test these propositions on the eighty-nine regional leaders of the Russian Federation, I use data on the degree of economic dependence/independence of the state on the federal center. Looking at the natural resource base of the regions is one way to examine whether elites are motivated by instrumental considerations in their bargaining with the center. Those with a strong natural resource base of tradable goods on the world market (i.e., oil, gas, diamonds, and gold) might be more likely to bargain for more autonomy. A cross-tabulation of resource base against the Median Autonomy Score seems to support this proposition, as Table 4.3 indicates. The state elites demanding a strong federation, that is, a strong center at the expense of regional state governments, are those from states with no known resource wealth. Of the 25 state elites opting for a 2 or 2.5 on the autonomy scale most of the time, 20, or 80 percent, are from states without any oil, gas, diamond, or gold reserves to speak of.

At the other end of the spectrum, however, things are not as clear. Of the seventeen 4's, that is, state elites advocating a very loose ethnic federation of states, ten are resource-rich and seven are not. Resource base is not an important predictor of this position, as it is for the strong federalist position. The one 5, Chechnya, is an oil-producing state. The overall correlation between natural resource wealth and the mean autonomy position of state elites is moderately positive at .295 (p=.001).

One additional way to determine the economic dependence of a particular state on the center is to examine the state's expenditures to revenues ratio. The World Bank has compiled a listing of the state budgets for 1992—their expenditures and resources. From these figures, I calculated the percentage of the local budget expenditures made up by federal subsidies. It ranges dramatically across regions from virtually nothing to well over 75 percent. Again, in a rational economic world, one would expect that those states least dependent on the center would be most likely to demand a loose federation, special autonomy, or outright independence.

The correlation between percent of local budget obtained from federal subsidies and the median autonomy index is statistically significant, but not in the expected direction. It is positive .172 (p=.043). Clearly, economic motivations alone are not determining state elite behavior with regard to the federal bargain. Those with little or no dependence on the center for subsidies are not more likely to demand autonomy; in fact, they are slightly less likely to do so.

Among the instrumentalist measures expected to predict demands for autonomy, then, only natural resource base is significant and predictive in the

Table 4.3
Natural Resource Base by Median Autonomy Score

	No Natural Resources	Oil, Gas, Diamond, Gold Reserves
2.0 Strong Federalists	(n=13)	(n=4)
2.5	(n=7)	(n=1)
3.0 Loose Federalists	(n=26)	(n=17)
3.5	(n=0)	(n=3)
4.0 Ethno-federalists	(n=7)	(n=10)
4.5	(n=0)	(n=0)
5.0 Independence	(n=0)	(n=1)

	Value	ASE1	Approx. Sign.
Kendall's tau-b Correlation Coefficient:	.29509	.08852	.001

expected direction. State leaders seem willing to use oil, gas, and diamond wealth as leverage against the center to obtain greater autonomy themselves over those same resources and other political and economic powers. This is true even in cases where the state has done well vis-à-vis the center in terms of what they have received relative to what they put in, and in cases where they appear to be dependent on the center for resources to cover local budget expenditures.

What it is about natural resource wealth above other kinds of wealth that makes local leaders more bold is not immediately apparent. Perhaps the marketability of these goods on a world market at values higher than they are likely to receive on the domestic market contributes to this phenomenon. Another possibility, worthy of further consideration at a later point, is more political. I can only begin to speculate here about the degree of influence that directors of natural resource extraction and production facilities (the profitable oil/gas ones, that is, not the forlorn coal mining facilities) in the states have on local leaders, but one could hypothesize that it is relatively strong and that they would tend to favor a loosening of federal authority over their prizes.

A final test of the instrumentalist position involves the reverse expectations. If the elite/managers/directors from the profitable firms are pushing for a looser federation with more local control, the reverse would certainly be true of those firms that are almost entirely dependent on the center for survival in the new marketplace. In this case, one can imagine that the advocates of a strong center at the localities' expense would be those states whose economy is almost entirely based on the center's continued strength—the defense regions. According to the logic of the instrumental approach, defense regions and their leaders are more likely to be hostile to attempts by other regional elites to jeopardize the territorial integrity of the Federation; defense regions would also resent the demands from resource-rich states for lighter tax burdens, greater revenue sharing, and economic decentralization.

The numbers do not support these expectations. In fact, there is no statistically significant relationship between defense regions and their position on the autonomy index.

Relative Deprivation

Moving next to an assessment of the relative deprivation school, I begin by attempting to measure relative deprivation in each state. The concept attempts to capture a psychological phenomenon that occurs when individuals, or groups of individuals, feel they are being mistreated relative to others. This situation comes to a crisis when there is a change in circumstance, when either the capabilities or status of a group experience a decline due to some outside force, or when the expectations of the group increase without a corresponding increase in their ability to fulfill those expectations.

I assume, at the onset, that the collapse of the USSR in 1991 and Yeltsin's victory over the putschists of August created a tide of rising expectations all over the Federation, which residents in some regions were more able to capitalize on than others. What is important in the relative deprivation school is the perception among large groups of people that they are doing worse than their neighbors, and that the center is somehow to blame, either from pursuing reckless policies, or more likely, from the sense that they are purposefully privileging some regions over others. In states experiencing a dramatic decline in the standard of living during this time period, leaders might opt to deflect the criticism from themselves by blaming the center and telling their constituents that they could do better without so much interference from the center. As a measure of change in the standard of living over time, I look at the level of change in income and unemployment from 1993 to 1994. Elites in those states experiencing slower income growth in the face of rampant inflation and a corresponding jump in the level of unemployment are more likely to demand autonomy from the center as a means of taking the heat off themselves.

The results do not bear this hypothesis out. Kendall's tau-b correlations between change in unemployment/change in income by median autonomy score do not yield statistically significant results. The correlation between level of unemployment and median autonomy score is negative (-.049), as expected, but not significant (p=.567). Likewise, level of income growth and median autonomy score are negatively correlated (p=-.030) so the higher the growth the less the deprivation and the less likely the leader is to demand autonomy. But this relationship, too, is not significant (p=.733).

An alternative to this measure of relative deprivation is one that measures whether or not the center considers this region to be a depressed region. In 1992, the President's Analytical Center identified twenty regions as economically depressed compared to the rest of the Federation during 1991-92. While this measure is only for a single point in time, and therefore, cannot measure the degree to which a state's capabilities have declined over this time period, if we take the collapse of the USSR to be a point in time at which all individuals' expectations were elevated, then we do not need to find a corresponding decrease in abilities. By the logic of the theory, the worse off regions would be more likely to opt out than the well-to-do regions, by virtue of the fact that they were worse off than their neighbors in a time when things were expected to improve (however unrealistic this expectation) for all.

The Kendall's tau-b correlation between depressed region and the state elite's median autonomy score is .284 (p=.004). The relationship is strong and positive, as the theory would have predicted. The fact that these regions were also identified publicly by the center as having been worse off than the average state in the Federation lends support to the relative deprivation theory. It is not enough that the region be depressed, but the population must also perceive this to be the case in comparison to some other. In this case, the comparison was made publicly clear for them.

The relative deprivation school, then, receives mixed reviews here. It finds little support when we use income and unemployment levels to measure deprivation, but when we consider a state's classification on a federal list of depressed regions, we find evidence of a relationship between those on the list and those demanding autonomy from the center. The most depressed regions are receiving subsidies from the center as the Central Asian states did under the Soviet system. However, these subsidies did not do away with the dramatic differences in quality of life between the peoples of Central Asia and the Baltics, for example, any more than they did away with the poverty afflicting the North Caucasus and the relative wealth of the Moscow suburban area under the Soviet system (Bahry 1987).

Resource Mobilization

The final test examines the proposition that those elites from states that were privileged under the old regime are most likely to demand increasing levels of autonomy on the basis that these elites gained in experience and networks the political skills and tools necessary to bargain effectively with the center. While the federalism that existed under the Soviet state was nominal in the amount of power it granted to state officials, it did allow for elite recruitment and some bargaining to go on between these local elites and the federal center. And it allowed this on an unequal, hierarchical basis. Elites from the ASSRs had more flexibility than those from the autonomous *oblasts*, who had more than those from the autonomous *okrugs*, who had more than those from the nonethnically defined *oblasts* and *krais*. This relationship should show up in an evaluation of the relationship between previous state administrative level and demands for autonomy under the new regime. Those from the ASSRs should be more demanding than those from the Autonomous *Oblasts*, *Okrugs*, and nonethnic states, and so forth.

The relationship is both strong and statistically significant. The higher in the administrative hierarchy (which I have divided into a rank-ordered four-fold classification: ASSR, Autonomous *Oblast*, Autonomous *Okrug*, Non-Ethnic State) the state was under the Soviet state, the more likely its current state elite are to demand special autonomy for themselves, if not outright independence.

Only three of the sixteen previous ASSRs are now demanding a federal arrangement under whose terms they are likely to give up some of their privileged status. Likewise, none of the territorial formations (nonethnic states) are demanding the kind of special status or independence demanded by the likes of Chechnya or even Tatarstan. Within the group of nonethnic states, however, there is disagreement about how strong a federal center should be created. Twenty-three of fifty-seven nonethnic states lean toward a very strong central state, while thirty-four others prefer a looser federation with more autonomy granted to the local leadership. This variation cannot be explained away in terms of the previous administrative status or nonprivileged status of the state under the Soviet system.

CONCLUSION

An understanding of the strategic preferences of both regional elites and their publics is prior to any investigation into the stability of the Russian state, its territorial integrity, and the prospects for the evolution of mature democracy. "Getting the institutions right" originates with an understanding the underlying interests of strategic actors in the transition process, such as the regional governors (*gubenators*).

However, prior to explaining the variation in the positions of state elites, we needed to classify where they stood with regard to the appropriate division of federal power and authority. While a number of studies investigate the disposition of individual regions and republics, and fewer others systematically classify the positions of the ethnic states, none have tried to put all eighty-nine states on a single autonomy continuum based on the behavior of elites in the regions (Sullivan 1995; Treisman 1997).

In examining major theoretical propositions from several competing perspectives to explain the behavior of both state elites relative to the re-distribution of authority in Russia, I find that cultural factors do matter. State elites with populations that have been able to maintain a strong separate national identity are more likely to continue to push for the maximum amount of auton-omy from the center, and for a continuation of their privileged status in the Fed-eration as separate ethnic nations. In fact, it might be a necessary condition to a state elite electing to opt out of the Federation altogether.

But as powerful a predictor of demands for autonomy as having a strong, separate, and distant identity is, it is not sufficient. A number of state elites adopt a strong ethno-federalist position despite the apparent weakness of the group identity of their populations, such as Karelia's Stepanov and Sakha's Nikolaev. Karelians and Yakutians have largely assimilated to Russian culture through conversion to orthodoxy and the adoption of Russian as their native tongue; the presidents of Karelia and Sakha have nonetheless been vocal in their advocacy of sovereignty, and critical of attempts by the Yeltsin administration to reassert federal control over the republics.

Are presidents of Republics such as Karelia and Sakha adopting such demanding positions out of their own instrumental and predatory concerns? Did they lead states with the potential for healthy economic development independ-ent of Moscow, which would allow each of them greater access to rents than they previously had? Among the instrumental variables that would support this interpretation, possession of natural resources is positively and significantly related to a state elite's position on the autonomy index, and is no doubt highly influential in the case of Sakha, rich in all categories, but especially diamonds and gold. It does not, however, help explain Karelia's Stepanov, however, whose region was rich in timber but little else.

Of the measures used to capture the position of the relative deprivation school, being publicly declared a Critically Depressed Region by the Center did seem to be related to a state elite's willingness to demand autonomy from the center, as does the previous administrative status of the region, which attempted to measure the political and organizational resources of state elites. However, while most of the approaches examined provided some insight into the behavior of the ethno-nationalists, in both their political and civic attire, they were much less helpful in differentiating between federalists and antifederalists, that is, between those adopting a two and a three on the autonomy scale.

The missing pieces of the puzzle are most likely found in the relation-ship between the masses and their local executives. Not only are elites not al-ways autonomous actors, free from public pressure either to be more demanding or to be cautious in asserting demands for autonomy, but certain aspects of the political process can be expected to play a role. Further research in the wake of elections in all the regions and republics would be required to note if popular election, rather than federal appointment, emboldens or quells the demands of regional elites. The defeat of over half the incumbent governors in 1996 and 1997, including several notable and visible autonomy seekers in the republics, may serve notice to those elites who had not correctly calculated the federal preferences of their constituencies.

Additionally, the individual political ambitions of the governors also need to be assessed as a potential explanatory factor. Ordeshook (1996) noted that an important element in the evolution to a stable federal republic involves the integration of local political leaders' ambitions into the national political arena. Local leaders with national ambitions must feel they have a stake in the federal system and that they can benefit from cooperating with the federal center, not just from challenging it. This may only happen when regional elites see governorships and senatorships as legitimate stepping-stones to a career in national-level politics, as Ordeshook claims they are in other successful federations. The recent electoral strategy of former presidential candidate Aleksandr Lebed to run for and win the governorship of Krasnoyarsk as he reaffirms his presidential aspirations may be indicative of the trend.

While the center continues to demand compliance with its decrees, condemning unilaterally the recent statements by Kalmykian President Iliumzhinov regarding his state's ability to secede if not heard, the Siberian states have already begun to develop independent means of cooperating and resolving local issues, especially as they pertain to the environment and foreign investment. Meanwhile, other local governors are issuing their own local *skrit* to deal with the payment arrears crisis in their regions, given financial collapse in Moscow. These governors' vision of the Federation's future is very far afield from that of the unruly parliamentary chambers of Moscow, and a thousand miles from the battlefields of the North Caucasus. In the current state of economic malaise, it is almost certain that this unsupervised differential federal evolution will continue until someone replaces the tired administration of Boris Yeltsin. Unfortunately, as this chapter indicates, the only viable alternative candidates are those with visions for a federal center much stronger than the average state leader.

NOTES

1. Riker (1964, 12-13) suggests that the center offers the bargain in order to expand without the use of force, usually because of a perceived threat. Those who accept the terms of the bargain, giving up some autonomy at the time, do so because they, too, perceive themselves strengthened against some military threat. He argues that these conditions are "necessary" for the striking of the bargain.

2. After the annexation of Tuva in 1944, the only territorial changes resulted from the wartime policy of deporting entire nationalities out of their ethnic homelands. Additionally, some autonomous entities were "demoted" and "repromoted" throughout

the Soviet era. An example would be Karelia, which from 1940 to 1956 existed as the Karelo-Finnish SSR, and was later demoted to an ASSR after 1956 (Sheehy 1991, 63).

3. See the following quotation attributed to Martin Malia in Fleron and Hoffman (1993): "It is precisely because during the past twenty-odd years mainline Western Sovietology has concentrated on the sources of Soviet stability as a mature industrial society with a potential for pluralist development that it has prepared us so poorly for the present crisis."

4. For purposes of clarity, I will use the term "state" whenever referring to any or all of the members of the Federation without reference to their administrative status or ethnic composition. The term ethnic state will refer to any of the three ethnic administrative units (ASSRs, autonomous *oblasts*, or autonomous *okrugs*). The term region or territorial formation will be used generically to refer to any of the nonethnic states in the Federation.

5. For more details on the range, standard deviation, and median states positions, see Dowley 1998, 359-380.

Chapter 5

Complexity Matters: The Re-distribution of Authority in Spain and Portugal

Jeanie J. Bukowski

The functions of governance in Europe increasingly are seen to be carried out by political and administrative units at a variety of levels, from the supranational European Union (EU) level to the local. The central state is seen by many analysts to be losing authority and competencies to other entities both above and below it. Myriad studies are devoted to ascertaining the particular distribution of competencies and governing authority among levels (both within states and considering the wider structure of the EU), explaining this distribution, and analyzing and predicting the possible effects of the distribution of authority for governance at all levels.[1]

Within European states, a general trend toward the creation and/or reform of substate governments, and the transfer of governing authority and competencies to those governments, has been documented.[2] France, Italy, Spain, and Belgium are but four European examples in which subnational governments have been created and/or reformed, and competencies transferred downward to these regional and local authorities, since the 1970s. Even in Britain, one of the most centralized of European governments, there is evidence that substate entities may be playing a more important decision-making role, particularly within the scope of EU initiatives (Marks 1993). These decentralizing trends, however, are not universal. A striking illustration of the continued consolidation of central authority is the recent rejection in a Portuguese national referendum of a plan to regionalize the country. Moreover, even within European states that have shown overall trends toward decentralization, the process is not always steady or uniform. Rather, there is pulling and tugging between the center and substate units, with the center at times reconsolidating authority in at least some areas of governance.

It is difficult to analyze the potential causes and effects of the diffusion of authority within the state because of the lack of a coherent approach to studying the phenomenon. A body of literature exists in several disciplines devoted to themes such as regionalism, federalism, decentralization, and territoriality. Yet there has been very little effort to develop a unified conceptualization. "Rather like guests at a badly organized dinner party," points out Christopher Harvie, extant studies tend to speak not to, but rather alongside one another (1994, x).

This chapter seeks to provide an analysis of the re-distribution of authority that takes into account both decentralizing and centralizing trends. An attempt will be made to cross the boundaries in the varied literatures by first identifying the main explanatory factors put forth in the most prominent works. Then, rather than determine the presence or absence of the explanatory factors indicated, it is more important to analyze how these factors interact to produce either centralizing or decentralizing tendencies in the distribution of authority.

These factors, and their interaction, will be evaluated through a comparative case study of the shifting of governing authority within Spain and Portugal from the end of their respective dictatorships to the present time. A comparison of Spain and Portugal is particularly useful. These states are similar in several respects: Both experienced nearly half a century of authoritarian, centralized government after long periods of monarchical rule and short-lived experiments with republican regimes. Both joined the European Community (EC) in 1986; both confront similar economic difficulties and structural problems (although Portugal is relatively less developed), and therefore both have qualified for high levels of EC/EU structural funds assistance. Against the backdrop of these similarities, differences in the speed and direction of decentralization in both of these states in the postauthoritarian period helps us to better evaluate the utility of the various explanatory factors examined.

A VARIETY OF LITERATURES AND OVERLAPPING EXPLANATORY FACTORS

The diverse literature that addresses the shifting of authority within and outside the state in Europe includes the work on decentralization, regionalism, federalism, and multilevel governance. An examination of these literatures shows that each contains explanations for the diffusion of governmental authority, and that these explanatory factors at times overlap.

Decentralization/Regionalism

The literature addressing decentralization and substate regionalism is diverse in its conceptualizations, approaches, and scope of analysis. Much of this body of work has been directed toward the study of Europe, and even within this area there is much diversity.

Several studies provide evidence that regional and local governmental entities in Europe have been created and/or reformed in ways that have increased their authority, as measured by the indicators of institutional capacity, functional scope, and resources, particularly since the 1970s (Bukowski 1996; Sharpe 1993b; Norton 1994; Engel and Van Ginderachter 1993). While substate authorities in some countries (for example Germany and Belgium) obviously have more governing authority than in others (such as the United Kingdom and Portugal), the decentralization trend generally obtains. The 1997 constitutional change in the UK that devolved authority to Scotland and Wales is an example of this trend in even very centralized states.

We can identify five general categories of explanatory factors that are hypothesized in this literature as contributing to regionalism or decentralization. They are: (1) a societal reaction against political, administrative, and economic centralism; (2) overload of the central state apparatus in the face of increasing service delivery, welfare, and efficiency demands; (3) territorially based differentials in economic development; (4) cultural, ethnic, linguistic, and/or religious cleavages within the state; (5) pressures leveled by substate (primarily governmental) actors against the central state apparatus. A brief discussion of each category follows.

Reaction to Political and Economic Centralism. This explanation for decentralization involves pressures on the central state from societal and governmental actors, stemming from an adverse reaction to administrative and economic centralization. This reaction may result from a desire to throw off the vestiges of authoritarianism. Sharpe, for example, cites the ideological association of decentralization with enhanced democracy (1993a, 14-15).

Furthermore, such pressures may arise from a more general reaction to the centralization in both political-administrative and economic structures that has characterized capitalist industrial development (Hueglin 1986, 448). Hueglin postulates that as the nation-state's role as guardian of its citizens' economic and security interests is increasingly challenged by the threat of nuclear weapons and global economic interdependence, the difficulties involved in running a "highly complex industrial democracy" under conditions of "turbulence"[3] increase. The only means of successfully administering such a society may be to create interdependent and nonhierarchical forms of interaction among "horizontally associated subsystems," rather than through a centralized organization of the state (455). Substate, societal pressures on the center, then, are a rational, logical response to the complexities of the modern state. Similarly, Keating argues that "peripheral regionalism" may well be "a mechanism used by dynamic, modernizing forces against an archaic center" (1988b, 18).

Off-Loading and Blame-Shifting. This category of causal factors is very closely related to the first. The first involves pressure from governmental and societal actors stemming from dissatisfaction with the economic and political centrality of the system, and the perceived inefficiencies and/or the lack of democracy that this system creates. Presumably the center will react to these demands by transferring at least some functions and powers to lower levels.

The explanation of off-loading implies a need on the part of the center to rid itself of duties and responsibilities that it cannot perform efficiently because of the increasing complexity of modern society and its demands. Blame-shifting is more explicitly political. The center may find it expedient to off-load politically distasteful functions, such as tax collection or certain types of service delivery, so that citizen dissatisfaction is directed at lower levels. The off-loading/blame shifting factor in decentralization would involve functions that the center may give up regardless of whether there exists specific substate pressure to do so.

Sharpe (1988, 1993a), for example, hypothesizes that the central government will find it necessary to create substate levels of government in order to cope with urbanization and new public service responsibilities of the modern state, such as education, health, and transportation. This type of analysis implicitly makes the assumption, maintained by Hayek and other neoliberal economists, that local knowledge, and thus decentralization, is necessary to the efficient functioning of the market (Hayek 1948, 55-64). Moreover, the center will find it expedient to "use" lower levels of government in order to avoid public resistance to increased taxation by divesting itself of many of these service responsibilities.

Territorially Based Economic Differences and Center/Substate Tensions. Another category of causal factors links decentralization to territorial differentials in economic development. Much of the literature is informed by theories of development economics and core-periphery analysis. Stohr and Taylor, for example, hypothesize that a necessary condition for the economic development of "disadvantaged" regions within the state may be to decentralize both economic and political decision-making power (1981, 10). The implication of this analysis is that poorer regions would have more of an incentive to demand decentralization, in order to take charge of policies that might improve their lot. Broadening the analysis, scholars such as Hebbert and Machin argue that, due to the rise of the "corporate economy," regional authorities (in both rich and poor areas) have the incentive to become territorial pressure groups, lobbying for "their" enterprises within the national and international economy, and also that there may be more opportunities for regional authorities to make economic policy due to the failure of national regional policy (1984, 9).

Keating (1988a) and Hueglin (1986) both provide evidence that it is the relatively richer, rather than poorer, regions that exert greater pressure on the center for decentralization of authority. Contrary to the core-periphery analyses, these studies suggest that better-off regions (such as Catalonia or Northern Italy) may have stronger incentives for pursuing a more independent policy of economic development than their worse-off counterparts, and also may be in a more advantageous position to make these demands on the center.

Ethno-nationalist Cleavages and Demands from Substate Units. This line of analysis seeks to determine the nature of territorial differences and how ethnic, historic, religious, linguistic, and/or cultural differences explain various types of demands and behavior (political pressure, protests, violence) directed toward the center. Further, this literature explores how these demands may affect the center's policies. This is different from the first category of causal factors. "Reaction to centralism" assumes a general backlash from societal actors (which presumably could include ethnic, linguistic groups) based on demands for increased efficiency in the delivery of services. The current category puts forth explanatory factors regarding why certain ethnic or cultural groups would react against the center and/or each other. The interrelatedness to the other factors already discussed again becomes apparent. The conditions put forth as explanations for ethnic group reaction include uneven economic development and perceptions of relative deprivation (Thompson and Rudolph 1989, 4).

Federalism

The federalism literature is diverse in setting forth definitions, characteristics, and explanatory factors. Whether one classifies particular states as federal depends largely on what one's initial assumptions are within this diverse literature regarding the definition of federation. For the purposes of this chapter, it is not so important to try to categorize states as federal or unitary. A more useful endeavor is to describe and explain how and why authority is distributed in these states the way that it is, and why this distribution might change. To the extent that the concept of federalism provides factors to explain this phenomenon, it is useful. Most of the factors that appear relevant, such as considering federalism as a means of accommodation and conflict resolution in ethnically, culturally, and/or linguistically diverse states (see, for example, Elazar 1987; Smith 1995; and Bowman and Dowley in this volume) are also encompassed in the regionalism/decentralization literature.

Federalism is useful in an examination of the cases discussed here, inasmuch as it helps us to understand the lines drawn and the political debates that have influenced the process of re-distribution. Whether or not Spain or Portugal can be categorized as "federal" is less important to the current study than how federalism has been used as a political argument to influence the distribution and re-distribution of authority.

Multilevel Governance

The multilevel governance perspective has been developed primarily in the context of the European Union, as a conceptual framework within which to analyze the apparent diffusion of authority from the central state both upward and downward, to suprastate institutions and substate entities (Marks 1993; Marks, Hooghe, and Blank 1996). The primary emphasis of this approach has been to demonstrate that multilevel governance indeed exists (that is, independent actors are operating above and below the state that constrain state action), and to determine the effects that the diffusion of authority may have on governance and decision-making in the EU. Regarding explanations for this diffusion of authority, multilevel governance is concerned largely with why states would allow competencies to shift to EU institutions, although some of these explanations are applicable to the transfer of authority downward as well.

In their "actor-centered approach," Marks, Hooghe, and Blank consider elected politicians in the central state executive, rather than a reified state. They cite two sets of reasons why these governmental leaders might shift decision-making authority to particularly the suprastate level. First, the benefits of reallocating competencies may outweigh the costs. While costs, especially loss of sovereignty, are present, the benefits gained, in terms of the "efficient delivery of collective policies," motivate leaders to transfer authority to the suprastate level. Second, there may be intrinsic benefits to reallocating authority upward (or downward). Leaders may do so, for example, to avoid responsibility for unpopular policies (blame-shifting) and/or to insulate the decision-making process from political pressures (1996, 347–350).

This approach is considered to be an alternative to intergovernmental bargaining or state-centric perspectives, and it has in the last few years become a routine part of the debate in EU studies fora. Multilevel governance does not deny the continued importance of the central state as an actor and decision-maker. It does, however, reject the assumption that central state governments have a monopoly on decision-making or the aggregation of domestic interests. Rather, the state must increasingly share decision-making competencies with actors at levels both above and below it. This view allows for the interaction of substate authorities (primarily regional governments and interests) both with the central state government in the domestic arena and also directly with EU institutions, other substate entities, and trans-state associations in the European arena (Marks, Hooghe, and Blank 1996, 346–347). The two processes of decentralization and integration affect each other in important ways, as direct links develop between suprastate and substate actors (see also Marks, Nielsen, Ray, and Salk 1996).

DECENTRALIZATION IN SPAIN AND PORTUGAL

It is well documented in the case of post-Franco Spain that authority has been transferred from the center to substate regional governments (for example, Cuchillo 1993; Maravall 1993; Martín-Retortillo ed. 1989; Morata

1991). In Portugal, while provisions for regionalization have been made in the postauthoritarian constitution, this process has proceeded much more slowly than in Spain. Moreover, limited authority has been transferred largely to the local, rather than the regional level (Opello 1993; Pereira 1991, 1995). This section will revisit and compare the process of authority re-distribution in both states, with the purpose of evaluating the explanatory power of the factors put forward in the literatures discussed above.

Spain: A Democratic Diffusion of Authority

Spain's conversion to democracy has been characterized as a *ruptura pactada* in the transitions literature; that is, the transition from authoritarian rule did not occur through a radical break with the previous regime, or because the authoritarian regime transformed itself. Rather, "it was the product of a series of pacts and negotiations in which several political actors were the key protagonists" (Maravall and Santamaría 1986, 73). The dynamics, causes, and consequences of the transition in Spain have been treated extensively and compared to the process in the other Southern European states, Latin America, and Eastern Europe (see O'Donnell, Schmitter, and Whitehead, eds. 1986; Diamond, Linz, and Lipset, eds. 1989; Karl and Schmitter 1991; Di Palma 1990; Linz and Stepan 1996). The focus here is on the decentralizing dynamic of the process.

One of the primary elements of the transition and consolidation of democracy in Spain has been a decentralization of the unitary state. Regional divisions figure most prominently here. The transfer of authority to the local level is also present, but regional decentralization was at the heart of the debate between opposing political actors during the transition period and the consolidation of democracy. This conflict continues to enter current political debates.

Pressures for decentralization came from a variety of sources during the transition period but may be characterized primarily as either general societal pressures in response to the economic and political centralism of the regime, or more specific regional autonomy demands, particularly from Spain's "historic nationalities." Many of the strict centralist controls on both political freedoms as well as the economy had been eased in reforms beginning in the late 1950s and early 1960s. These reforms were not enough, however, to avoid a widespread challenge to the legitimacy of the regime, which intensified in the early 1970s. Support for decentralization existed to a large extent in most sectors of Spanish society—centralism was associated with the repression of the Franco regime and therefore devolution of authority with democracy.

More specific regional autonomy demands accompanied the general sentiment in favor of decentralization. The historic nationalities (Catalonia, the Basque Country, and Galicia) that had been granted autonomy during the Second Republic (1931-1936) pressed for an arrangement that would devolve powers to regional assemblies.   While the nationalist movements demanded increased autonomy at the regional level, local government officials and supporters envisioned an increased political role in the new democracy as well.   Regional autonomy has been given priority over increased local powers, however, which has created tensions among these substate levels.

Opposition to the devolution of authority, particularly greater regional autonomy, came primarily from members of the armed forces and the conservative "Bunker" of centralist politicians who viewed themselves as guardians of the territorial integrity and unity of the Spanish state.   National politicians and bureaucrats, fearing infringement on their policies and power bases, also opposed increased decentralization of authority (Keating 1988a, 187).

Given the strong forces with varying opinions on how to deal with the so-called regional problem in the transition, the political actors engaged in negotiation and compromise.   The result of this political pulling and hauling was a solution whose basis was institutionalized legally in the constitution and in subsequent basic laws and statutes.   The ambiguity of the formal legal structure necessitated by the delicate balance of opposing political forces is still apparent in the debates among actors at various levels regarding distribution of competencies, authority, and finances.

The constitution became the primary tool for building the agreement among opposing groups regarding the re-distribution process in Spain.   Right-leaning elements would not accept an explicitly federal solution or the immediate restoration of the Basque and Catalan autonomy statutes from 1931, but there was a consensus among politicians in most of the major political parties that the regions should have access to at least limited autonomy (Clark 1987, 144).   The result of negotiations was the *estado de las autonomías* (state of the autonomies).   This compromise was enshrined in the 1978 constitution and subsequent autonomy statutes, and provided avenues through which all regions, not just the historic nationalities, could attain autonomy.

This arrangement was palatable for nearly all actors concerned.   Some nationalist parties considered the generalization of the process to all regions as a way of neutralizing the opposition of the armed forces to possible Basque and Catalan separatism, while allowing these regions to push for special privileges in the subsequent statutes.   Most of the conservative elements did view this generalization as a way of diluting Basque and Catalan nationalist aspirations and subsequently promoted the equality of all regions.   Other areas in Spain supported the opportunity to gain autonomy, and the leftist parties saw the decentralization process as a means of making the regime more democratic by dismantling the centralized structures of the state bureaucracy.   The constitution was passed almost unanimously by the *Cortes* (the Spanish parliament), with only members of the Basque Nationalist Party (PNV) abstaining and some conservative Popular Alliance (AP) members opposing it (Maravall and Santamaría 1986, 87-88).

The Spanish constitution rests on a fundamental contradiction by guaranteeing two potentially conflicting concepts of the Spanish state: "the indissoluble unity of the Spanish Nation" as well as "the right to self government of the nationalities and regions of which it is composed" (Intro., Art. 2). The tension between center and peripheries has driven Spanish politics since the consolidation of Spain as a nation-state, but particularly since the late eighteenth century. This contradiction was brought to the legal and political center of Spanish politics for the first time through the 1978 constitution. Political compromise resulted in a document that laid out a fluid process of decentralization. This flexibility, a major factor in the peaceful transition to democracy, subsequently has resulted in ambiguities and conflicts among the central and various substate governments and in continuous negotiations within the basic legal framework.

The process of decentralization in Spain continues to be characterized by political pulling and hauling and shifting of relative authority among the national, regional, and local levels, but the long-term general trend has been toward greater substate autonomy. This process has had a piecemeal nature. The transfer of competencies to the various Autonomous Community governments has not been uniform; rather it is based primarily on bilateral negotiations with the central state. While Spain displays federal characteristics, there is disagreement regarding whether or not Spain is a federal or even a "federalizing" state.[4]

Once the initial bargain was in place specifying how regions could obtain autonomous status and which competencies in general would be eligible for transfer from the center,[5] a period of "autonomy fever" ensued, as both the regions with a tradition of nationalist sentiment (especially Catalonia and the Basque Country), as well as those without such a tradition (for example, Andalusia and Extremadura), rapidly moved forward with their autonomy statutes. By early 1983, statutes had been approved in all seventeen autonomous regions, and regional government structures were in place (Clark 1987, 148).

In very general terms, the subsequent process of re-distribution can be characterized by the central state government proceeding cautiously and attempting to limit and "homogenize" the process, on the one hand, and the regional authorities demanding the transfer of authority in more policy areas, on the other. The process slowed considerably after the 1981 coup attempt by conservatives in the armed forces, which led the major national parties to sign an Autonomy Pact proposing to limit the powers that could be devolved to the regions. The law resulting from this pact (LOAPA) was largely rejected as unconstitutional by the Constitutional Court in 1983 (Cuchillo 1993, 220).

The period since the early 1980s has been characterized by continued negotiation among the various parties as well as conflicts regarding state versus regional authority, evidenced by the large number of appeals brought before the Constitutional Court by both central and regional institutions (Barnés Vazquez

1994). Progress was made on devolving further competencies specified in the constitution in a 1992 Autonomy Pact between the governing Socialists (PSOE) and the opposition Popular Party (PP). In 1994, a historic Senate session approved, in principle, amending the constitution in order to allow this body to become a chamber of regional representation (Romero 1994, 11).[6]

The changing electoral fortunes of Spain's major national parties, and the rise in prominence of the Catalan regional nationalist party, Convergence and Union (CiU), have been a major catalyst in shifting the balance of power toward those who support further transfer of authority to the regions. The PSOE failed to win an overall majority in the *Cortes* in the 1993 elections. Jordi Pujol, CiU leader and president of the Catalan regional government, the *Generalitat*, engineered a legislative pact between the PSOE and the CiU, giving the Socialists a governing coalition with a slim majority. The CiU withdrew its support in 1995, due partly to a series of scandals involving PSOE officials and the decline in popular support for the Socialists. In the subsequent 1996 elections, the opposition PP finished ahead of the PSOE, but fell twenty seats short of an outright majority. After two months of bilateral negotiations, PP leader José María Aznar secured the support of the CiU, the Basque Nationalist Party (PNV), and the Canaries Coalition (CC), in return for promises of greater regional autonomy. Notably, the PP agreed to transfer more powers to the regions in several policy areas as well as modify the system of taxation and financing (Enesco 1996). It is perhaps ironic that the PP, which has traditionally opposed Basque and Catalan nationalism and upheld the ideal of Spanish unity, now finds it politically necessary to agree to measures that are likely to enhance regional authority.

The political pulling and hauling between the center and substate levels continues. In September 1998, the principle nationalist parties of Catalonia, the Basque Country, and Galicia conceived and signed the so-called Barcelona Declaration, in which they proposed a reform of the Spanish Constitution that would expand the possible competencies to be transferred to the Autonomous Communities. An initial draft of this document even called for the transition of the Spanish state from a "federal" to a "confederal" system, but this language was dropped in the final version. Both the PP and the PSOE have rejected a modification of the constitution, with the only exception being the adaptation of the Senate to convert it to a body of regional representation. The focus of these two parties is on the "finalization" of the state of the autonomies, resulting from the transfer to the regions of a few remaining competencies (such as public health) specified in the constitution, a modification of the system of regional finance, and further transfer of competencies from the regional to the local level (Aizpeolea 1999).

Portugal: Failed Regionalization?

Portugal's transition from dictatorship to democracy is also analyzed extensively and is usually compared to that of Spain. The former's conversion was also a *ruptura*, or a break with the past, in which the coup d'état carried out by the left-wing Armed Forces Movement (MFA) effectively neutralized the far-right elements of the *Estado Novo* dictatorship (1933-1974). After a rocky period of transition (1974-1976) which included three elections, six transitional governments, and two failed coup attempts, Portugal's political and military elites agreed on the formation of a Western-style democracy (Manuel 1998).

The Portuguese transition is characterized by the lack of an urgent, strong, and united elite and societal demand for decentralization, particularly on an ethnic, linguistic, or historic basis. In comparison to Spain, Portugal is characterized by a great degree of ethnic and linguistic homogeneity.[7] Historic differences have tended to be based more on economic factors, as economic hardship and opportunities tend to fall unevenly across the Portuguese territory. There is a north-south division: the north is more densely populated, with a low rate of urbanization, while the south tends to be more sparsely populated (with the exception of the coastal Algarve), and more urbanized. An even more important dichotomy exists between the coastal fringe (between Setúbal and Braga, and including the major cities of Lisbon and Oporto), and the interior. Encompassing only about twenty-nine percent of the total surface area of the country, the coastal fringe contains approximately two-thirds of the population and employment opportunities, and three-fourths of the gross value added (Gaspar 1976; Regional Disparities 1994; Covas 1997).

Some scholars have disputed the "homogeneous Portugal" characterization on the grounds that there are very strong cultural and ideological cleavages that tend to be drawn along territorial lines, as evidenced by differences in ideological leaning, party identification, and religiosity (see Baum 1998). Others have pointed to a long history of federalist proposals and writings in mainstream Portuguese politics, although these suggestions have rarely been put into practice (Martins 1998). Portugal does have a long tradition of varying degrees of local governmental autonomy, particularly at the level of the municipality (Birmingham 1993, 13, 20). During the *Estado Novo*, however, provincial and municipal structures were utilized strictly as a means of local implementation of national policy, notwithstanding administrative codes that granted a significant amount of decision-making authority to substate governments (Opello 1993, 162-163).

Despite similar economic problems and inadequate provision of public services in Spain and Portugal, the latter experienced much less effective societal mobilization and public protest than had arisen in Spain in the later years of the Franco regime. Opposition to the *Estado Novo* came largely from the elite—both exiled opposition leaders (such as Socialist Mario Soares) and from within the corporatist structure. The immediate cause of the Revolution of 1974 that brought down the forty-eight-year dictatorship was the frustration engendered in the Portuguese Army by the continuing wars against independence movements in the African colonies (Maxwell 1986, 109).

Decentralization demands, while clearly not as strong or urgent as those in Spain, did affect the immediate transition agreements. As in Spain, the constitution of the newly democratic Portugal, promulgated in 1976, specified a transfer of authority to local governments, as well as the creation of a system of regional government. The 1982 and 1989 constitutional reforms confirmed these specifications, and for much of the postdictatorship period there has been general support among many of the political protagonists and elites, again as in Spain, for a process of decentralization to counter the political and economic centralism of the dictatorship.[8] Reforms have been implemented granting authority to local government. The mainland regional reforms, however, have not yet been realized, due to political and technical disagreements that persist among the major actors, which apparently to date outweigh the concerns for the re-distribution of authority downward.

The 1976 constitution describes Portugal as a unitary state, but allows for decentralization of the state and autonomy for substate units. Specifically, it provides for autonomous regions on the Azores and Madeira islands and maintains the existing local divisions of municipalities and parishes. The local government structures were to be reformed, however, in order to make them truly representative and answerable to their publics, rather than simply implementers of central government policy, as they had been during the *Estado Novo*. The constitution also calls for the creation of administrative regions on the mainland, which were designed as self-governing regional entities, but with less political autonomy than the autonomous island regions. "Other forms of autarkic territorial organization" in the "large urban areas" are also permitted (Article 238; see also Opello 1978; Opello 1993).

The Autonomous Regions of Azores and Madeira were created immediately after the 1976 constitution was approved, and their powers were developed through subsequent statutes of regional autonomy. These regions have both legislative and administrative power, along with the ability to collect and spend their own revenue (although their budgets are still largely determined by the central government). The Portuguese autonomous regions are more limited in their authority than their counterparts in Spain. The central government maintains control of the regions through its representative, the *Ministro da República* (Minister of the Republic), assigned to each region. The *Ministro* serves as the center's watchdog through his authority to countersign all legislation passed by the regional assembly and to veto and send back legislation to the assembly. Moreover, the Portuguese Constitution prohibits the formation of regional political parties (Opello 1993, 165).

The existing local governments were quickly given a democratic base after the transition, with elections first held in December 1976 under the Local Elections Act. Subsequent legislative action (such as the 1977 Local Government Act and the 1979 Local Finances Act) began to delimit the functions and autonomy of local government. Self-governing "metropolitan areas" were established in Lisbon and Porto in 1991. In reality, however, the central government has largely ignored the Local Finances Act, with the result that local governments are chronically underfunded.[9] Moreover, while there has been almost continuous discussion and debate since 1976 regarding the mainland administrative regions, these have not yet been created.

In addition to the association, in both elite and public opinion, of decentralization with democratization, the other major reason for the general consensus regarding a regionalization of Portugal has been the need to develop ways of dealing with the country's economic development problems, particularly the severe territorial inequalities that still persist (Opello 1993, 164). The agreement seems to stop there, however. The form that decentralization should take has been debated extensively, and involves almost all sectors of society, including the political parties, representatives of industry, the universities, public administrators, local authorities, and the media (Pereira 1995, 273).

A variety of political and technical reasons have combined to make the implementation of administrative regions impossible to this point. What the territorial composition of these regions should be has been one major stumbling block, with several different divisions of the country being proposed and discussed. In contrast to the Spanish case, support for decentralization from substate actors in Portugal, such as the National Association of Portuguese Municipalities (ANMP), has thus far failed to provide sufficient pressure to move the process forward.

The major national parties have in general been reluctant to strongly back regionalization, in part for fear that the administrative regions would give the opposition the opportunity to develop additional bases of support. This has been especially true in the case of non-Communist party leaders. The concern is that the region of Alentejo, in which the majority of municipal support still goes to the Communists, would provide the latter with a significant power base.[10]

The Social Democrats (PSD), who formed a minority government from 1985-1987, and a majority from 1987 until their defeat by the Sociality Party (PS) in 1995, consistently have opposed regionalization. Many members of the PSD express opposition to the idea of administrative regions altogether, not just disagreement with their form, arguing that Portugal is a homogenous, unified state without regional tensions and that the formation of administrative regions would promote divisiveness. They contend that regional development can be promoted without administrative regions, and that such regions would result in a significant increase in expenditure and duplication of services (Covas 1994). Despite this view, however, pressures from opposition parties, substate elites, societal actors, and EU initiatives resulted in the unanimous passage in 1991 of the Framework Law for Administrative Regions (Law 56/91) by the National Assembly. This law designated the creation of regional assemblies on the mainland and specified the constitutional articles for the regions (Pereira 1995, 269).

The Socialist Party (PS) adopted a pro-regionalist stance during its years in opposition. One of the party leaders' first actions after taking office in 1996 was to attempt to pass the enabling legislation needed to implement the 1991 framework law. The government, which is four seats short of an absolute majority, relied on the Communist Party (PCP) to pass a draft law in the face of opposition from the PSD. The law would have created nine regions with elected regional assemblies possessing power over local issues but without the right to raise taxes (McArthur 1996).[11] A law based on this draft was finally passed in 1998 (Law 19/98), which provided for implementation of Law 56/91, and specified eight territorially based regions as well as the competencies to be transferred to them (see Baum and Freire 1999; Kahan et al. 1999). It also called for a national referendum on the question of whether or not to establish these regions (the Portuguese Constitution had been revised in September 1997 to allow the referendum to decide the regional question).

The November 1998 referendum subsequently failed, primarily due to lack of support from most of the major political parties, even those who had at one time or another supported regionalization. The PSD engaged in active campaigns against the referendum, in a political move to try to discredit the PS's policies and improve their own political fortunes. Even the PS, a proponent of the reform while in opposition, was deeply divided, with eminent party member Mario Soares (former president of Portugal) lending his support to the "no" campaign. The PCP was the only party united behind creation of the regions, and even some of its more prominent members came out publicly against the idea. Public support of the measure declined in the face of negative television advertising on the part of decentralization's opponents, as well as voter confusion and uncertainty on the issues (Baum and Freire 1999).

So despite support, in principle, of the general public as well as many local elites for the idea of re-distribution of authority in Portugal,[12] opposition and/or ambiguity on the part of national political actors has thus far prevented regionalization. Another important factor here is that, unlike in Spain, where particularly the historic nationalities provided unquestionable boundaries for territorial division, in Portugal how to draw the map of decentralization is also contested.

In addition to the proposal for nine regions and the compromise choice of eight regions presented in the referendum (which was bitterly contested by some local leaders and residents), much discussion focuses on basing regionalization on the five already existing Commissions of Regional Coordination (CCRs). To many, these entities seem to be the logical basis for the territorial division of Portugal. The Salazar regime created the CCRs in 1979, in an attempt to improve economic development planning across Portugal (Opello 1993, 167-168). The CCRs are responsible for planning projects on a regional level, supporting municipalities, and coordinating activities with universities and business associations. Legally, they are strictly extensions of central government, but in practice they have taken on a regional identity and have to a certain extent served as a lobby for their territorial area at both the national and European levels. They have executive functions in urban and rural planning and coordinate their activities with municipalities in the selection of local projects to be financed by national and EU development funds, and they are involved in the implementation of these funds. Despite this activity, however, they are not locally elected or appointed, and remain units of the central government (Pereira 1995). Moreover, they are widely criticized for their bureaucratic complexity and inefficiency (Baum and Freire 1999, 7).

Antiregionalists tend to think that many CCR activities represent an extralegal exercise of competence, that they have promoted a regional identity that did not exist previously, and that they should be reined in. Some proregionalist politicians, on the other hand, believe that the CCRs may be delaying the implementation of the administrative regions by filling the gap with their current activities (Pereira 1995, 277-278).

Another political factor that may have affected the nonimplementation of administrative regions, at least in the earlier years of the Portuguese transition, is the initial opposition to these by many local authorities who feared that they would be more tightly controlled under regional authorities than they were under central authorities (Covas 1994; Pereira 1995). Support on the part of local elites for regionalization has steadily increased, however. Given the perceived failure of the current centralized system to meet the needs of the localities and their citizens, elites see reform of the system as more of an opportunity than a threat (though they continue to disagree on the exact form decentralization should take) (Baum and Freire 1999). A conflict among levels may still be witnessed in the autonomous island regions, where there is ongoing disagreement among the regional and municipal governments, with the latter at times accusing the former of excessive control (Nunes Silva 1994).

As the dust from the referendum on regionalization settles, it is not at all certain that the constitutional imperative of regionalization will someday be realized. The issues surrounding, and the pressures for, a re-distribution of authority are of course still present.[13] Whether the multidimensional political disagreements regarding the actual regionalization reform can be overcome in the future, however, remains to be seen.

RE-EVALUATING EXPLANATORY FACTORS: THE CASES OF SPAIN AND PORTUGAL

Upon application to the cases of Spain and Portugal, the lines blur among the explanatory factors set forth above. It is therefore not useful to try to study these factors separately. Rather, a more important endeavor is discerning their patterns of interaction. Toward this goal, a more helpful differentiation may be between the structural, not explicitly political factors (overload, inefficiencies of centralization, territorially based economic differences, and ethno-nationalist cleavages) and those factors involving political agency (societal reaction to centralism, demands from substate units, blame-shifting, interaction among levels). The patterns emerging from the study of postauthoritarian Spain and Portugal indicate that the structural or background factors create the conditions under which political actors (political parties, national and substate governmental and societal leaders) make demands on the system. These demands may produce either decentralizing or centralizing tendencies. Moreover, the differences in the scope and pace of decentralization in the two states may be explained largely through differences in the structural factor of ethno-nationalist cleavages and the agency factors of societal reaction and substate demands.

Economic Inefficiencies and Overload/Societal Reaction

The decentralization of Spain was an essential component of the postauthoritarian transition. As we have seen, strong societal pressures against both the economic and political centrality of the Franco regime contributed to the regionalization process. These pressures stemmed from a variety of concerns on the part of societal and governmental actors at all levels. In Portugal, societal reaction against the dictatorship was neither as strong nor as unified as in Spain. Decentralization in Portugal was not as crucial to the transition process as in Spain. Nonetheless, increased local autonomy and proposed regionalization have figured prominently in Portuguese governance and politics since 1974.

The economic conditions and difficulties in both the Franco and Salazar regimes were very similar and elicited largely the same policy responses from these very centralized regimes. Early on, both leaders followed strategies of economic nationalism and autarky, with disastrous consequences. Through the 1940s and 1950s, both economies stagnated, industry developed slowly and erratically, and misallocation of resources, balance of payments constraints, and inefficient production prevailed (Donges et al. 1982, 33-34).

Both regimes ended their experiments with autarky in the late 1950s. In Spain, the goals of the subsequent Stabilization Plans (beginning in 1959) were to speed industrialization and to reintegrate Spain into the world economy.

The ambiguous attitude of the national government toward substate levels—the need for development plans that could be implemented at a level below the center, but the fear of ceding any type of authority to the local or regional levels—is illustrated in Franco's National Plans for economic development in the 1960s and 1970s. These plans deliberately left out any mention of the word "region," but they were in reality based on a need for implementation at a regional level.[14]

Similarly, the various national economic plans implemented in Portugal recognized regional disparities and included a regional component. In the Third Plan (1968–1973), the government organized bases for regional planning policy due to pressure from national technicians, rather than as a result of any local or regional demands. The regional planning committees created had no autonomy or local participation. Most of the regional development projects were drawn up in Lisbon, a few of which were then implemented through the national structures located at the local or regional level (Gaspar 1976, 32).

In Spain, the inability of the centralized system to meet increasing demands for efficient delivery of services was demonstrated even more toward the end of the regime, particularly in large urban areas. The reforms managed to spur economic growth, but the centralized structures of the regime were incapable of handling the increasing social welfare and functional demands brought on by this growth. Rapid industrialization, migration from rural areas, and accelerated urban expansion contributed to demands for new public services and better infrastructure in almost all functional policy areas, including education, housing, social welfare, health, and transportation. Regional economic disparities also increased during this period (Cuadrado Roura 1981). Well-organized protest movements encompassing a wide variety of groups (such as urban neighbors' associations, trade unions, and students) were prevalent in the early 1970s. The regime intensified repressive tactics from 1968 to 1973, which curbed the union and working-class movements but had the effect of mobilizing larger societal groups, such as elements of the Church and university students and faculty (Clegg 1987, 132; Maravall 1993, 5-6; Maravall and Santamaría 1986, 78).

After Franco's death, the historic nationalities effectively incorporated these service delivery and efficiency concerns into their political demands for decentralization. Regional political reaction was mobilized not only against economic centralism and inefficiencies but also against the suppression of minority rights. Regional politicians generally were supported in their initial demands for decentralization by their own publics as well as societal and political elites, especially in major urban areas, who were dissatisfied with the economic situation and associated devolution of authority with democratization.

Despite some positive effects of the Portuguese development plans during the *Estado Novo*, economic indicators (such as per capita income, health services, and education) remained the worst in Western Europe, and territorial differences also persisted or were aggravated. What gains were made in areas such as wages, better medical facilities, and greater educational opportunities were increasingly concentrated in the two urban industrial areas of Lisbon and Porto, while "change, in the rural areas [as well as in the Azores and Madeira] was principally associated with people leaving them."[15] Development in the cities resulted in the same kinds of inadequacies in providing public services in these areas as the problems witnessed in the large urban areas in Spain, such as insufficient housing and transportation systems and lack of adequate sanitation. During the final years of the dictatorship, Salazar's successor, Marcelo Caetano, (in his attempt at "renewal in continuity" and "evolution without revolution"), implemented reforms that allowed more political freedoms and attempted to improve living standards, but these were largely viewed as too little too late (Robinson 1979, 165-173).

Persistent economic difficulties, as well as suppression of political freedoms, did elicit a significant societal response, especially on the part of student and church groups in the 1970s (Raby 1988). Unlike in Spain, however, the ethnic homogeneity of the Portuguese state precluded mobilization along ethnic or nationalist lines and protests in favor of minority rights, an element that appears crucial to the re-distribution process in Spain.

It is clear that the inability of the centralized systems in both Spain and Portugal to perform many of the essential functions of government, especially as economic development progressed, contributed to decentralization of many of these functions. Both the Franco and Salazar/Caetano regimes saw the need for a substate focus in their development programs, particularly to address territorial inequalities. It is likely that even in the absence of any societal pressures, the central government in both states would have found it necessary to deconcentrate or further off-load certain responsibilities to lower administrative levels after the demise of the dictatorships.

We see significant differences in the two states with regard to the factor of societal reaction to centralism. In Spain, high levels of societal mobilization, especially along regional and nationalist lines, contributed to the urgency of the decentralization process and the necessity of the constitutional compromise. Demands and protests from a wide cross-section of societal actors contributed to pressures on the central government to decentralize. Regional actors utilized this general discontent in order to support their demands for autonomy, which were based on concerns regarding both economic inefficiencies and political repression and discrimination. Because of such demands, as well as their effective utilization by political forces in the historic nationalities, the resulting compromise went much further than simply devolving or deconcentrating some functions. It moved the state toward a system of regional autonomy.

Despite similar inefficiencies and economic difficulties caused by Portuguese centralism, the extreme core-peripheries tension and mobilization of substate interests seen in Spain was not present in the relatively homogeneous Portuguese state. Reaction against the dictatorship was based more generally on economic development difficulties and suppression of political rights as well as opposition to the colonial wars; not on any perceived violation of minority, ethnic, or territorial-based rights. The difference in societal reaction to similar difficulties engendered by economic, and political centralism, then, helps to explain the difference in the pace and scope of the decentralization process in Spain and Portugal. The center-peripheries tension in Spain threatened the stability of the political, economic and social system, and therefore required an urgent solution. Portuguese elites and citizens also associated decentralization closely with the democratization process, and regionalization is, as in Spain, specified in the constitution. Despite this general consensus, pressures for decentralization have not been as intense in Portugal, because center-periphery conflicts historically have not been strong. In contrast to Spain, the structure of the Portuguese polity would not collapse even if the decentralization process did not proceed quickly.

Economic Efficiency Imperatives/Interlevel Tensions
and Blame-shifting

A few additional points must be made regarding economic efficiency imperatives and the political arguments that may accompany such imperatives. These may provide both decentralizing and/or centralizing (or re-centralizing) pressures, as well as conflict among and within levels of government. In Spain, the ambiguities of the constitutional compromise have made conflicts inevitable, and negotiations necessary, among the center and substate governments to decide which competencies would be transferred from the center to lower levels. The major argument of each governmental entity is that it will most efficiently manage the disputed competence. These same types of disagreements are also evident in Portugal. In the recent referendum, for example, supporters of regionalization argued that it would be a means of correcting regional economic development gaps and reforming the inefficient bureaucracy, while opponents maintained that only the central government had the ability to correct territorial economic disparities, that competition among different regions would reinforce these gaps, and that regionalization would increase and complicate bureaucracy rather than simplify it (Baum and Freire 1999).

That economic and/or service delivery imperatives may cause centralizing, as well as decentralizing pressures, and therefore partially account for the dynamic nature of the re-distribution process, is illustrated by the controversy over allocation of scarce water resources in Spain. The constitutional division of competencies grants overlapping and somewhat ambiguous authority to both the central and regional governments. During water shortages of the mid-1990s brought on by several years of drought, regional governments in the drier south of the country lobbied the government to develop a plan to transfer water from reservoirs in the relatively wetter north.   Madrid developed both long- and short-term plans that would involve this type of transfer and give the central state tighter control over policy and resource management of Spanish rivers and waterways.   This plan became subject to a high-profile conflict among three Autonomous Communities on the giving and receiving ends of the proposed water transfers.   The central government overruled the complaints of the northern Autonomous Community of Castilla-la Mancha, which then threatened to take the matter to the Constitutional Court (Mardones 1994).   Nature temporarily solved the problem with increased rainfall, but the debate continues.   Political and societal actors at all levels are pressuring the central government to develop a comprehensive water plan to avoid this type of conflict in the future, and leaders in the central government also have looked to the EU for aid in a long-term solution to water shortage and distribution problems (*European Report* 1995).

Economic Differentials and Ethno-Nationalist Cleavages/Interlevel Tensions and Substate Demands

It is too simplistic to attribute substate demands, the effectiveness of these demands, or the re-distribution process to center-periphery tensions based on economic differences.   In both Spain and Portugal there exist several peripheries, as well as peripheries within the periphery (that is, localities within the regions) which may be at odds over the decentralization process itself as well as competencies and policy.   A more realistic conceptualization might be that of changing coalitions, agreements, and conflicts among entities at various levels, depending on the issue being considered.   Moreover, territorial economic differences (either relative affluence or relative poverty) can interact in a complex way with ethnonationalist cleavages to produce varying demands on the central state for increased autonomy and varying responses by the center to those demands.   Based on these two cases, there is also evidence that both the presence of ethnonationalist tensions, as well as the influence of regional-based political parties and their ability to capitalize on these tensions, result in more rapid and far-reaching decentralization of authority.

Many Peripheries, and Both Centralizing and Decentralizing Pressures. In Portugal, the local level is more important than the regional because of the homogeneity of the state, the historical administrative division of the country along local rather than regional lines, and the ongoing inability to regionalize the mainland.   Indeed, some of the arguments against forming administrative regions are that their creation would promote unnecessary divisiveness in the homogeneous, unified state (Nunes Silva 1994).   Some of the earlier debates on regionalization involved a fear on the part of local government officials that regional authorities might constrain local autonomy to a greater extent than the central state, although this fear has abated more recently. The debates regarding the 1998 regionalization referendum indicated fairly widespread support on the part of local elites for decentralization, but there is still much disagreement over both the form this re-distribution of authority should take and the reasons why it should be implemented. Most local leaders express the hope that economic development and efficiency would improve with the reform. Others see regionalization as a way to counter what they perceive as the ability of the autonomous island regions to unfairly gain more than their share of the national budget by virtue of their constitutional status and ability to lobby the national and European levels (Nunes Silva 1994).

In Spain, both rich and poor regions have pressured the central government for more authority in relation to regional development and other policies, but the richer regions have been the most influential in the decentralization process. Moreover, we see even greater conflicts among the peripheries in Spain than in Portugal. An example of how the process of decentralization has been slowed by this type of internal substate disagreement in Spain is the ongoing debate regarding the percentage of income tax to be ceded to regional authorities. The central state has retained responsibility for a majority of total revenues, particularly income taxes, but this situation began to change because of regional pressure, first with agreements among central and regional officials in 1991, and more recently with the pact made by the central PP government with the regional CiU. A new financing system is being discussed, but an important obstacle to an agreement has been conflict among the regions themselves regarding the plan, primarily drawn along the lines of rich and poor regions.

The most recent proposal involves the central government ceding to the regions thirty percent of income taxes raised in their respective territories. The poorer regions argue that this plan is flawed because the thirty percent figure is based on averages over the entire state, not taking into account regional economic disparities or differences in levels of taxable income. Therefore, the uniform rate may favor the richer regions whose populations generate more income. The plan also specifies that at least thirty-five percent of new central state investment be channeled through the Interterritorial Compensation Fund (designed to redistribute resources to poorer areas), but the disadvantaged regions argue that this is not enough and that the proposed system will serve only to widen the economic differences that already exist between rich and poor Autonomous Communities (Aizpeolea 1998, 1994; Alavedra 1993; Díaz 1992).

Mobilization of Substate Demands and the "Creation" of Nationalism. In Spain, ethnic, nationalist differences have been a key variable in the decentralization process, particularly when these have been emphasized and utilized by effective territorially based political leadership. As we have seen, the longstanding conflicts between the center and particularly the historic nationalities, and these regions' demands in the transition period, contributed to the urgency of the decentralization process and the constitutional compromise. Subsequently, the influence of regional political parties has played an important part in the continuing process of transfer of authority to lower levels.

Political resources, such as public support for regional and local governments and the structure of the party system that has developed in the substate areas, also are important in the re-distribution process in Spain. Specifically regionalist parties have formed and are active to varying degrees in nearly all regions, campaigning at all levels of government.[16] During the transition years even national parties attempted to distinguish themselves as separate entities at the regional level; the Spanish Communist Party in the regions recast themselves as Andalusian or Valencian Communist Parties, for example. In most Spanish regions, national parties tend to dominate even in the Autonomous Community governments, but these parties must accommodate regionalist interests (Keating 1988a, 199). The only regional-nationalist parties that have been able to convert their regional dominance into a significant source of power at the national level, however, are the Catalan CiU and, to a lesser extent, the Basque PNV.

It also must be noted that while the constitutional compromise allowed for a peaceful transition, the Basque separatist movement ETA, supported by the political party Herri Batasuna (HB), has continued its demands for independence and its terrorist campaign against the central government (although a "cease fire" has been called by ETA during the past year). ETA has steadily lost public support, even within the Basque Country, since the fall of the dictatorship and the establishment of the system of Autonomous Communities. Citizens in all parts of Spain increasingly reject ETA's goals and tactics, and, if anything, the continued ETA demands and actions actually strengthen the central government's hand and result in support for centralizing measures emphasizing the unity of the Spanish state.[17]

The opportunity for regional parties, particularly the CiU, to enter national politics in the position of power broker since 1993 has had a major impact on the decentralization process. Advantageous political circumstances have allowed the CiU to effectively make autonomy demands on both the Socialist and Conservative governments. While there is disagreement among the regions regarding whether that which is good for the Catalans is also good for other regions, it is indisputable that the decentralization process has been accelerated because of the political deals that first the PSOE, and later the PP, have been forced to make with the CiU. Pressures for increased regional autonomy, regardless of ethnonationalist or economic bases, appear to be most effective under this type of enhanced political bargaining situation at the national level.

In Portugal, there is some territorial basis for political party support, but this is necessarily among national political parties, since the formation of regional parties is still prohibited by the constitution. With the exception of a brief period of separatist fervor in Azores and Madeira after the end of the dictatorship (Gallagher 1979), there are no important regional or local parties or movements in Portugal, as in Spain.

To summarize, in Spain, the presence of ethnonationalist divisions, coupled with economic inefficiencies and societal reaction to centralization, provided the conditions under which regional political parties could effectively use nationalist claims in addition to economic grievances to further decentralization. Indeed, the presence of ethnonationalist cleavages and the emergence of effective regional-based parties in Spain, and their absence in Portugal, helps to explain why the decentralization process has moved much more quickly, and is much more extensive, in the former state.

Nevertheless, while historic ethnic, nationalist-based territorial differences may be important, they are not a necessary condition for a region or locality to pressure the center for more autonomy. Rather, this is a dynamic process. In Spain, ethnonationalistic factors were quite significant during early stages of the transfer of authority, but once institutional units were established at lower levels, they provided a mobilization point and incentives for developing a regional consciousness even in areas that have no historic nationalist claims. Once developed, this newfound nationalism may in turn be used by political leaders to legitimize their demands on the center for further autonomy.

Rapid initiatives toward autonomy by the nonhistoric regions in Spain had been largely unanticipated. The necessary concessions to allow the historic nationalities to pursue the fast track to autonomy had the unintended consequence of creating tensions with the nonhistoric regions. The political elites in the latter regions, as well as the media, portrayed the two-tier system as offensive and discriminatory to those regions that would achieve autonomy through the "slow track" of Article 143 (Pérez Díaz 1990, 29-31).

A new regional consciousness, based on the desire for equal status with the Basque Country, Catalonia, and Galicia, emerged in areas of the country that had no previous experience with self-government or any significant ethnic, cultural, or linguistic differences from the center. In both poorer and richer areas, regional pride was accompanied by economic motivations and the belief that development would be better served at a lower level. Regional elites also anticipated the receipt of national and EU regional development funds. Supported widely by their publics, leaders in nonhistoric regions, not wanting to fall further behind the Basque Country and Catalonia either politically or economically, seized the opportunity presented by the constitutional structure to "ask for everything, if only to see, in the next moment, what this everything would consist of" (Acosta España 1981, 15).

In attempting to homogenize the process and curb the strength of the historic nationalities, centrist forces during the transition in Spain supported the autonomy demands of all regions. This in turn created a system in which it was possible for regional leaders to mobilize substate demands in areas that had no separate ethnic, linguistic, and/or historic claims (in the same sense as the historic nationalities). These leaders were able to create a regional consciousness in these areas, which in turn has been used to legitimize and strengthen further demands for autonomy.

As is reinforced by the Portuguese case, heterogeneity and historic regional conflict is not a necessary condition for efforts to decentralize. The devolution process in Portugal has moved at a much slower pace than in Spain, but has occurred to a certain extent, with the creation of the autonomous island regions, and the debate regarding further decentralization continues. Even a limited transfer of authority creates institutions around which local and regional political interests can mobilize, as evidenced by the activities and demands of the CCRs in Portugal. The formation of these bodies has given officials on these committees both an incentive and an organizational base from which to represent the interests of "their" region (Nunes Silva 1994). Given the cultural, economic, and social cleavages identified by Baum along geographic lines (1998), it is certainly possible that local elites with an interest in increasing the authority of their territory may in effect utilize these differences, along with economic grievances, to promote a sense of "nationalism" or substate identity in order to further the cause of greater regional or local autonomy.

A Role for the EU? Opportunities for Multilevel Interaction

It is undeniable that the EC/EU has played a role in the democratization of both Spain and Portugal.[18] The role of supranational institutions and integration in the decentralization debates and processes in these two states, however, is less clear. The EU has made explicit efforts to include substate entities in the decision-making processes. These efforts are encompassed primarily in the EU's regional development policy and programs and in the doctrine of "partnership" (which requires regional input in all stages of policymaking). Moreover, the stated goal of increased substate involvement was embodied in the creation (with the Treaty on European Union) of the Committee of the Regions as a formal EU institution, albeit without much real authority. Despite these efforts, member state central governments remain the only official representation in the main EU decision-making institutions (with the exception of the German *Länder* in some circumstances), and are largely the most influential.

Informal arrangements, however, especially between EU institutions and substate lobbying groups, and also the nature of implementation of EU policy, has allowed interaction between actors at the substate and suprastate levels that may be influencing the distribution of authority within states. More policy decisions are being made at the EU level that have a direct impact on regions and local areas, thereby giving actors at these levels an incentive to become involved in the policy process. The development of EC/EU regional policy since the mid-1970s, with increased opportunities and incentives for participation of substate actors, roughly parallels the decentralization of authority in European member states. There is thus a greater incentive and opportunity for substate actors to participate directly and indirectly in EU decision-making processes.

One example of this contact between suprastate and substate actors is the growing number of substate "information" offices in Brussels. There are over 100 offices representing local and regional interests.[19] None of these offices serves in any official government capacity, nor are they provided for formally in the EU institutional structure. They are organized under a wide variety of legal structures, many times incorporated as private development agencies or consortia bringing together representatives of the regional government with private sector interests, and they range widely in size. Nine of the seventeen Spanish Autonomous Community governments operate such offices in Brussels. The Basque and Catalan offices are the largest and best-organized, with the Basque office structured almost as a mini-embassy, and openly claiming to be representing the regional government, which has caused conflicts, and a legal battle, between the regional and the central government (see Coates 1998).

Regardless of their structures, the main functions of these offices are to serve as "antennae" for their regions or localities in Brussels and to promote their interests directly to the EU institutions, particularly the European Commission. Commission officials stress that they deal officially only with member state delegations in making policy decisions, since the internal structures of most states do not allow for representation outside these Brussels delegations (with the notable exception of the *Länder*). Nonetheless, they maintain frequent, direct contacts with the substate offices. The Commission staff is relatively small and must rely on information provided by member states. The regional offices often can provide the type of detailed information on local impact of projects, for example, that is not available from other sources. Moreover, Commission officials seem to welcome input from regions and local authorities as a counterbalance to information provided by member states.[20]

In turn, regional and local leaders view the EU as another channel of influence, outside of, and in addition to, their national government. Some of these leaders also envision the EU as providing a wider context within which nationalist or even separatist demands could be accommodated. The logic here, as argued in various forms by regional leaders in the Basque Country, Scotland, Northern Italy, and to some extent in Catalonia, is that in a free market not demarcated by state boundaries, in which decisions regarding foreign policy and defense eventually will be made at the EU level, and in which powers for policies such as education, health, and welfare have already been devolved to the substate level, autonomy or even independence is now possible for these smaller entities (Walker 1993). Central state leaders would hardly accept the argument that they have lost authority to the point that they are practically obsolete and unnecessary to the functioning of their substate components. Nevertheless, integration appears to have bolstered the arguments of regional leaders for increased autonomy, providing what these leaders see as a positive incentive for decentralization, as well as continued European integration.

The primary effect of the EU and the integration process on the re-distribution of authority within states appears to be to provide substate leaders both incentives and opportunities for mobilizing around regional policies and issues. It may also serve to add legitimacy to nationalist leaders' claims that their region could "go it alone" within the wider structure of the EU. EU efforts to enhance regional participation do not appear to be a sufficient factor in influencing decentralization within states. As we see in the case of Portugal, these efforts and incentives have not been an important consideration in the regionalization debate (and certainly did not prevent the recent failure of this initiative). But in Spain, where regional and local governments have been established and strengthened, EU institutions, policies, and initiatives provide substate leaders with a channel of influence outside the national government and a further means of legitimizing demands for increased autonomy.

RE-DISTRIBUTION OF AUTHORITY: TOWARD A NEW CONCEPTUALIZATION OF A COMPLEX PROCESS

It is impossible to separate causal factors into rigid categories and still have a realistic picture of the re-distribution of authority. All of the factors outlined in the literature have an effect on the process in Spain, and all but ethnonationalist cleavages are operating in Portugal. Within each of these states, however, the factors overlap and interact in ways that are not discerned in most analyses, and the same types of factors may result in either centralization or decentralization. Moreover, differences in the factors outlined can explain differences in the scope and extent of decentralization in the two states.

From the cases presented here, we may construct a model (pictured below in Figure 5.1) for evaluating this interaction of explanatory factors. Overload and inefficiencies associated with centralization, territorially based economic differences, and/or ethnonationalist cleavages (structural or background factors) result in societal reaction and tensions between the center and substate units and also among substate units (mediating factors). The presence of EU integration and institutions and EU incentives for regional actors also may be considered a mediating factor. How the various political actors at different levels utilize the conditions created by these tensions, responses, and opportunities in making their demands then determines whether decentralization or centralization occurs. This is a dynamic process. The mediating factors and the independent variable may have reciprocal effects (e.g., demands of regional leaders can rally public opinion and increase the intensity of societal reaction). The independent and dependent variables may also have reciprocal effects (e.g., greater centralization may result in a change in regional actor demands).

Moreover, as a result of governmental decisions and compromises, the structural or background factors may change. The conditions under which political actors can make demands then also may shift, resulting in decentralizing or re-centralizing pressures at different points in time.

Figure 5.1
Re-distribution of Authority: Model of Explanatory Factors

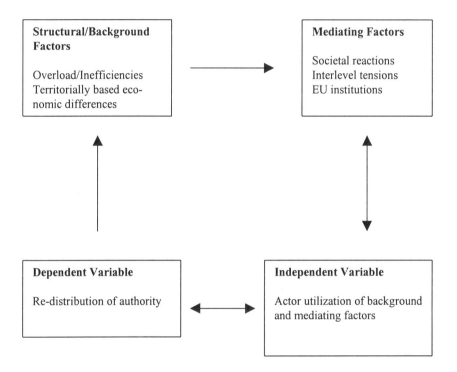

In both Spain and Portugal, the presence of the economic inefficiencies of centralization, overload, and territorial economic differentials contributed to the center's need to at least deconcentrate some functions, even during the dictatorships. In Spain, the presence of ethnonationalist cleavages and past suppression of the historic nationalities resulted in a strong societal reaction and gave particularly regional political actors the opportunity to utilize both economic and political grievances to pressure the center for decentralization in the post-Franco period. The urgency of the situation for the political stability of the country resulted in the constitutional compromise and the creation of the "State of the Autonomies." The absence of such ethnonationalist cleavages and the relative homogeneity of the Portuguese state resulted in a much weaker societal reaction. As in Spain, however, there was a general consensus that decentralization should occur, for both political and economic reasons. Authority was therefore transferred to local governments and to the autonomous island regions and provisions were made in the constitution, as in Spain, to regionalize the Portuguese mainland. The political stability of the country was not threatened by the lack of progress toward this stated goal, however, and there has been significant counterpressure for continued centralization, especially from parties and politicians at the national level, and lack of agreement on the formula for decentralization. Thus, regionalization did not occur after the fall of the dictatorship, and, indeed, still has not been implemented.

The initial constitutional compromise in Spain defused ethnonationalist tensions (with the exception of ETA) by granting the regions autonomy, but it also had the effect of providing a point of mobilization around which regional leaders could "create" a regional identity where none had existed previously, thus contributing to pressures from even more actors for further decentralization. Regional elites also have utilized EU institutions and opportunities for participation in policy making as another point of mobilization and influence outside the national government, as well as to further legitimize their demands for greater autonomy. In Portugal the transfer of authority to local governments and the CCRs also created new points of mobilization. Substate demands in Portugal are much less effective than those in Spain, however, because of the homogeneity of the Portuguese state, the lack of legitimate grievances regarding minority rights, the fact that regionalization has not been legally implemented on the mainland, and the fact that regional political parties in the island regions are prohibited. The central government in Portugal can therefore more easily resist pressures for decentralization.

Even in Spain, however, the re-distribution of authority is a dynamic process, and the constitutional compromise has not resulted in linear progress toward ever greater decentralization. The central government generally has tried to put a brake on the decentralization process. Moreover, while many functions are performed more efficiently at lower levels, in some areas, such as water distribution, the inefficiency in the delivery of services was increased by decentralization, resulting in recentralizing pressures.

The structural factors are continually modified by the results of prior political decisions. Under these changing circumstances, how authority is re-distributed is determined largely by the ability of political actors to utilize these factors and conditions to further their goals of either more diffused or more concentrated authority. Indeed, the most important determinant of a likely greater decentralization of authority in the near future in Spain is the ability of the Catalan and other nationalist parties to translate regional discontent into electoral support, which has allowed especially the CiU a crucial place at the national bargaining table. In Portugal, the defeat of the regionalization referendum shows that structural imperatives for decentralization such as economic efficiency can be overcome by a concerted political effort on the part of actors and parties opposed to the re-distribution of authority.

NOTES

1. For a detailed treatment of decentralizing reforms in major European states, see Assembly of European Regions 1989; Bukowski 1996, 53-132; Engel and Van Ginderachter 1993; Norton 1994. Studies of "multilevel governance" in the EU arena present evidence of an increasing diffusion of governmental authority among the supra-state, state, and substate levels and examine both causes and effects of this perceived trend. See, for example, Constantelos 1995; Marks 1993; Marks, Hooghe, and Blank 1996; Hooghe 1995.

2. In this chapter, "state" refers to the central government apparatus. "Sub-state" government refers to any governmental or administrative units established at a level below the central state, including the regional and local levels.

3. This analysis is similar to the ideas presented in Rosenau 1990.

4. Agranoff, for example, argues that while Spain is an "incomplete federation," it is nonetheless moving toward federal democracy (1996, 1997). He analyzes the evolution of institutional arrangements and competencies, including fiscal arrangements, among the central and substate governments in Spain to provide evidence for the increasing de facto federal character of the country (despite the prohibition in the Spanish constitution against federation). Conversely, other analysts argue that since federations are defined as contractual, that is, presumably "sovereign" units or states coming together in an agreed-upon arrangement, the initial and subsequent bargains in Spain's evolution cannot be considered federal (Guibernau 1995).

5. For details on the "two-track" system developed, see the Spanish Constitution, Articles 143 and 151; Clark 1987; Pérez Díaz 1990; Valles and Cuchillo 1988. For more information on the actual distribution of competencies as it has evolved, see Bukowski 1996, 77-82, 101; Engel and Van Ginderachter 1993, 70-74.

6. This session was historic in that it allowed the presence and participation, for the first time, of all regional executives. The only concrete follow-up action that was taken, however, was to appoint a committee of experts to study the matter and make recommendations regarding how to implement the approved reforms. The major national parties appear to be willing to amend the constitution for the purpose of making the Senate a body of regional representation. In a recent proposal, the major opposition party, the PSOE, proposed a pact with the PP government that, among other things, allows for such a modification, presumably by 2004, when the proposal specifies that the process of "autonomic development" would be "culminated" (Aizpeolea 1999).

7. Linz and Stepan, for example, argue that because Portugal consists of a relatively homogeneous society and has no significant linguistic or ethnic minorities, it does not demonstrate the same problem with "stateness" evident in, for example, Spain (1996).

8. Walter Opello, for example, in a 1989 survey among interest group leaders in Portugal, found that a large majority were dissatisfied with the prevailing distribution of authority and thought that it would be a good idea to create autonomous regions on the archipelagos and administrative regions on the mainland (Opello 1993).

9. Local government in Portugal receives about eight percent of total government spending, among the lowest amounts for local government in the European Union (Kahan et. al. 1999).

10. The Communists are the majority party in twenty-nine of the forty-six municipalities of Alentejo, and even in the metropolitan area of Lisbon, eighteen of the municipalities are pro-Communist. These fears are reminiscent of the arguments against redistribution in Italy for fear of the "red belt" regions of Tuscany, Umbria, and Emilia-Romagna. (Pereira 1995, 275).

11. The PCP subsequently disagreed with the PS over the proposed division of Alentejo into two regions (Correia 1997). In the summer of 1997, the Socialists and Communists reached an agreement to consider only one region in Alentejo, creating majority support in Parliament for the creation of eight regions.

12. Baum and Freire observe that the most important local government group in Portugal, the National Association of Portuguese Municipalities (ANMP), supported the proposed regionalization and that many local governments in Portugal have already moved in the direction of bottom-up regionalism, forming regional associations for the purpose of solving common problems (1999, 14).

13. This is demonstrated most recently by the approval, in the wake of the referendum defeat, of a plan that would grant approximately one million escudos to reinforce the work of the Local Development Associations (ADLs), which are quasi-statist nongovernmental organizations (Rocha 1999).

14. The Development Plans referred to *polos de desarrollo* (development poles), for which programs such as economic incentives for the development of industry would be created and implemented. These were organized around distinctly geographic points (such as "Mediterranean," "Ebro," and "Madrid-Catalonia"), explicitly avoiding historical ethnonationalist configurations (Lorca Corrons, Martínez Estévez, and García Menéndez 1981, 614).

15. Emigration, both internal as well as international, has long been a major characteristic of the Portuguese economy. Between 1950 and 1970, for example, approximately 2 million Portuguese emigrated abroad or to the Portuguese colonies (which was the equivalent of sixty percent of the labor force in 1970) (Robinson 1979, 156, 160).

16. For example, several parties and groups have been active in trying to cultivate an "Andalusian identity," despite the fact that there is no historical nationalist or separatist tradition in this region. What binds Andalusians together tends to be a state of relative economic inequality. In the 1995 mayoral elections in Cordoba, for example, three different "regional-nationalist" parties presented candidates (*La Voz de los Barrios*. 1995. Election publication, Cádiz, Spain, 15-30 May, 1995 18-19).

17. For a history of ETA, and more recent issues and developments, see Douglass 1985, Clark 1990, Aulestia 1993, and Sullivan 1999.

18. Indeed, the major rationale used by EC officials for allowing these relatively less-developed states into the integration scheme (even though it was almost universally admitted that their economies were not prepared for accession) was that it was in the interests of the EC members to do what they could to help these transitioning states become stable democracies. Public support in both Spain and Portugal was largely in favor of accession primarily because it was viewed as a way of throwing off the dictatorial past and taking their "rightful" place as part of democratic Europe.

19. Information provided in author interviews (1993-94) with officials in the Association of European Regions and Directorate General XVI, Commission of the European Communities, in Brussels. See also Marks et al. 1996.

20. Author interviews (1994) with officials in the Spanish regional offices and Directorate General XVI, Commission of the European Communities, in Brussels.

Chapter 6

Decentralization in Senegal: Reordering Authority or Reinventing Past Reforms?

Amy Patterson

By the 1980s, many African countries had begun to redesign the relations between local and central governments. This chapter will examine decentralization efforts in the West African country of Senegal. Decentralization includes either devolution of power to legally established, locally elected government authorities that have clearly differentiated legal powers and responsibilities, or deconcentration of administrative authority to representatives of central government agencies (Conyers 1983). Devolution is a more radical form of decentralization, but most forms of decentralization in Africa have more closely resembled deconcentration. I use the term decentralization broadly to include both deconcentration and devolution.

This chapter argues that although decentralization in Senegal has led to the creation of new regional development and electoral institutions, these institutions have only marginally increased the power of rural citizens and local organizations. Decentralization has most closely resembled deconcentration, not devolution. I assert that decentralization policies in Senegal have little potential to foster democracy and improve local development. In making my argument, I illustrate that throughout its postcolonial history, the Senegalese state has used decentralization policies to stem societal pressures for economic and political change. At opportune times, state authorities have proposed top-down decentralization reforms that are neither rooted in society nor able to empower society.

Roughly seven million people live in Senegal, the Wolof ethnic group being the largest with forty-three percent of the population. However, ethnicity has rarely played a role in politics, because ninety percent of Senegalese are Muslim, a fact that unifies the population (Villalón 1995). The national economy centers around tourism, phosphate exports, fishing, and the peanut cash crop. Senegal is often praised for its stable and relatively democratic political system, though the same political party has won control of government from independence in 1960 until the present. Multiparty elections were instituted in 1980, and recent reforms have helped to make these elections more competitive (Villalón 1994). Senegal provides an ideal case to study the reconfiguration of state power because numerous decentralization reforms have been instituted throughout the country's postcolonial history. Though many aspects of decentralization in Senegal are not unique to the country, the case was not chosen with the specific intent to generalize my findings across many venues. The case study presented here examines specific reforms and reactions to those reforms. The case provides a starting point from which to critically evaluate the larger implications of decentralization efforts in Africa.

The work is divided into four sections. First, I frame my argument about Senegal in the context of the social science literature on state–civil society relations in Africa. Decentralization efforts throughout Africa must be understood as part of the dynamic interplay between a weak and authoritarian state and a weaker, though more legitimate, civil society that lacks resources, organization, and multiple links between its members. Second, the chapter outlines Senegal's historical experiences with decentralization. I illustrate that Senegal's decentralization efforts from independence until the present reflect a continued legacy of French colonial centralization and despotism. Third, I analyze the most recent efforts at decentralization in Senegal—the proposed regional assemblies, the reform of electoral laws, and the development of state-sanctioned local development organizations. I argue that these efforts to devolve state power are examples of deconcentration because these strategies have remained under central state control. In the conclusion, I summarize the explanatory variables that have shaped Senegal's decentralization experiences and question the effectiveness of decentralization when the state and civil society are weak.

DECENTRALIZATION: A TRENDY SOLUTION TO COMPLEX PROBLEMS?

Theda Skocpol (1985) defines the state as an administrative, legal, coercive, and autonomous actor, not an arena in which other political groups act. The autonomy of African states is rooted in their colonial legacy and has enabled them to initiate top-down political, economic, and social reforms (Callaghy 1984; Mamdani 1996). Autonomy, however, is not synonymous with strength. African states are juridical, but not necessarily legitimate. The idea of nationhood and the loyalty it brings to the territorial entity and its government apparatus are largely absent in Africa, since the African state did not rise from societal forces and lacks support in society. Without ties to social classes, ethnic groups, or interest organizations, the state's policies are not grounded in social realities. The disconnection between the state and society serves as a source of weakness for the state (Jackson and Rosberg 1982; Bratton 1989).[1]

Because the African state is weak, a political space develops in which societal forces can operate and, at times, challenge the state (Bratton 1989; Bayart 1986). Civil society is composed of independent businesses, grassroots associations, opposition parties, local political institutions, and traditional organizations. Civil society can either engage with the state or disengage from the state (Chazan et al. 1988). Through the black market or tax evasion, civil society disengages, while it engages the state via patronage ties (Bunker 1987; Azarya 1988). African civil society is often more legitimate to citizens than the state is. Local organizations provide for their members, represent specific interests to the state, provide a forum for learning democratic values, and counter state despotism (Bratton 1989; Sklar 1987; Putnam 1993; Diamond 1988). However, civil society in Africa is often considered to be weak. It often lacks the resources needed to be effective, and its members may be divided by class, ethnicity, or gender (Patterson 1996; Patterson 1998b; Fatton 1995). Unless they are traditional associations, groups in civil society may also be the creations of the postcolonial African state. Political parties, women's federations, and large peak associations may not be rooted in larger social realities (Fatton 1995; Mamdani 1996; Boyd 1989).

In the context of a weak state and a weak civil society, the relationship between these two entities is dialectical. As societal organizations demand more resources and power, the state may attempt to centralize its authority. It may limit contestation and participation or build up state institutions such as the army or bureaucracy (Chazan et al. 1988). On the other hand, the state may willingly relinquish some control in order to gain legitimacy with citizens and to relieve pressures from civil society (Bratton and van de Walle 1992). Decentralization reforms in Africa occur within the context of this interplay between a weak and illegitimate state and a weak but more legitimate civil society.

Recently, decentralization has received much attention from international donors, societal organizations, academics, and even state officials who espouse its numerous benefits (Olowu and Smoke 1992; Conyers 1983). They claim that the failure of African centralized planning in the 1960s and 1970s necessitates that local governments oversee economic and social development. Local governments can more efficiently administer development programs because their members better understand local problems and the solutions to those problems. Decentralized agencies can respond to demands from citizens and other local agencies. Decentralization aims at weakening vertical control and increasing horizontal control in the arena of development (Mutizwa-Mangiza and Conyers 1996). David Leonard and Dale Marshall (1982) assert that decentralization of state power allows local governments to better design development initiatives. In turn, local governments will be directly accountable to individuals for their decisions, a fact that will force them to consider the ideas of those who elect them (Clark 1990; Esman and Uphoff 1984; Nzouankeu 1994; Ostrom 1990).

In contrast, the Senegal case illustrates that decentralized agencies may not necessarily be more efficient on development initiatives. In order to address development problems, local governments need resources. The central state has often been unwilling to devolve access to resources as it devolves administrative authority. William Tordoff (1994) finds that in Ghana's decentralization program in the early 1980s, local governments were not given adequate resources to implement their policies. Local governments also may not be more efficient because they continue to be controlled by central state authorities (Ribot 1995). The central government may continue to check the decision-making power of local authorities, as has been the case in Tanzania and Zimbabwe (Tordoff 1994). Development policies that emerge may meet the goals of the state, but not of the supposed beneficiaries.

Another positive outcome that is often attributed to decentralization is its ability to foster democracy. Many policymakers and scholars have argued that the reason African countries have not grown economically since independence is because development initiatives have not been participatory (Conyers 1983; Esman and Uphoff 1984; Leonard and Marshall 1982). The state and international aid donors have devised development programs without the input of local citizens (van de Walle and Johnston 1996; Sy 1988; Patterson 1998a). Local individuals do not have the opportunities to voice ideas and learn the value of local participation and leadership accountability. Without the existence of these democratic values at the grassroots level, democratic citizenship at the national level is more difficult to sustain. Compromise, legitimacy, participation, and trust in government will not exist if people feel isolated from politics at the local level (Putnam 1993).

I argue that decentralization efforts may not be sufficient to encourage grassroots democracy. One problem is that the party that controls the central state and its resources often dominates local governments. Multiparty elections in Africa have produced few turnovers in power; ruling parties continue to win elections and control access to state resources (Bratton and van de Walle 1997). In an era of partisan competition, ruling parties have used decentralized institutions to maintain support among populations. William Tordoff (1994) finds that the ruling party in Zambia controls the appointees to district governorships and many of the positions in local institutions. In Senegal, the state controls the individuals who allocate forestry resources and make local forestry regulations (Ribot 1999). The state can limit the accountability, transparency, and independence of decentralized government through its control over the personnel and resources of local institutions. Such institutions are neither democratic nor able to challenge state policies.

Another reason that decentralized state institutions may not encourage democracy is because they perpetuate social inequalities and political exclusion.

Patron-client relations, class cleavages, gender inequalities, and ethnic divisions may limit the ability of local political organizations to be democratic (Patterson 1998b; Patterson 1999; Fatton 1992). For example, Aili Tripp (1998) illustrates that decentralization in Uganda has not had the effect of increasing women's participation in local government, despite the fact that the 1995 National Constitution stipulates that women must hold thirty percent of all seats in local government. Though decentralization in Uganda has opened up opportunities for women, larger societal institutions such as marriage, gender norms, and women's access to education have limited their ability to utilize these opportunities. Decentralization reforms do not guarantee that local decision-making bodies will be democratic.

Robert Bates (1981) maintains that African leaders make policies after they calculate the risks of those policies to their political power. Using this rational choice perspective, the state's decision to decentralize power must be understood within the political and economic context in which it has occurred. In 1990, societal organizations in many African countries challenged centralized state authority and demanded democratic reforms such as freedom of the press and multiparty elections (Bratton and van de Walle 1992; Heilbrunn 1993). Through protests, marches, and riots, civil society organizations were able to gain some democratic concessions in countries such as Benin, Cameroon, Kenya, Niger, and South Africa. One way state governments reacted to this democratic pressure was to reconfigure their relations with local governments. State officials argued that decentralization was a way to increase opportunities for participation and state accountability.

Decentralization also occurred in the context of economic uncertainty in Africa. The debt crisis in the early 1980s caused most African states to adopt structural adjustment programs (SAPs) in order to receive further loans from the International Monetary Fund (IMF) and World Bank. SAPs have included liberalization of trade, privatization of state-run industries and state-controlled agricultural markets, and austerity measures. These reforms have hurt the legitimacy of the African state, because the state can provide fewer jobs, subsidies, and patronage than in the past. In response, citizens have become angry. Many of the democratic protests of 1990 began as protests over austerity measures (Bratton and van de Walle 1992). In order to keep power, state officials have looked to other ways to appease citizens. In some cases, such as Zaire and Zambia, the state has simply reneged on its SAP agreements (van de Walle 1998). This, though, is a temporary solution. African states have also used decentralization as an avenue for relieving pressure on the state. Dele Olowu and Paul Smoke (1992, 3) point out that decentralization can help "to mitigate the negative effects of structural adjustment programmes for the poor." Decentralization is a means by which the African state can maintain some level of power and stability in a period of economic and political uncertainty. I will now examine the political and economic reasons for decentralization in Senegal and the democratic and developmental limits of Senegal's decentralization program.

DECENTRALIZATION IN SENEGAL: THE SENGHOR YEARS (1960-1979)

Senegal has undergone several types of decentralization reforms in its postcolonial history. To understand these reforms, it is necessary to briefly outline the colonial legacy in Senegal. The French divided the country into fifteen administrative districts (*cercles*), each of which was headed by an authoritarian French official (*commandant*) who received his orders directly from Paris. In the system of native justice (*indigenat*), the commandant had the right to arrest African subjects, to force Africans into work crews or military service, to collect taxes, and to confiscate land. Below the *cercle*, the main administrative unit was the *canton*, which was administered by African canton chiefs who were named by the colonial administration and directly incorporated into it. They tended to have French language skills and education in order to communicate with their French superiors, and they served as the link between the rural population and the colonial government (Gellar 1995). The colonial administration was very centralized and hierarchical.

French centralization was exemplified in the metropole's control over the Senegalese economy. The French worked through canton chiefs and religious leaders to encourage peasants to grow the cash crop of peanuts. Rural farmers were at the mercy of colonial traders and transporters, who determined the price for agricultural commodities and controlled access to markets (Cruise O'Brien 1971; Gellar 1995; Behrman 1970). Central authorities guided economic development and the cultivation of the peanut, which dominated the economy. At the time of independence, peanuts amounted to two-thirds of all Senegalese exports. As we shall see, the postcolonial state in Senegal also tried to control rural cultivation.

Though similar to other French colonies, Senegal had one major difference. After 1848 France granted French citizenship to males living in the four Senegalese coastal cities of Dakar, Rufisque, Gorée, and Saint Louis, the so-called *quatre communes*. These citizens could vote in elections and hold electoral office. Though this group was less than five percent of the Senegalese population, it became an important force in colonial and postcolonial politics. The disparity between the urban citizens and the rural subjects is a legacy of colonialism that continues to shape attitudes about state and societal power. Today it is primarily urban elite citizens who guide development and democratization policies, while the vast majority of rural individuals are subjects who follow the decisions of these elites (Fatton 1987). Mahmood Mamdani (1996) uses the term decentralized despotism to describe this bifurcated political system, in which rural institutions continue to be limited in their resources and power and urban elites control decision making because of the colonial legacy.

After Senegal gained independence in 1960, the country ventured to reconfigure the relations between the urban-dominated central state and the rural-based civil society through the ideology of African socialism. Educated in France and a former member of the French Parliament, Senegal's first president, Léopold Sédar Senghor, claimed that the centralized African state had a key role to play in development, yet the structures of that development were to be decentralized. The role of the state was to create institutions that fostered local democracy and controlled the rural economy (Gellar, Charlick, and Jones 1980). A direct reaction to centralized colonial control, African socialism espoused a rhetoric of authentic decentralization and empowerment of Senegalese rural society.

To implement the ideas of African socialism and to bring the state closer to the rural populations, then–Prime Minister Mamadou Dia proposed four overall changes in central government authority. First, the former colonial administrative districts were redrawn and their number was expanded. Senegal was divided into seven regions that governors administered, twenty-five departments that prefects administered, and fifty-five provinces (*arrondissements*) that sub-prefects administered. Despite the rhetoric of decentralization, however, these officers remained agents of the state. They implemented policy decisions made at the central state level and were accountable to central government ministries (Gellar 1990). This first reform did not devolve authority, but rather deconcentrated it.

Second, Dia proposed that seven regional assemblies composed of popularly elected individuals be instituted. Unlike the postcolonial urban decision-making bodies that were grounded in the citizen experience of the *quatre communes*, these regional assemblies did not have roots in the colonial historical experience. Few peasants elected to the regional assemblies had gained decision-making experience under French colonialism. As institutions, the regional assemblies also had few powers and very small budgets. They functioned under the tutelage of the Ministry of the Interior, and the Senegalese Constitution did not recognize the power of regional institutions to make, implement, or enforce policy (Gellar 1990). The regional assemblies were ineffective and were completely dismantled by the early 1970s. They exemplify Senegal's postcolonial deconcentration of power, not devolution.

A third aspect of African socialism was the development of a network of rural cooperatives. Imposed by the central state, the cooperatives became a means by which the state controlled and encouraged the production of peanuts. Cooperatives bought and sold peanuts, dispersed state fertilizers and seeds, provided farmers with low- interest loans, and organized transport for agricultural commodities. State agents supervised the cooperatives, and rural citizens grew to despise the organizations, over which they had no control (Boone 1992). Highly inefficient, the cooperatives stifled the initiative and productivity of farmers. And they contributed to the peasant malaise of the 1970s, in which farmers decreased their production of peanuts in favor of subsistence crops (Gellar 1995). The disengagement of farmers from state-controlled markets led to the decline of the Senegalese economy. By the late 1970s, peanuts accounted for only forty percent of all Senegalese exports. As was the case with administrative redesign and the regional assemblies, this decentralization reform did not devolve state authority, promote grassroots democracy, or foster economic development.

A final reform was to devise a state bureaucracy intended to foster rural development, the Rural Expansion Centers (*Centre d'Expansion Rurale*-CER) and the Rural Animation (*Animation Rurale*-AR) program. CERs were supposed to provide technical assistance to rural peasants in the areas of forestry, women's development, health care, agriculture, and water resources (Schumacher 1975). Situated in *arrondissement* capitals, these government officials were intended to be accessible to the rural population. In reality, the resources for CER activities were (and still are) limited. Transportation for aiding villagers, materials for rural projects, and training of officials are minimal, which makes the CERs very ineffective (Chef du CER, Ndoulo *arrondissement*, 2 March 1995; Gellar, Charlick, and Jones 1980). Because the CERs are unable to provide benefits, they have lost legitimacy in the eyes of rural peasants. The president of a village women's group in the Diourbel region commented in 1995, "They [the CER officials] do nothing. They never have resources and are unwilling to help us" (Ndoulo women's group president, 12 June 1995).[2] Additionally, the CER has been more concerned with carrying out central government economic policies and enforcing state regulations than promoting participatory development (Gellar 1990). CERs may be viewed as deconcentrated, not devolved, agencies.

The AR program was supposed to encourage the peasants to participate in the cooperatives and to utilize the CERs. On the positive side, the program identified and trained over 3,500 villagers to lead rural development initiatives. AR was based on the assumption that the peasants could organize and guide development. However, AR leaders were accountable to state officials, not local citizens, and they continually lacked the support of local elites. AR did not contribute to rural development, foster grassroots democracy, or disperse state power. Rather, it exemplifies the state's desire to deconcentrate, not devolve, authority (Gellar, Charlick, and Jones 1980). "Animation had originally intended to change the entire nature of traditional Senegalese society. It started to make vital changes in the principles basic to the structure of society, yet it ended by merely increasing the power and jurisdictions of the central authority" (Markovitz 1991, 80).

Though ambitious, the reforms initiated after independence exemplified the colonial legacy of decentralized despotism. The state controlled local institutions, and the involvement of rural Senegalese was minimal. Despite the rhetoric of participatory development, state officials and the ruling Socialist Party (*Parti Socialiste*-PS) did not relinquish much power to society. They did not provided needed resources and clarify the powers of the regional assemblies. They did not allow for local control of the cooperatives. While it appeared that power had been decentralized because of the newly established administrative divisions, this was not actually the case.

After 1962, centralization of state authority became more overt. President Senghor concentrated political power in his hands after ousting Dia for an alleged coup attempt. By 1966, while not creating a de jure one-party state, Senghor created a de facto one by making it impossible for other parties to win election. He strictly limited the rights of citizens to form political, economic, and media organizations. At the local level, the prefect played a larger role in supervising local affairs. Regional governors began to oversee local administration and were made directly accountable to the president. The cooperatives became more closely allied with the state's peanut marketing board, and their legitimacy further declined (Gellar 1990, 138; Ndoye, Gaye, and Tersiguel 1994; Sy 1988).

Senghor's decentralized despotism reflected a desire to maintain power in an increasingly uncertain political and economic environment (Bates 1981; Mamdani 1996). Politically, Africa had begun to experience military coup d'états. Economically, it was evident that participatory development plans were not successfully increasing rural production. State elites ignored the fact that local institutions lacked the political and economic resources to foster development, and they dismissed the argument that central state policies had incapacitated local institutions. Rather, local institutions were deemed to be inefficient and backward; increased centralization was believed to be the best avenue for development (Gellar 1990).

Senghor's centralization of power was not without political costs and societal reactions. By the late 1960s, urban and rural constituencies began to demand more political space. Student unrest in Dakar in 1968 and the growing peasant malaise forced Senghor to introduce political, administrative, and economic reforms. Here I will concentrate on the administrative reforms. In 1972, the Senegalese state designed the rural community (*communauté rurale*-CR), as the lowest level of administrative structure between the *arrondissement* and the village. Today there are 319 CRs in Senegal, each of which is composed of between ten and fifteen thousand individuals.[3]

An elected rural council governs the CR. Intended to increase participation in local development and encourage grassroots accountability, the rural councils have suffered from a wide array of problems. As a form of decentralized despotism, the rural councils are under the supervision of an official who is accountable to the state, the sub-prefect. The rural councils lack needed funds for development projects and have little autonomy in decision making. Rural councils can assess a tax on local peoples, the proceeds of which the CRs can manage and budget. But until 1990, the council could not determine the rate of taxation, which was fixed by the state (Bouat and Fouillard 1983, 59).

Even with more ability to determine taxation rates, the councils have had continual problems collecting tax revenues, and they must rely on the sub-prefect to enforce tax regulations. The number of peasants paying their taxes varies widely among rural communities and often depends on the legitimacy of the rural council and the willingness of the sub-prefect to enforce local tax ordinances. In two CRs in the Diourbel region, less than half of the households paid their taxes (Chef du CER, Ndoulo *arrondissement*, 22 May 1995). An additional limitation is that until 1990 each CR had to contribute twenty-five percent of its annual rural tax to the National Solidarity Fund for the development of rural areas. While this money was intended to be redistributed back to villages, between 1972 and 1985, no rural communities received funds (Vengroff and Johnston 1987). The lack of resources, and ability to collect those resources, has hampered the capacity of the councils to promote rural development.

Rural councils lack power because they are often manipulated by state officials and ignored by international donors that work on village development projects. International donors, rather than seeking the advice and cooperation of rural councils, tend to sidestep these local institutions, unless they need specific permission for access to land or water resources (Peace Corps volunteer, 30 July 1995; Peace Corps official, 4 January 1995; UNICEF official, 31 December 1994). Dependent on international donors to finance development projects for which they do not have funds (Patterson 1998a), local council members have little choice but to permit the curtailment of their authority. Rather than being incorporated into the development process, rural councilors are often unaware of the development projects that exist in their own communities.

Though part of the justification for the 1972 reforms was that the rural councils could promote democracy, the councils are not inclusive, representative, or accountable. Until 1996, elections to the council were conducted using a winner-take-all party list system. This system insured that the councilors in a given rural community would always be from the same party, particularly the well-organized PS. Additionally, the population elected two-thirds of the council and peanut cooperative members selected the remaining third. This arrangement guaranteed that state authorities working with the cooperative could influence at least one-third of seats on the council (Vengroff and Johnston 1987). Richard Vengroff and Alan Johnston (1989) discovered that the rural councils also were not very representative of society in terms of age or gender. Forty-three percent of these officials were village elders over fifty-five years old, despite the fact that more than twenty percent of Senegalese are under 20 years old (United Nations 1992). Few councils had more than one female member. The lack of societal representation has made it more difficult for rural councils to build support for their decisions.

The attitudes of rural council members have distanced them from the local populations. Vengroff and Johnston (1989) report that councilors often seek the opinions of only the village chief, heads of local organizations, and other opinion leaders. A few quotations from rural Senegalese illustrate the distance between the fiscally weak and somewhat illegitimate rural councils and the peasants they are supposed to represent. One rural woman in the Diourbel region said, "The council is worthless—just a bunch of people with money and power who ignore the rest of us" (Female peasant, 25 February 1995). Another farmer in the Louga region said, "Talk, talk—that is all the council does. When have they helped people and done development projects? They just get together with the sub-prefect and steal our money" (Male peasant, 28 April 1995). While these are only the opinions of two individuals, they do provide a perspective about how rural citizens perceive the rural councils. Because they do not represent and include all citizens and because councilors are often not accountable to the larger community, rural councils are less likely to be a forum for learning democracy than advocates of decentralization often argue.

The 1972 establishment of rural councils did not devolve state power, increase democracy in local decision making, or facilitate the management of local development initiatives. At best, the 1972 reforms, and those that preceded them in 1960, can be defined as deconcentration of state power. Power was not devolved from the state apparatus, and local structures gained few institutional capabilities. They lacked resources, autonomy, power to enforce and implement their decisions, and legitimacy from the people they were intended to serve. Rather than constituting a major change in power between the central government and societal institutions, these efforts acted as what Richard Vengroff (1993) terms a "safety valve." "As Senegal's leaders have found themselves confronted with economic conditions beyond their control, increasing societal pressures, and political challenges, they have moved to calm the waters by allowing for increasing levels of local participation, albeit under the watchful eye of a parallel prefectorial administration under the tutelage of the Ministry of the Interior" (Vengroff 1993: 162). The uncertain economic situation of the 1970s and the increased demands by civil society for democracy were factors that contributed to the reforms of 1972. The most recent set of decentralization reforms that Senegal has undertaken can be viewed in much the same manner. It is to these reforms that I now turn.

DECENTRALIZATION IN SENEGAL: THE DIOUF YEARS (1980 PRESENT)

Eager to portray himself as independent from Senghor and the PS hierarchy, President Abdou Diouf (Senghor's chosen successor) responded to societal pressures for political liberalization when he came to power in 1980. He permitted the formation of political parties and lifted regulations on independent media outlets and civil society organizations. Societal organizations flourished and new radio stations and newspapers developed (Villalón 1994; Gellar 1995). Yet political liberalization has not meant there has been a change in which party controls the state. In the first multiparty election after 1980, the ruling PS maintained control of the presidency, with eighty-three percent of the vote (Villalón 1994). In 1988, President Diouf again won reelection against Abdoulaye Wade of the Social Democratic Party (*Parti Démocratique Socialiste*-PDS) in a competitive contest that was situated around economic issues. Senegal had accumulated a substantial foreign debt, and in 1979 the country had agreed to implement SAPs in return for additional loans from the World Bank and the IMF. SAPs included liberalization of trade and the agricultural commodity market, cuts in state spending on health, education, and employment, and decreases in food subsidies (Delgado and Jammeh 1991). These policies especially hurt urban populations, students, and lower-level civil servants. In the 1988 election, Wade capitalized on the negative impact of SAPs and motivated individuals with his slogan of *sopi* (change in Wolof) (Villalón 1994; Vengroff and Creevey 1997). When Diouf was reelected with seventy-three percent of the vote, disaffected youth in urban areas rioted. The government declared a state of emergency, imposed a curfew, and arrested Wade and other opposition party leaders. Senegal had never experienced such political violence before, and these actions caused some international donors to reevaluate their loans and aid projects in Senegal (Villalón 1994; Vengroff and Creevey 1997).

In addition to the political unrest and economic decline that had developed in Senegal, the country faced a growing separatist movement in the southern region, the Casamance. Beginning in 1982, the Movement of Democratic Forces of the Casamance (*Mouvement des Forces Démocratiques de la Casamance*-MFDC) organized antigovernment rallies and began armed attacks against civilians and Senegalese soldiers. While predominantly composed of Diola ethnic group members, the movement has sought to address larger economic and political considerations. The Casamance is separated from Senegal by Gambia, and its citizens feel distant from political and economic decisions made in the capital of Dakar. The infrastructure of the Casamance, especially in the areas of communication, health, and education, is much less developed than in the rest of Senegal, and local commerce and civil servant jobs have been controlled by "Northerners." However, of all regions of Senegal, the

Casamance shows the most potential for economic development, since it receives the highest rainfall levels, has the most fertile soil, and holds offshore oil reserves. The people of the Casamance fear that these resources will be squandered by Northern politicians (Coulon 1988), and this fear and isolation has contributed to the separatist movement. Despite a peace agreement in 1990, violence has continued in the region. The numerous rebel factions have been unwilling to give up their various demands for autonomy, more state resources, or for some, complete independence from Senegal. The separatist movement has hurt the Senegalese economy, since many tourists who visit the country go to the beautiful beaches of the Casamance. After four French people were kidnaped in 1995 in the region, tourism has lagged. Senegal's international reputation as a peaceful and welcoming place to visit has suffered (Vengroff and Creevey 1997).

Several factors culminated to pressure Diouf and the ruling PS to further democratize the political system in the 1990s. First, the 1988 postelectoral riots encouraged Diouf to look for more peaceful ways to incorporate the opposition into politics so that such destruction would not occur again in the future. Second, the separatist movement led to a feeling of instability and uncertainty in national politics, and tarnished Senegal's image abroad. Third, the economic situation of Senegal had not improved despite the implementation of SAPs in the 1980s. In fact, rumors circulated that Diouf would permit the devaluation of the *Communauté Financière Africaine* (CFA) currency, which is tied to the French franc. The World Bank and IMF advocated devaluation, but Diouf realized that such a move would be politically unpopular, as it would increase the price of imports. Though devaluation did not occur until 1994, citizens blamed Diouf for the precarious economic situation that has existed in the country since the 1980s.

In addition to domestic economic and political pressures, Diouf faced an international community that was pushing African states to democratize. After the end of communism in Eastern Europe, international donors and scholars began to speak about the spread of global democracy (Huntington 1991). Beginning in 1989, Africans began to topple authoritarian rulers and civil society organizations called for democracy. By 1991, many West African Francophone countries such as Togo, Benin, Niger, Cameroon, and Mali held national conferences in which civil society organizations and state elites agreed on multiparty elections and new constitutions. Senegal appeared to be left out of this movement to further democratize its political system.

The late French President François Mitterand also pressured former French colonies such as Senegal to democratize. Because France is the major trading partner and aid donor to its former colonies (Schraeder 1995), leaders in Francophone Africa cannot disregard French policy. At the Franco-African summit at La Baule, France, in 1990, President Mitterand threatened African leaders who did not implement political reforms with economic retribution. The so-called "La Baule doctrine" was viewed as a means to pressure authoritarian African leaders to liberalize politics. A year later, Mitterand spoke again of the importance of human rights and the democratic process in Africa (Takougang 1997). Though Senegal was not as authoritarian as other Francophone countries such as Togo or Cameroon, Mitterand's statements pressured Diouf to further liberalize the political system. International donors began to advocate decentralization and more democratic electoral rules in order to decrease the power of the Senegalese state and facilitate alternation in political power.

In response to these internal and external pressures, Diouf invited Wade to become part of a government of national unity in 1991. Many Senegalese viewed this government to be beneficial, since it allowed for greater compromise and peaceful discussion between political elites (Schaffer 1998). Over the next two years, Diouf and the PS-dominated government proposed several reforms to reconfigure the power relations between the state and society. By including Wade in some of these decisions, Diouf hoped to build legitimacy for state policies and to relieve societal and international pressures for democratization. As in the past, these reforms were initiated from above, not below, and have helped to relieve some pressure on the state.

The first proposed reform was the reestablishment of the regional assemblies. Diouf announced this initiative in a message to the nation on April 3, 1992, and then proceeded to assign a cabinet member to be in charge of studying and implementing the decentralization proposals. In words reminiscent of previous decentralization efforts, the government explained that the regional assemblies will serve the development needs of the country and increase rural participation (Vengroff and Creevey 1997). After almost two years of study, several specific proposals were made about the regional assemblies. Their members will be elected through universal suffrage, with half elected through winner-take-all and half elected through proportional representation. The size of the assemblies will vary, depending on the population of the region, with the smallest being twenty-two members and the largest being fifty-two. The assembly will manage development projects, control urban and rural affairs, coordinate development initiatives with international donors, and oversee local resources such as water, land, and forests. In addition, the regional assemblies will work closely with an appointed economic and social council, composed of rural council presidents, mayors of local cities, and nongovernmental organization (NGO) representatives. Funds for the regional assembly will come from local taxes, regional tariffs on timber and resources, and other license fees (Ndoye, Gaye, and Tersiguel 1994).

It is too early to assess the regional assemblies and their impact on development and democracy, since elections for assembly members have yet to occur. However, one can speculate on the possible outcomes of this decentralization reform. This top-down policy exemplifies decentralized despotism. The central state will continue to control development, since an officer of the state—the regional governor—will oversee the functioning of the regional government. And the regional governments will have legislative, but not executive, functions; their ability to implement and enforce their decisions will be limited (Vengroff and Creevey 1997; Ndoye, Gaye, and Tersiguel 1994). It is also not clear that the regional assemblies will receive the resources needed to be effective. State revenue for the project has been minimal, with a significant portion of the finances coming from donors such as the US Agency for International Development (USAID). Further, it is necessary to think about the opportunities for democratic participation in the regional assemblies. Will those elected be representative of the entire society? If the level of representation in the rural councils is any indication, the regional assemblies may underrepresent women and young people. Only the future will determine if the regional assemblies have the resources and capacity to foster democracy and development.

The second set of decentralizing reforms that Diouf has instituted relates to the electoral code. It is possible that these reforms will reconfigure the relationship between the state and civil society, because they will give opposition parties a better opportunity to win elections. Under pressure from opposition forces, the PS agreed to rewrite the electoral law in 1992. The new electoral code mandates the secret ballot, the use of voter identity cards, better oversight of ballot boxes, a decrease in the voting age from twenty-one to eighteen, the use of indelible ink to prevent multiple voting, and the representation of all political parties at voting sites. The electoral reforms made the 1993 presidential election more competitive, though President Diouf was reelected with fifty-eight percent of the vote (Villalón 1994). While the reforms have hurt the PS, they have not caused it to lose control of political power. The ruling party continues to win rural support, because of its strong organization, its ability to dominate rural councils, and it access to patronage.

Because of the winner-take-all electoral system, and the subsequent PS control of rural councils, opposition parties tended to boycott local elections. The opposition used its meager resources to compete in national elections or to win mayoral positions in urban areas where it had greater support (Vengroff and Ndiaye 1998). In an attempt to decrease PS dominance of rural councils (and the party's support in rural Senegal), the opposition parties pushed to further reform the electoral code. In the 1996 elections for rural councils, the electoral system was changed so that half of the seats are allocated based on winner-take-all, while the other half are allocated using proportional representation. With control of half of the seats determined by proportional representation, opposition parties were able to compete in 1996. The PDS won seats in eighty-one percent of the country's 319 rural councils. The other major national opposition parties, the Unity Party (*And Jef*-AJ) and Democratic League (*Ligue Démocratique*-LD), won seats in every region, including twenty-three percent and thirty percent of the rural councils, respectively. Because opposition parties now have a core group of local officials, they can begin to build party organizations and to dole out patronage to build a body of local supporters. In the long run, being represented in local government should enable opposition parties to mount more competitive challenges in national elections. Richard Vengroff and Momar Ndiaye (1998) argue that the electoral rules, and the dispersal of power from the ruling party to opposition parties in local governments, is a positive step in Senegal's democratic decentralization.

In contrast, I assert that the aftermath of the 1998 legislative elections illustrates that the state still holds power, while civil society must react to state-imposed decentralization. To understand the aftermath of the 1998 elections, it is necessary to explain that the electoral code of 1992 changed the allocation of the 120 seats in the National Assembly. At that point, fifty of the seats were allotted using a winner-take-all formula, a system that benefited the PS and its rural organization. The remaining seventy seats were elected nationally using proportional representation, to the advantage of the opposition parties.[4] After opposition parties won representation in the 1996 rural council elections, however, the PS-dominated national legislature voted to expand the number of seats in the National Assembly to 140 from 120 (*Sud quotidien*, 3 June 1998). Now seventy seats are allocated using winner-take-all while seventy are decided based on proportional representation. These rule changes benefitted the PS in the 1998 election, in which the party won 93 of the 140 seats, the PDS won 23, the Union for the Democratic Renaissance (*Union pour le Renouveau*-URD) won 11 and other parties, the remainder. The PS won almost all of the twenty new districts. Given the sizeable win of the PS, it will be difficult for the PDS and other parties to shape legislation or to change the formula for allocating seats in the near future. The actions of the central state have served to counteract the gains of opposition parties in the 1996 rural council elections and the subsequent political support these parties might derive from those gains (*Sud quotidien*, 30 May 1998). The actions of the PS-dominated state illustrate the unwillingness of the state to fully relinquish power, especially in the electoral realm.

I argue that the Senegalese state's electoral reforms are a reaction to the political instability that developed after 1988, the Casamance separatist movement, the uncertain economic situation, and international pressures. As such, the reforms helped to relieve some of the pressures on the state from internal and external forces. But the state has been unwilling to give up too much control over the elections and their outcomes and has centralized power when it felt threatened. The changes in the electoral code enabled opposition parties to gain representation in 1996 and decentralized the dominance of the state by the ruling party. The 1998 reaction by the state shows that the state may feel threatened and insist on more control of national and local institutions. While the 1992 electoral changes facilitated democratic competition, the 1998 changes did not.

A final aspect of recent decentralization efforts in Senegal is the liberalization of societal institutions intended to foster development. Since the mid-1980s, it became apparent that the rural cooperatives did not encourage agricultural productivity or facilitate development. As a response, the National Assembly passed the New Agricultural Policy in 1984, a law that enabled the state to gradually pull back from the agricultural market and dismantle the cooperatives. The state stopped setting the market price for commodities, and only provided a floor below which prices could not fall (Ka and van de Walle 1992). One of the most successful aspects of the New Agricultural Policy has been the establishment of economic interest groups (*groupements d'intérêt economique*-GIE). By 1990, there were over 5,000 GIEs in Senegal. Any number of individuals can form a GIE, though they must pay approximately 50,000 CFA ($100) to register with the state. Recognition as a GIE enables an organization to obtain bank loans, licenses for trade and transport, assistance from CER officers, and CER recommendations for access to international donor funds (Peace Corps official, 30 June 1995; *Chef du CER*, Ndoulo *arrondissement*, 22 May 1995). Several local organizations have been empowered through GIE status, and the program has helped to devolve some power from the state to civil society.

However, there have been limits to this devolution. Some rural citizens, development workers, and scholars (Sy 1988; Ka and van de Walle 1992; Club du Sahel 1987) argue that in one sense the program removes the pressure from the central state to provide for basic development needs for its people, since GIEs are now responsible for development. On the other hand, the requirements of registration and fees enable the state to better control rural populations and development. The Club du Sahel (1987) writes that while the GIE program had the appearance of creating more economic possibilities for more associations, the reform has really enabled the state to control local economic movements. One group president in rural Diourbel said the program was "simply a way for the state to make money, without really providing any benefits to its rural citizens" (President Patar men's group, 12 April 1995).

Also, the money needed for registration has been prohibitive for some organizations (Peace Corps official, 30 June 1995). The president of a women's group that wanted to gain GIE status but did not have the money said, "The GIE program rewards wealthy groups with more access to state resources. Poor groups that most need state help to further the economic goals of their members are left out" (President Ndoulo women's group, 16 February 1995). The lack of GIE status has prohibited some rural citizens from accessing state resources and international donor assistance. Rather than foster societal equality and access to the state, the GIE policy may actually increase inequality. In doing so, this state-initiated program has not increased democracy or development.

From a preliminary examination, it appears that the post-1990 decentralization policies in Senegal have been somewhat shallow. The reforms have been portrayed as something that will increase the power of civil society, but in reality they have not helped to foster democracy or development at the local level. Granted, it is impossible to evaluate the effect of the regional assemblies. However, since the central state faces increasing economic problems, it is difficult to believe that the state will be able to provide the resources needed to develop and sustain institutional capacities at the regional level. The slow pace at which the regional reforms have been implemented also does not attest to the state's commitment to them. Electoral reforms have been more likely to be instituted, though the changes in the electoral codes did not fully enable civil society to counter the state. Even the GIE program, while enrolling many groups, has not increased the power of a large number of rural citizens and has not markedly improved rural development. The recent decentralization reforms, like those that preceded them, are best understood as central state reactions to increasing local, national, and international pressures.

CONCLUSION

There are several explanations for why the Senegalese state has attempted to re-distribute authority since independence. First, the Senegalese state and the international donors that have provided it resources have been guided by the argument that reconfiguring power and resources from the central state to civil society institutions will increase democracy and development. Local institutions can best understand development problems and have the most appropriate solutions to those issues. They permit participation and accountability, two aspects of democracy often lost in African national politics. Decentralization has been viewed as a remedy for the failure of colonial and postcolonial state policies.

The second explanation for the decentralization efforts in Senegal is the French colonial history of centralized economic and political power. As a reaction to French authoritarianism, Senghor sought to disperse power, incorporate rural individuals into the public realm, and facilitate economic development. However, even Senghor's postcolonial decentralization efforts were controlled by urban elites, who had a history of citizenship in the *quatre communes*. The relationship between the state and civil society continues to be shaped by the citizen-subject mindset present during colonialism. Subjects, or the peasants in rural areas, are to accept the rule of urban elites. Even policies that appear to incorporate the input of "subjects," such as AR or the rural councils, are patrimonial in nature. Yet it is necessary to realize that leaders in Senegal have not purposely emulated French colonialism. While devolution of power in Senegal has been unable to completely facilitate rural democracy and development, leaders of independent Senegal have sought to move beyond the centralization of French colonialism.

A third factor that has pushed state elites to attempt decentralization has been the political climate. The political unrest in 1968 led to the formation of rural councils. The 1988 postelection riots caused Diouf to reform the electoral system. The separatist movement in the Casamance pressured Diouf to set up regional assemblies, which then could provide the Casamance some level of autonomy from the state. The country's economic situation has contributed to this political instability. SAPs and the 1994 devaluation have increased public cynicism and decreased trust in the state and President Diouf. In response, Diouf has sought to release pressure through decentralization efforts.

A final factor that has contributed to decentralization in Senegal is external forces. French actions and the spread of democratic movements throughout West Africa encouraged Diouf to further liberalize the political system in the 1990s. International donors have pressed African states to devolve authority (Conyers 1983), arguing for the positive democratic and development outcomes it can bring. Donors such as USAID have spent money to facilitate the process. Donors often fill the space left when the state devolves its responsibilities to develop a country but does not provide the resources and power to local institutions to do those tasks. Because they have resources, donors may help shape the development initiatives, priorities, and programs of local citizens, either independently or in conjunction with local NGOs. In doing so, they may ignore the participation of rural individuals and may not encourage grassroots transparency or accountability (Patterson 1998a). Though not purposely authoritarian, international donors may become like the patrimonial state as they control democracy and development.

Decentralization in Senegal has always been instituted from the top as a means to release political, economic, and social pressures on the state. The resources necessary for local institutions to facilitate effective and efficient development have been lacking, either because local elites cannot collect them (as in the case of tax money for CRs) or because the state has not provided them (as in the case of AR, regional assemblies, or GIEs). Rural citizens have viewed local institutions as an arm of the central state, as they did during the colonial period. And local government organizations, such as the cooperatives, the AR program, and the rural councils, have been under the tutelage of state agents such as the sub-prefect.

It is apparent that decentralization in Senegal has only partially achieved its goals of increasing democracy and development. Why have decentralization efforts had only limited success? I argue that the success of decentralization relates to the nature of the state in Senegal, and more broadly in Africa. Because the African state is weak, its attempts at decentralization are often piecemeal and viewed with suspicion by citizens. The institutional and political weaknesses of the African state make decentralization that effectively devolves power rather than deconcentrates it more difficult, because the state is afraid of losing control of resources and authority. Decentralization through devolution may inadvertently weaken the state, whereas what may be most needed in Africa is a strong and legitimate state. By a strong state I do not mean an undemocratic state, rather a state that can effectively provide development resources and support to its people, and one that has the legitimacy of its citizens. "[Decentralization] demands more centralization and more sophisticated political skills at the national level" (Tendler 1997, 143). In reality, decentralization does not force the state to become more accountable, participatory, or transparent in its financial affairs. Decentralization does not require the state to initiate the institutional reforms that are necessary to facilitate development and democracy locally and nationally.

The weakness of civil society in Africa compounds the weakness of the state. Because of its lack of resources and underdeveloped networks of communication, civil society is unable to force the state to be accountable or to encourage the state to institute needed reforms. A weak civil society also is easily captured by international donors and it may be suspicious of state attempts to build networks to civil society. Yet it is precisely the linkages between the state and civil society that are necessary to facilitate state legitimacy and accountability. Decentralization in Africa will be more likely to succeed when both the state and civil society in Africa are strengthened.

NOTES

1. In contrast, Robert Fatton (1992) uses neo-Marxist analysis to argue that the African state is partially captured by the ruling class. The state has ties to society, though even Fatton argues that the links between the dominant class and the institutions of the state are incomplete.

2. I interviewed individuals from primarily the Diourbel region during 1994 and 1995. Interviewees were assured that their names would not be included in any publications.

3. Though there are also ninety-eight municipalities in Senegal's cities, there are several reasons why I will focus on the rural communities. First, the majority of Senegal's population is situated in rural areas. Second, the Senegalese state and international donors have viewed rural development as central to the development of the country. Consequently, decentralization efforts have focused on empowering rural areas, not urban areas. Third, Senegal's colonial history divided urban and rural areas and their populations. Because of this legacy, Senegal must incorporate its large rural population into the public realm in order to increase democracy and development.

4. Prior to 1992, sixty legislative seats had been allocated through proportional representation and sixty through winner-take-all. The 1992 changes reflected the aftermath of the 1988 election riots, when the opposition was able to convince the PS to equalize the rules of the electoral game.

Chapter 7

Re-distribution of Authority in South Africa: Centralizing the Government; "Rainbowing" the Nation

Eleanor E. Zeff and Ellen B. Pirro

In a number of respects, South African re-distributions of authority have made headlines more often and more dramatically than contemporary alterations of power in other parts of the world, even Eastern Europe. High voter turnout, relatively peaceful majority elections in 1994 and 1999, and the charismatic leadership of Nelson Mandela and F. W. de Klerk made the whole world take notice of South African politics. South Africa has recently and profoundly changed its entire political system. Few imagined, even in the 1980s, that this deeply divided country would have been able to move so smoothly from rule by an "ascriptive racial minority" (the whites) (Friedman 1995, 531) to a majority elected government that is mainly African.

The previous government used a comprehensive political, social, and economic system, apartheid, based on separation of the races, to keep control over the majority of nonwhite South Africans. Ethnic divisions among the nonwhites further compounded the complexity of the situation, leading many to fear that the only way to change authority would be through violence. Yet this scenario did not occur. Re-distribution of authority began in the 1990s, when President de Klerk and the National Party dissolved the apartheid system and the old constitution, recognized the African National Congress (ANC) and other political parties, freed Nelson Mandela and other black political leaders, and opened elections to all South Africans, including the formerly disenfranchised two-thirds of the population. The first elections were held in 1994; the second ones in 1999. The 1990s have seen steady change and progress toward a racially integrated society with a new government representing the entire

The authors wish to thank Clayton J. Cleveland for his help with this research.

society. Authority and citizenship has been extended from the white minority to all citizens.

This chapter describes how two differing and seemingly contradictory processes, popular enfranchisement and centralization, are combining to create a new South African state where authority has recently changed hands and the electorate has grown considerably. Centralization and popular enfranchisement traditionally do not go together. Because centralization indicates that the national government is focusing its power, there are usually fewer opportunities for citizen participation. To some, enfranchisement means simply the ability to vote. In South Africa, its meaning is much broader and includes not only increasing political participation but also the expansion of economic and social opportunities at all levels of society.

This chapter briefly outlines South Africa's recent history and then examines two major research questions. The first question asks why and how popular enfranchisement occurred. Four major explanatory factors are discussed: economic factors, external pressures, internal pressures from political and social groups, and the leadership of Nelson Mandela and F. W. de Klerk.

The second question examines why the South African political system, contrary to current global trends, is engaged in centralizing power in the national government. Four possible explanations emerge: economic development imperatives, security imperatives, the ANC's political philosophy and objectives, and deconcentration of functions such as territorial restructuring and administrative "rainbowing" to diversify and expand the leadership of the country.

Like the fall of communism, the fall of apartheid was largely unpredicted. Most observers believed that South Africa could "hold out" for years. Throughout the years of major change, 1989-1995, scholars applauded the leadership for its willingness to negotiate, to foster peace, and to move within the context of a democratic system (Bratton 1998, 214). Few have looked beyond these obvious elements to investigate what is happening within the structure of the country. It is the contention of this chapter that although South Africa has undergone significant change, there are many pitfalls along its chosen route as the country seeks to reverse its economic downslide while expanding political, social, and economic benefits to all citizenry. South Africa's future prospects are by no means rosy unless it successfully moves through these present dangerous times. It is also significant to note that because the South African case is so new, there are few concrete outcomes and research is limited to the immediate past. Although it is difficult to attribute results concretely to the new governments, it is important to examine the process of re-distribution of authority in order to understand where the new South Africa is heading.

BACKGROUND

South Africa is a medium-sized nation of thirty-eight million inhabitants located on the southernmost tip of the African continent. South Africa remains a highly diverse and complex society composed of many different ethnic groups.[1] The new Constitution of 1996 designates eleven official languages, including Afrikans, English, and nine major African languages. South Africa's history is an account of the coming of group after group. Dutch Boers (Afrikans) arrived in 1652 and displaced several nomadic groups. They were followed by the British, while at the same time Bantu tribesmen were moving southward into South Africa. Gold and diamonds were discovered near Johannesburg in the 1860s and quickly became the backbone of the economy, although various types of farming also continued. The British gained control of these precious resources, winning the Boer War in 1902 and establishing the semi-independent Union of South Africa in 1910. The Union introduced the Westminster model of parliamentary democratic government to Africa. Like Canada, the Union remained in the British Commonwealth with self-government and increasingly loose ties to Great Britain.

The apartheid system came into effect only in 1948 when the Afrikaner-dominated National Party gained the parliamentary majority. From the 1950s until the late 1980s, this party continued its de facto single party rule, using the police and the military to enforce separation of the races, repression, and censorship. Government was strong, authoritarian, and centralized under the Nationalists. The fabric of apartheid laws governed every aspect of life. The majority of the nonwhite population were required to live in restricted areas, were disenfranchised, and had to carry passes at all times. While the government retained the traditional colonial provinces, they carved out of them "African homelands," the Bantustans, foreseeing a future when all blacks would return to their homelands to live. White South Africans alone had the vote, despite numbering less than a third of the total population. Apartheid was an ambitious experiment in social engineering (Ottaway 1993, 18). It permeated all aspects of life in South Africa. To dismantle apartheid would entail major changes throughout the entire social, economic, and political arenas.

International pressures for change began to develop in the 1970s and intensified in the late 1980s. The international community became familiar with South African atrocities such as the Sharpeville and Langa killings, the Church Street bombings, the Soweto uprising, the killing of Steve Biko, and the so-called "black on black" violence. The National Party, first under President P. W. Botha (1983-1989) and later President F. W. de Klerk (1989-1994), began to modify the apartheid system and make overtures to the West and to the banned South African parties, especially the African National Congress (ANC), the Pan Africanist Party (PAC), the South African Communist Party (SACP), and the Inkatha Freedom Party (IFP). In February 1990, de Klerk lifted the ban on all political parties and released Nelson Mandela, the ANC's acknowledged political leader, who had been in prison for twenty-seven years.

With the lifting of the ban, the political parties began competing for political power using centralization/decentralization as a major distinguishing issue. F. W. de Klerk wanted to negotiate for a power-sharing form of government in which the National Party could still play a part. Although the Nationalist government had been strongly centralized, de Klerk thought a decentralized system would maximize Nationalist strongholds in the Cape and elsewhere. He proposed various consociational schemes and forms of proportional representation to assure white citizens that they would continue to play a part in the government.[2] The IFP was also interested in power sharing and submitted its own proposals for decentralizing power and allocating it to the provinces. In contrast, the ANC was the only major negotiating force advocating a strongly centralized form of government. Despite the disparity in viewpoints, enough compromise occurred to allow the adoption of the Interim Constitution (December 1993), the first national constitution to include all ethnic groups, in time for the first major nationwide elections in 1994. These elections were fair according to international standards, and voter turnout was high, with violence held to a minimum. The ANC won major victories and Nelson Mandela became president. South Africa began its re-distribution of authority in a surprisingly peaceful manner.

Once elected, the new government immediately began work on the permanent constitution, which was passed in 1996, taking effect in January 1997. In January 1998, Nelson Mandela stepped down as head of the ANC and was succeeded by Thabo Mbeki. Mandela then announced he would not stand for reelection. In the first national elections under the new constitution, on June 2, 1999, Mbeki was elected president with a majority of sixty-five percent. Mbeki is widely believed to have a more technocratic leadership style and his big majority allows him to increase the size of the presidential office, get rid of some of the less effective ANC leaders, and more directly control the government (Daley 1999b). With this election, the South African government passed a major hurdle: the peaceful transition of authority through the electoral process.

FROM APARTHEID TO A MULTIRACIAL GOVERNMENT

Why did re-distribution of authority and massive popular enfranchisement occur in South Africa? What are some of the explanations, and why, in an otherwise violent society, did this change occur so peacefully? Considered here are four major explanatory factors: economic factors, external pressures, internal pressures from political and social groups, and the leadership of Nelson Mandela and F. W. de Klerk.

Economic Factors

The downward spiral of the South African economy was the major factor that ended apartheid. South Africa, alone among the African states, moved into the modern era with multiple technological advances. Most of the world, and South Africa itself, has considered South Africa "developed." After the fall of apartheid, it became apparent that there were two South African economies: a first world, developed, white economy and a third world, lesser developed, nonwhite economy.

It has been the task of each South African government to keep the national economy functioning at a high level. During much of the apartheid era (1948–1989), the South African economy prospered and government involvement was minimal. The international changes of the 1980s altered everything. The end of the Cold War, worldwide recession, and the computer revolution spurred the downward turn of the South African economy. There were three reactions: The South African government took a more active role in "managing" the economy; as conditions worsened, internal support for the apartheid regime weakened; the South African government and economy became more vulnerable to external economic pressures, which ultimately doomed the apartheid system.

South Africa's exports, especially in the area of minerals, were very important both to South Africa's GNP and to the Western nations during the Cold War. In the 1970s and 1980s, the price of gold on the world market stayed high and diamonds were in demand. South Africa supplied the major portion of both of these products to the rest of the world. In addition, South Africa also mined a number of specialized metals such as chrome and argon, which were greatly needed by the Western powers for their super weaponry as they prepared for the later stages of the Cold War. Much of the West, including the United States under the Reagan and Bush administrations, turned a blind eye to the excesses of South Africa's apartheid policies and argued that the need for the minerals South Africa could supply outweighed any political considerations. This picture changed in the 1980s. First, the price of gold fell and did not recover. With the downslide of the Soviet Union and the end of the Cold War, the need for South Africa to supply other strategic minerals declined as well. Unfortunately, South Africa needed these international earnings to continue to purchase oil, the one major commodity vital to continued technological advances that was not produced domestically.

Also, South Africa had become deeply involved in Cold War military ventures in a number of neighboring countries in the name of anticommunism. The price tag for these adventures was steep. According to an article in the *Wall Street Journal*, (5 September 1985), in order to finance its military operations, South Africa had contracted a large amount of short-term debt, placed by one source at around $22 billion (US). Ultimately, it was these loans and the action of United States' banks that turned the tide against the apartheid regime.

Despite large trade surpluses, financial market experts became concerned about the safety of investments and loans in South Africa. International pressures on the economy increased, as did the flight of capital, which was estimated at about $2 billion a year through the 1980s (Lewis 1989, 167). Banks in the United States decided to cease their lending in late 1985. They demanded that the South African government make major concessions toward the black population to turn around the economic crisis. Instead, the Botha regime reaffirmed strict apartheid principles. US banks began to ask for loan repayment and refused to extend further credit and loans, triggering a lack of confidence, which soon spread to financial institutions throughout the world. The South African economy went into a downward spiral, where change was necessary to avert total economic disaster. Finally, in 1989, Botha was forced to resign, and de Klerk took over and began to dismantle apartheid.

External Pressures

During the 1980s, at the same time as the economic downturn, the international community created pressure to stimulate change in South Africa. Forming a group to end the apartheid system and re-distribute South Africa's leadership authority more equitably, the nations participating in this international effort created pressure in three ways. First, the United Nations voted a series of sanctions against South Africa, which were designed to isolate the country, economically and socially. Countries participating in applying sanctions included the nonaligned states at the UN and former Commonwealth colonies. A number of these countries were the frontline states, which were dependent on South Africa for both exports and imports. For these countries especially, upholding sanctions caused hardships and forced sacrifices. Second, and partially in line with the sanctions, the United Nations and the British Commonwealth expelled South Africa from membership. Other international groups also expelled or excluded South Africa from major international cultural and sporting activities. Third, a number of nongovernmental groups within the United States and other nations, such as the labor unions, various churches, the National Association for the Advancement of Colored People (NAACP), etc., began campaigns against the apartheid South African government, seeking pressure for changes by having corporations divest themselves of their South African holdings. Members of these groups and others attended the stockholder meetings of large businesses and solicited proxies for divestiture. They also pressured colleges and universities to divest from South Africa. All these steps contributed to South Africa's increasing isolation and exacerbated a strong economic downswing.

These international pressures culminated in a reversal of US policy, which proved to be critical for South Africa. Before then, the United States had continued its tacit support of the apartheid regime.   Under the Reagan administration, the official US policy toward South Africa was titled "constructive engagement," which meant continuing to interact with the country both economically and politically while trying to push for South Africa to change its internal policies.   By the beginning of Reagan's second term, however, it was evident that South Africa was not moving away from its apartheid system and that US policies were not expanding democracy there. Despite opposition from the Reagan administration, a bipartisan coalition in the US Congress passed the Comprehensive Anti-Apartheid Act in 1986.   As directed by Congress, the United States ceased trade and official communication with South Africa.

As the Cold War ended, it became obvious that the United States and the Western world no longer needed South Africa as an ally against "communist aggression," and that African nations could no longer be used by one side against the other. The end of the Cold War meant that many African conflicts, including some with direct impact on South Africa, could be and were resolved. The fact that South Africa fought "communist aggression" had previously allowed the South African military to intervene in many of the conflicts of its neighbors.   South Africa had fought in Angola since the beginning of the Angolan civil war in 1981.   In 1986, South Africa used force to change the government of Lesotho. In its efforts to eliminate the guerrilla camps of the ANC, South Africa launched attacks against Zimbabwe, Botswana, and Zambia. It was also known that South Africa's military played major roles in the Namibian and Mozambique conflicts. With the end of the Cold War, South Africa became vulnerable to pressures from other African and developing nations to stop interfering in the internal affairs of its neighbors. When these additional pressures combined with existing international, antiapartheid forces, the apartheid government in South Africa, with no remaining room to maneuver, had little choice but to change.

Internal Pressures

Within South Africa, various political movements worked to dismantle apartheid and enfranchise the majority of the population, but these groups were severely limited by the activities of the repressive regime.   Religious leaders filled the leadership vacuum when political leaders were jailed or exiled. Even peaceful protests resulted in severe repression in events such as the Sharpeville massacre. In the Cold War atmosphere, guerrilla movements were very small and poorly funded and supported. Only small bands of the ANC's Spear of the Nation managed a few guerrilla activities on South Africa's border.

Furthermore, the apartheid government successfully stimulated the fear among all sectors of the society that even their neighboring countries were dangerous.

Much of the frustration expressed by black South Africans against the apartheid regime was economic in nature. Despite the fact that, in general, black Africans were better off economically in South Africa than they were in other parts of Africa, they were limited in their ability to advance to top positions and compete economically with white South Africans under the apartheid regime. The desire for change and for the re-distribution of economic power grew as black South Africans confronted their economic limitations. Yet South Africans were careful because no one, including the black political movements, wanted to endanger the developed nature and position of the South African economy or destroy the economic well-being of its citizens.

Although South Africa has a history of violence, and there were great internal pressures for change, spearheaded by various political movements among black Africans, much of the political activity was not violent. The roots of African political involvement extend back to the founding of the Union of South Africa in 1910. The ANC is more than eighty years old, and although it was banned by the government in 1960, it continued to exist underground and in exile. The Inkatha Freedom Party (IFP) originated as a Zulu cultural movement in the 1920s, and the Pan African Congress and the African Communist Party both have long South African histories. By the end of the 1980s, most of the black electorate, with the exception of several Zulu groups, supported the ANC in its attempts to pressure the apartheid National Party government to re-distribute power (Giliomee 1998, 131).

While each of these groups sought change in South Africa, the pervasive and coercive structure of the apartheid police and military prevented much of the violence that accompanied other "liberation movements" in Africa. The military and police under the National Party government had two major occupations: repression of other than white racial groups and protecting the national borders. The police enforced the hated "pass" laws and harassed and arrested black Africans. They infiltrated the change movements and incited intertribal rivalries as well. Both police and military were highly trained, with up-to-date equipment and large salaries. The results were a series of severe repressive measures against those who dared seek change. The police arrested black demonstrators, even nonviolent ones. In jail, a number of leaders "disappeared," or like Steve Biko, died mysteriously. Others, like Mandela, received long sentences with little hope of release.

Under these conditions, internal protests came largely from the clergy and religious movements. Bishop Desmond Tutu, Alan Boesak, and others came to prominence by speaking for South African freedom. Some peaceful protests occurred in boycotts, strikes and nonparticipatory actions, especially among renters and students. When conflict erupted, it was mainly between various black ethnic groups, such as between the Inkatha Party and members of the ANC.

There are several explanations for why major internal conflict did not occur. First, the apartheid government created a "siege mentality" internally and provided an external outlet for people's aggressive tendencies by engaging in many conflicts on its various borders. Most South Africans, black and white, believed that their country was under attack from communist neighbors and that the nation had to be strong in the face of potential foreign aggression. Second, many black South Africans feared that a large influx of Africans from the poorer neighboring countries would mean a loss of jobs and decreased wages for themselves. In addition, according to polls taken at the time (Mattes and Thiel 1998, 102), when most South Africans, black or white, thought of the political system, they defined government and politics in economic ways. Indeed, much of the frustration experienced by black South Africans under apartheid came from their low wages, their inability to get an education, training or promotions, as well as their lack of basic life needs such as housing, clean water, electricity, and garbage collection. At the same time, most blacks realized that living in South Africa meant having a standard of living far exceeding other Africans in neighboring nations. Despite massive poverty, the potential for growth and prosperity within South Africa has traditionally been far greater than it is outside the country, and most South Africans appreciate this fact. To prevent violence the system has always maintained some outlets for frustration among the nonenfranchised black and colored population, by providing the means for limited economic well-being and limited access to modern amenities.

These two considerations do suggest a future danger. Now that the leadership has changed and the electorate has expanded, the population expects governmental and political re-distributions to result in rapid and major economic changes. However, in most developing nations it is necessary to endure a period of continued and in some cases increased deprivation, in order to put development into effect (Shils 1960, 329-68). Although South Africa has long positioned itself as developed and not part of the third world, the majority of black Africans, who make up about two-thirds of the population, have a standard of living more in line with people in other third world countries. All South African citizens are now constitutionally able to share fully in the nation's economy, but that economy is not growing very fast. The system itself has been slow to change, and continued high unemployment, crime, lack of capital investment, and sluggish foreign trade may forecast upcoming frustration and potential internal conflict. South Africa clearly needs time to make substantial gains in the economic sphere and to solidify the re-distribution of authority to an expanded electorate and to the new ANC leadership. Many feel that time is too short and may be running out.

The Leadership of de Klerk and Mandela

The nature of South African leadership arises as an additional explanation for why power re-distribution occurred in South Africa and why the process of popular enfranchisement and leadership change was largely peaceful. South African leaders, and in particular Nelson Mandela and F. W. de Klerk, played important roles in preventing conflict and in influencing the way re-distribution of authority occurred.

It is widely believed that the charismatic leadership of Mandela helped create the so-far successful governmental change. He has also been widely praised for his forgiveness of the apartheid leaders and others who were his oppressors, for his extraordinary push for reconciliation, and for his willingness to compromise. He did not seek revenge on those who imprisoned him for twenty-seven years, nor did he seek wide-scale retribution on the police and military who were the arms of repression. Initially, he embraced power-sharing in government, in order to give the former white rulers a continuing role and speed the process of re-distribution. Mandela has been able to unify the people of all races in a way that no one else has as yet accomplished. His charisma is such that at a recent rugby game he donned the Springbok shirt, symbol of the once all-white national team, and was resoundingly cheered by the entire stadium of mainly white spectators (Issues of Rugby and Race 1996). De Klerk also deserves his share of praise for his willingness to abandon the past, his power to convince other members of his party to create change, and his ability to work together with his former "enemy."

Several elements of both men's leadership styles have contributed to the shaping of these major national changes. First, both leaders emerged as highly pragmatic. They recognized that the country's success depended on maintaining economic growth and development in the modern, technological world and in continuing the relatively high standards of living for all the citizens of South Africa. They realized that revolution, bloodshed, and even a series of legal trials or lengthy legal battles would disrupt the economy. Furthermore, unrest would probably exacerbate the flight of capital investment from abroad and the emigration of white South Africans, who are the most skilled and technically advanced people in the country. As leaders they recognized that both elements were badly needed to keep the nation on course, and they have worked hard to entice both money and people to remain in South Africa. Second, neither leader wished to fight. With numerical superiority on one side and superiority in technical weaponry on the other, both foresaw a huge bloodbath, should change be attempted through conflict. The outbreaks of violence that did occur convinced both men that fighting was not the pathway to success.

Third, both leaders are somewhat authoritarian and view government as a strong central force that should take decisive action for the nation as a whole.

De Klerk received his political training under the highly centralized apartheid regime. His philosophy viewed the national government as the one agency that can control the economy and maintain security. Mandela's ANC has traditionally been a highly centralized political party. He has viewed centralization as the best method to unify the various ethnic groups and prevent the emergence of challenges to the ANC. Thus, both before and during the Government of National Unity, there was agreement between these two leaders on many of the basic principles of the new constitution. Even today, with the National Party in opposition, there is still widespread agreement among most of the leadership on the basic structures and principles for governing, and centralized government is at the heart of these beliefs (Giliomee 1998, 131-3).

CENTRALIZING AND "RAINBOWING" THE GOVERNMENT

As South Africa approaches the millennium, it will confront many problems, including demands for economic development and for integrating and empowering millions of newly enfranchised citizens into all realms of politics, economics and society ("rainbowing"). Currently, events, actions by the Governments, and the political literature demonstrate a consensus among leaders, citizens, and parties that the best way for South Africa to achieve its many goals is by centralizing authority. Thus, at this time, but unlike some other countries that are also re-distributing authority, South Africa is moving toward administrative and territorial centralization (Giliomee 1998; Lodge 1997). "To achieve the policy goals fed by this interpretation of reality, South Africa's government became highly centralized" (Vale 1999, 14). Simultaneously, South Africa is also trying to "rainbow" the nation by opening all levels of government and all areas of administration to all races. A series of factors explain these choices: economic development imperatives; security imperatives; the African National Congress (ANC) political philosophy and objectives; and de-concentration of functions only (rather than transfers of real power).

Economic Development Imperatives

Two major economic goals faced the new government of Nelson Mandela in 1994: turning the economy around and restoring the "good times" of the 1970s; and economic enfranchisement and opening all levels of the economy to all races. Achieving these goals is proving much more difficult than expected.

The economic system the ANC inherited was in chaos. When the government changed, it became apparent that the sanctions had taken a heavy toll on the South African economy. The first years of the new era, 1990 to

1992, saw negative economic growth in the country. Over fifty percent of the population lived below the poverty line and most of these people were black Africans. Over the prior ten-year period, a significant amount of capital fled South Africa and few investors came forward to put money in the country after apartheid. In this tense atmosphere, a significant number of white South Africans, including many skilled and valuable technocrats, left the country (White South Africa on the Wing 1998). During the crisis years of isolation (1980–1990), South Africa was cut off from all kinds of technological advances and fell behind the rest of the industrial world by about ten years (Simkins 1996, 82).

In this situation of economic crisis, the Mandela government felt that only the national government was in a position to take the drastic measures designed to turn around the economic downslide. Centralizing economic functions in the government was widely accepted as the appropriate choice given the crisis nature of the economy. A number of initiatives have been attempted, but the results have not all been as beneficial as desired. Currently, the economy suffers from high interest rates, low gold prices, shortage of skilled workers, and low savings rates. These are mostly problems that could be helped by strong central planning and good leadership. The new administration, with its increased mandate under ANC leaders President Thabo Mbeki and Finance Minister Trevor Manuel, will have more direct control over the economy with the increased power of the presidential office (Funky for a Day at Least 1999).

Soon after the 1994 elections, the new government began centralizing its control over the economy and pushing for economic growth by putting the Reconstruction and Development Program (RDP) into effect. This program addressed some of the major national needs and focused on formerly disenfranchised Africans. In 1996, a newer program, GEAR (Growth, Employment and Re-Distribution) was instituted to move the nation more quickly along the development path. Some significant gains have been made. Under the RDP, three million children had school lunches, 1.7 million people got water benefits, 1.2 million citizens were connected to electricity for the first time, and a great number of houses were built (Handley and Herbst 1997, 225; Bratton 1998, 216). However, within a short time after enactment, the GEAR program turned the national focus away from the social needs of the people to the overall economic development of the nation. GEAR is economically conservative, which has alienated the major labor unions. It is also fiscally cautious, partially in response to the fluctuations of the rand (South Africa's currency) in 1996 and 1998, to the limited foreign investment, and to the restricted budget. Hoping to improve the levels of foreign investment, GEAR seeks to recreate the booming times of the 1960s and the 1970s by creating a similar economic climate.

Until the sanctions era, South Africa had enjoyed high levels of commerce with a variety of nations. There was an assumption that when the government changed, South Africa would be "back in business" and involved in the high levels of trade it had enjoyed in the past. This situation did not develop. During the ten years when South Africa was isolated from the rest of the international community, former buyers found alternative supplies and suppliers. After the 1994 elections, South Africa largely started from the beginning to build up trade. In 1998, the government took a leading role in targeting growth with former partners Japan, Australia, New Zealand, the European Union, and the United States (South Africa and the EU 1996). Currently, South Africa has a negative balance of trade with many countries such as Germany. It hopes to redress this current trade imbalance with its recent trade initiatives. As in the past, the South African government is again a major player in negotiating trade deals, stimulating trade, and being generally involved in the management of its economy. The government feels that playing a central role in international trading is vital to the expansion and balance of national trade and also should stimulate the entire country's economy (South Africa and the EU 1996).

Furthermore, the Mandela government felt that many concerns such as land reform were so bitterly divisive and so variable from one section of the country to another that they had to be taken over and handled centrally by the national government. Under apartheid, Africans could not own property. Over the years, in many areas of the country, traditional and tribal lands were appropriated for various agricultural and business reasons. Now black Africans and Coloureds are demanding restoration of property, division of property, etc. These demands range all the way from Bushmen suing for traditional tribal lands to residents of Soweto purchasing their shanties. The worst problems come with the distribution of agricultural land. There are well-documented accounts of black Africans being moved off their lands and into "Bantu homelands," but the government cannot easily remove Afrikaner farmers from lands where their families have lived for several generations and that they consider to be their ancestral homes. (Under Threat 1998). Much of the agricultural basis of the economy and a major source of South Africa's earnings come from these large-scale farms, which have belonged to and are run by Afrikaners. The typical African small holding is neither efficient nor economically effective and usually operates at subsistence level or below even in the best farming areas.

The Mandela administration placed land questions into a centralized, federal arena but has moved very slowly, allocating only limited funds to purchase land from those willing to sell and reforming legislation on home ownership in the towns (Under Threat 1998). Very few Africans have benefited to date and there are many pressures to move land re-distribution ahead at a faster pace. Land re-distribution decisions are important because agriculture is one of the major areas of the economy, employing a sizable proportion of the population. South Africa had traditionally supplied Western Europe, Japan,

Australia, and New Zealand with agricultural commodities until the sanctions started. Now the agricultural sector must be "jump-started" and these markets reconstructed. Land re-distribution is also a major concern, but the government is limited in what it can do without disrupting too drastically the former structure while at the same time meeting the strong needs of the national economy. Furthermore, "land reform might help ease tensions in the countryside, but the government does not have the cash" (Under Threat 1998).

Security Imperatives

The security area provides a clear illustration of the ways the new government is using centralization to enfranchise new portions of the population, as well as reduce challenges to the new regime. Security in South Africa remains the prerogative of the military and the police. The apartheid regime centralized the police force and created a national cabinet ministry for each security force. The Mandela-Mbeki governments have continued this policy. There are several areas of concern for the new regime, including police and military personnel, reduction of crime, and modernization.

Personnel situations have high priority for the new administration. Both the police and the military have large numbers of Africans, but the majority are outside the officer corps, which continues to be white and Afrikaner dominated. Also, these Africans are disliked by the majority of the population because they were used to enforce the hated apartheid laws against their fellow Africans. Because the police organization is centralized, the government has been able to take decisive actions: promoting Africans into the officer corps, moving unpopular personnel to different parts of the country, and seeking retraining. The military also agreed to ANC proposals to amalgamate the former armed forces of the liberation movements and the "homelands military" into the newly formed, regular defense forces, now known as the South African National Defense Force or SANDF (Kynoch 1996, 441). But, even with these assertive steps, there is a general consensus that change has been slow in coming, and much of the security operation is simply business as usual (Kynoch 1996, 457).

While providing an opportunity for some increased participation, the present security forces contain too many officers and personnel from the previous apartheid era to be able to absorb many new recruits. Under apartheid, South Africa maintained one of the largest per capita security organizations in the world. The Mandela-Mbeki governments are seeking ways to reduce the size of the security forces without leaving large numbers of former police and soldiers without a job. Security takes large chunks of the national budget that would be better diverted to development now that both internal unrest and threats on the borders are greatly reduced. Both the military and the police have retained their technological superiority, their equipment, prestige, and large salaries, and they are reluctant to give up their privileged positions (Kynoch 1996; Lodge 1997; Good 1997). South Africa is now trying to both "rainbow" its once paramilitary police force and turn it into a service group that is also friendly and efficient (Your Friends, the Police 1997). It will take a lot of cautious and delicate maneuvering for the government to achieve these goals.

The high crime rate remains a big challenge for the government. Under apartheid, the police were trained to control, harass and repress the black majority. Military forces were trained in antiguerrilla warfare and destined to fight in foreign wars. Neither police nor military were trained to investigate, solve, or prevent crimes. Thus, they have been unable to stop the huge growth of criminal activities. Johannesburg has the highest murder rate of any city in the world not involved in a war. Over 19,000 people were murdered in South Africa during 1995, and this rate had increased to seventy-one murders a day by 1996 (Good 1997, 549). The number of car hijackings, rapes and armed robberies has also increased and severely threaten the country's political and economic development. Many educated and talented people, whom the country can ill afford to lose, are moving to other countries because of their fear of crime.

The inability of the government to fire former bureaucrats including the police, and the lack of education and training of many people seeking work, have combined with the sluggish economy and other structural problems to increase unemployment levels to all-time highs, and to limit the amount of "rainbowing" which can be accomplished. Unemployment has increased the gap between rich and poor and has been a contributing factor to the rising crime rates. To date, there has been no reversal of the crime rate and policing has not noticeably improved. Instead, there is also widespread corruption of security forces and many crimes are being committed by service and ex-service personnel themselves (Lodge 1997, 15). Although some retraining is occurring, lack of funds severely limits such education. It is hoped that a better economic situation will reduce crime as well as provide resources to successfully restructure police work (Lodge 1997, 15).

The GNU made a number of administrative changes to "Africanize" the administration of security and to ensure central control by the government (Kynoch 1996, 441-57). It also developed more distinct divisions between military and police. ANC ministers took over portfolios of both units. The Mbeki administration has continued this policy. The monopoly of weaponry in these two administrative units always poses a potential challenge to constitutional authority, especially in Africa, with its history of military coups. The new government has not yet reduced the military nor cut its budget significantly, although it has stated that it intends to do so (Maphai 1996, 72). Both organizations are still top heavy and have highly centralized bureaucracies. These issues will become significant in the upcoming years. Continuing the centralized security forces has helped maintain political control over these units but has not improved their functioning within the new national situation. The country is hopeful that the recently appointed Minister of Security, Steve Tshwete, will improve the effectiveness of the security forces (Mandela's Heir 1999). The ANC administration supports a centralized security organization as the best route to achieve needed changes, including mandating procedural changes throughout the country, establishing national training programs, and continuing to ""rainbow"" the personnel at all levels. Mr. Mbeki has promised that the ANC will deliver (Mandela's Heir 1999).

ANC Political Philosophy and Objectives: The Centralization Choice

The African National Congress (ANC) faces crucial challenges as it moves from nationalist liberation movement to ruling party, trying to govern a land of tremendous diversity, with major ethnic groups vying for governmental attention and resources. The ANC is more like a revolutionary movement than it is like a political party. Its members are often uneasy with the idea of limited government, and presidential advisers have suggested that the ANC should extend its control over even more of the government (Mbeki's South Africa 1999). Despite a highly centralized organization and widespread support for the ANC, the party itself remains an umbrella organization with many different elements, including the powerful trade unions, business interests, various ethnic associations, and so on. "South Africa needs a dominant party to preserve stability, consolidate democracy, spur socioeconomic development, narrow class cleavages and contain populist pressures" (Giliomee 1998,132).

When the apartheid system ended, there were many calls for decentralization. Three major groups made demands. The Inkatha Freedom Party (IFP) under Buthelezi sought self-determination for the Zulu peoples. Chief Buthelezi wanted the Zulu areas to be as independent of the central government as possible. Also, the National Party (NP), which represented a majority of the white Afrikaner population, wanted to maintain its political involvement and economic supremacy. Finally, the homeland chiefs, individuals put into positions of power by the apartheid government, sought to retain their privileges among their ethnic groups.

One of the biggest problems for the ruling ANC government was to bring unity to the regions in spite of challenges posed by these three disparate groups. A brief description of the party system, the electoral system, and the final federal compromise helps explain the centralizing decisions taken by the ANC for governing South Africa.

Political Parties. Although the political party system in South Africa is currently undergoing a period of great change, its roots extend back to the beginning of the Republic in 1910. At the end of the apartheid era, there were already several established political parties that took part in the early negotiations for the Interim Constitution. The National Party (NP), which controlled the South African government from 1948 until the 1994 elections, was and still remains largely a party for white Afrikaners, with a current power base in the Western Cape. The ANC is also more than eighty years old, and although it was banned by the government in the 1960s it continued to exist in exile. By the end of the 1980s, "the ANC remained the unchallenged political home of most Africans," with the exception of conservative Zulus (L. Thompson 1995, 268). It received sixty-two and a half percent of the vote in the 1994 elections and was only one vote short of a two-thirds majority in the June 1999 parliamentary elections. Its popular support under both President Mandela and recently elected President Thabo Mbeki remains high. The Inkatha Freedom Party (IFP), which had originated as a Zulu cultural movement in the 1920s, was another big player in the constitutional negotiations. It continues as a powerful force under Chief Buthelezi in the KwaZulu Natal province. Other parties are quite small and their future is uncertain, given the centralizing tendencies of the new government and the ANC party. Because of the current strength of the ANC and despite the use of proportional representational voting, which is supposed to prevent single-party domination of the government, the South African regime is moving toward a dominant-party system similar to those in India and Mexico (Gilomee 1998, 128).

Elections and Political Enfranchisement. The de Klerk regime faced considerable difficulties when dealing with the issues of elections and political participation. A majority rule system meant that black Africans, with the largest number of people, would become the controlling force in any government, and this dominance was greatly feared by the existing white leaders. No fewer than nineteen political parties, as well as business and civic groups, participated in various stages of the discussion on these issues. Major and sometimes conflicting considerations were: how to divide the existing power among the many diverse groups in South Africa; how to share power fairly with these different groups while retaining the expertise of the people who had previously been in power; and how to peacefully enfranchise two-thirds of the population. Of particular importance was the prevention of any ethnic or other grouping developing a regional "island" apart from the rest of the country.

To solve these problems, the constitutional working groups suggested that voting for representatives to the South African Parliament be changed from direct voting to proportional representational voting (PR) in order to account for the more diverse opinions and parties in the greatly enlarged electorate. The party lists would be closed, and each voter would have two votes: one for a single party or organization on the national lists, and one for a single party or organization on the provincial lists (*Africa Research Bulletin* 1994, 11385). A PR voting system would theoretically allow white and other ethnic minority parties to have representation in both the legislature and the cabinet. The 1994 elections successfully used this system to elect a government of National Unity which included not only the majority ANC party representatives but also representatives from the National Party, the South African Communist Party (allied with the ANC along with COSATU) and the Inkatha Freedom Party. Marginalized by the new constitution, the National Party pulled out of the GNU in order to go into the opposition before the 1999 elections. These June 1999 elections, using PR voting, gave the ANC an even larger majority, although the party is still just short of the two-thirds majority needed to make constitutional changes. The NP's vote decreased from twenty-nine percent to less than eight percent. These election results confirmed the electorate's confidence in the ANC and will allow the party to continue its consolidation of power and centralization policies (Daley 1999a).

Between the elections of 1994 and 1999, the ANC was able to consolidate and centralize its authority so that there are currently fewer effective parties and less opposition. Results of the 1999 elections indicated that even parties with long histories in the country were dying (Daley 1999c). Despite the diversity of the population, the enlargement of the electorate, and the centralization of authority at the top, voter turnout for both the first election under the new system and the June 1999 elections was exceptionally high and amazingly peaceful under the circumstances; clear evidence of successful enfranchisement. Voter apathy was not a factor in the 1999 elections as had been predicted (Daley 1999a; 1999c).

Deconcentration of Functions: Territorial Restructuring and Administrative "Rainbowing"

The new South African government has also tried to cope with national diversity by changing the administrative divisions created under the apartheid system. The Union government had divided the country into fifteen provinces based on the original colonial divisions, and all subsequent governments including the apartheid regime left this structure intact. The apartheid regime had also created ten Bantu "homelands" by taking territory in various provinces and assigning it a tribal identity and maintaining a tribal "government." In 1994, the government of National Unity quickly eliminated the homelands as symbols of the repression enforced by the apartheid system, but it was harder to know what to do with the Bantu "chiefs" and "headmen" and the numerous bureaucrats who had "ruled" these areas and who wanted to retain their privileged positions and economic benefits.

South Africa made two major compromises that will have lasting impact on the future of the country. The Federal Compromise restructured the provincial boundaries of the entire nation. The Bureaucratic Compromise has had lasting implications for the civil service and for administrative implementation throughout the country. In both cases, the choice for centralization has meant retaining power in the federal government. Even where decentralized structures, such as provincial legislatures, continue to exist, real power is centralized. These local and provincial structures are becoming the focii of blame when malfunctions occur and the recipients when the federal government off-loads administrative tasks.

The Federal Compromise. It was apparent that the nation could not remain structured as it had under the "homelands" system. Not only did the hated homelands restrict a single ethnic group to one region, but the fifteen original provinces had ethnic bases within them with a potential of developing challenges to national authority.

The decision was made to centralize authority and redraw the provincial boundaries. First the homelands were dissolved and consolidated within their provinces. In most cases each homeland had been entirely encompassed in one province. Second, the fifteen old provinces were merged into nine new provinces, with only two of them similar to what they were under apartheid (Lyman 1996, 110). The 1996 Constitution lists these new provinces: The Eastern Cape, the Free State, Gauteng, KwaZulu-Natal, Mpumalanga, Northern Cape, Northern Province, North West, and Western Cape (34).

It is noteworthy that the provinces have "governments" and bureaucracies, but in most cases, they are allocated functional authority only, and are strictly limited in their capabilities. Chapter 6 of the Constitution discusses the rights and the legislative authority of each province (34-44). It states that each of the provinces has its own legislature and constitution. However, the provinces are functionally limited. The Federal Constitutional Court must certify any law passed by the individual legislatures (42). In most cases when there is a conflict between the national and provincial governments, the national government prevails (43).

Part of the constitutional debate involved the question of how the provinces should relate to the center and how much power and independence they should have. The result was to make the Federal Compromise three-tiered. The three tiers consist of the central government, the newly created nine provinces, and hundreds of local governments. Chapter 7 of the Constitution describes the functions and powers of the local governments. It states that the objects of local governments are to provide democratic and accountable government and promote social and economic development for local communities (45–48). The compromise gave the provincial governments joint responsibility with the central government for managing education, health, roads, and welfare issues, but the provincial governments were given no power (South Africa's Profligate Provinces 1998). They can neither create policy nor tax.

The major restrictions on the provinces are in the areas of raising revenues. Under the new Constitution, the provinces must receive all revenues from the federal government and cannot levy taxes themselves. This provision opens all activity at the provincial level to federal scrutiny and oversight. It also pits province against province in the competition for scarce revenues.

The Federal Compromise creates political artifacts, the provinces, which are designed to maximize the ruling authority of the new government and maintain ANC dominance. After the 1994 elections, the ANC party controlled seven of the nine provinces. In fact, several provinces were specifically "gerrymandered" to allow the ANC to gain control. The former Cape Province was split into two parts. The National Party controls the Western Cape province, which was split off from the Eastern Cape, an ANC stronghold. Similarly, the new KwaZulu-Natal province takes the former Natal province and links it with former homelands to create a province that came under the Inkatha Freedom Party control in the 1994 elections. The ANC isolated its major political opponents by giving them dominance in two provinces and secured its own continued supremacy in the other seven.

Under the Government of National Unity, Buthelezi, who headed the Inkatha party and was also Minister of Home Affairs, sought a devolution of power to the provincial level. Thwarted by ANC moves, he threatened secession and was supported by a number of Zulu chiefs. To date, nothing concrete has materialized from these threats but the possibility hangs over the ANC government. The fear is that Zulu success could open the door for other possible secessionist groups, including Xhosa, Tswana, Pedi, Venda, and Tsonga chiefs (including those who did well in the homelands but are now struggling) and, of course, white racists (L. Thompson 1995, 272).

Through the Constitution, South Africans have established a relatively unitary state, despite using terminology such as "federalism." The provinces have been created as a powerless buffer between the population, the local governments, and the federal government. The main function of the provincial governments is to implement policies and deliver services, despite lacking the ability to create the policies or even determine how the implementation will take place (Giliomee 1998; the 1996 Constitution). Because of this federal structure, the government can insulate itself from many of the day-to-day dissatisfactions with governmental operations. Furthermore, the federal government may view the provincial government as a logical site of blame for many problems (South Africa's Profligate Provinces 1998). So the federal compromise works to the advantage of the ANC politically and the federal government administratively.

The Bureaucratic Compromise. Part of enfranchisement includes opening all levels of government employment to all ethnic groups, ("rainbowing" the administrative services). Unfortunately, the bureaucratic compromise has effectively limited the extent of "rainbowing" that can occur. Before the 1994 elections, a promise was made that all members of the civil service would be retained. No one could lose a job because of restructuring, downsizing, or governmental change.

This compromise was made to facilitate the end of apartheid and to reassure white South Africans that they would still have a voice in the new government and still be employed. Neither the changes in government personnel nor the centralization of authority has opened up enough new civil service jobs to effectively "rainbow" the bureaucracy or enfranchise large number of Africans as part of the government.

Until the mid-1980s, South Africa was known for its developed infrastructure system, its well-trained bureaucrats, its relatively efficient bureaucracy and its wide administrative reach (Good 1997, 547; Lodge 1996, 196). However, since 1994, there has been a noticeable decline in the capacity of the state administration, both at the national and especially at the provincial levels of government, and administrative corruption has grown massively (Good 1997, 547; Lodge 1996, 196). Major problems with the bureaucracy are only beginning to emerge. As a part of the moves to gain support for a new constitution, to allay the fears of the white population who dread massive layoffs, and who constitute much of the bureaucracy, and to avoid resulting unrest, a promise was made before the 1994 elections to retain all former bureaucrats in the new government. Consolidating provinces and local systems has led to inflated numbers of bureaucrats who cannot be fired. New provinces often inherited bureaucrats from several former provinces. Because of the large numbers of "leftovers," who are largely white, it has become exceedingly difficult to find room for any new, ethnically diverse bureaucrats.

There is also a lack of newly trained and ethnically diverse individuals to fill the jobs of those civil servants who leave their government positions, especially at the higher and more technical levels. Throughout the country, education and training, especially in technical areas, have been suffering for lack of funding. The end result is inflated governmental bureaucracies, "54,000 who are paid but not needed; the Eastern Cape alone has 15,000. Yet one provincial minister argues that it would be 'immoral' to sack them" (Mbeki's South Africa 1999). Keeping the pre-1994 promises means that the government cannot fully restructure the bureaucracy and eliminate waste, lower civil service wages, make administration more efficient, or provide more ethnic diversity within the bureaucracy (Lodge 1996, 1997).

CONCLUSIONS

The relatively peaceful end of the repressive, and often violent, apartheid system, the change in leaders and parties, the acceptance of a new and liberal constitution, and the enfranchisement of millions of new voters has caused the world to take notice of South Africa. The apartheid system fell, as has been described, because of internal and international pressures, especially in the economic area. That these changes occurred peacefully is due in large part to the extraordinary leadership of the two major politicians, Mandela and de Klerk. It is also due to their dominant guidance that South Africa has remained highly centralized.

Here is a country that has experienced drastic re-distribution of power in a relatively short period of time. On the one hand, there has been a massive and relatively peaceful re-distribution of authority from an elite, centralized, racially repressive regime to an inclusive, participatory government that includes over thirty million newly enfranchised citizens. On the other hand, the new governments in both 1994 and 1999 are demonstrating a desire to centralize authority in their elected leadership and the dominant ANC party, despite greatly expanding the electorate. With high levels of participation by these newly enfranchised voters, national elections took place in 1994 and in 1999 with notable success. The Constitution of 1996 created new institutions, redivided the country into nine new provinces, and provided for safeguarding basic human rights for all races. In 1999, leadership passed from Nelson Mandela, the liberation leader and first president, to Thabo Mbeki, the technocrat and second president. Both men have supported strong centralization of the government in the name of protecting these hard- won changes.

Since the end of the apartheid regime widespread popular enfranchisement has occurred as the country moves toward its goal of becoming a "rainbow nation." Enfranchisement means a lot more than simply the ability to vote, although both national elections saw record turnout in all parts of the country. In South Africa, it means eliminating race as a basis for participation in all aspects of society: political, social, and economic. There are suggestions that "rainbowing" is beginning in many levels of private business, as well as in sports, recreation, and other aspects of daily life.

The ANC has opted for centralized control to easily mandate changes in both the security and economic areas, where potential crises may be developing. Furthermore, the situation is anything but static. One government official noted that it takes time to get things established, and at this early stage of the regime, it is very important for the government to speak with one voice on matters like education and the police (Van der Merwe 1999). The Constitution is flexible enough to allow for changes in the future, such as decentralizing some of its authority to the provinces. After governing becomes more routine, the ANC may well decide to loosen its grip on power and let some of this decentralization take place.

Yet many danger signals also exist. The 1999 elections saw South Africa come close to a one-party state with the ANC clearly dominating. The fear is that the ANC will use its monopoly of power to eliminate opposition and consolidate power as a single-party state. Already the ANC controls seven of the nine provincial governments. Indeed, the election victory shows that the

ANC is de facto the only political force in the country, although a number of smaller parties continue to sit in the legislature on the opposition side.

Other danger signals include an economic system that has not made dramatic gains and that is developing too slowly to keep up with the demands of the newly enfranchised citizens. Unemployment and crime are also rampant. There are enormous needs for education and training. Unless economic recovery improves, many remedies for society's ills simply cannot be funded and the worsening situation could lead to political unrest.

The verdict is still unclear about whether South Africans can defer benefits until the country advances economically and whether the average South African will continue to feel enfranchised and have opportunities to participate in this increasingly centralized system. It is also uncertain whether the ANC will continue to centralize its authority or whether the provincial and local governments and other political parties will demand more power.

South Africa continues to surprise the world with its emphasis on peace and forgiveness. It is hoped that current fears will prove groundless, that the economy will improve, and that the nonracial, nonsexist, nondivisive, and democratic tendencies existing in the system will continue to influence the leadership and the direction of the country.

NOTES

1. Out of a population of around 38 million people (1996 census) 29 million were Black Africans and about 60.5% of them were living below the poverty line (Sisk 1995, 12). There were also several million Asians and "Coloureds," who were disenfranchised under the apartheid system.

2. Consociational democracy is a form of governing in divided societies where power at the upper levels of government is shared among the contending groups, i.e., the president comes from one group and the prime minister comes from another group, etc. See Lijphart 1977.

Chapter 8

Conclusion: Re-distribution of Authority in Comparative Perspective

Jeanie J. Bukowski and Swarna Rajagopalan

The case studies presented in the preceding chapters have yielded a wealth of data on the causes and consequences of the re-distribution of authority and allow us to posit five general statements regarding this phenomenon that go beyond the conclusions of existing research:

1. Re-distribution of authority does not necessarily take place in one or the other direction. That is, it includes centralizing and decentralizing changes.
2. Re-distribution is an ongoing, indeed unending, process in every polity.
3. Re-distribution of authority takes place between all levels of governmental activity—the substate, including local (village, tribal, county, municipal, provincial, district and divisional) and regional, state, and suprastate (international, intergovernmental) levels. Authority need not be re-allocated from one level to the very next one, but may in fact bypass levels.
4. Re-distribution of authority is not "zero-sum." That is, a loss of authority by one level does not necessarily result in a corresponding and equal gain by another level.
5. There is no single, isolated factor that causes authority to be re-distributed. Instead, we hold that the re-distribution of authority from one case to another depends on the interaction of a particular set of factors.

We also are able to identify four explanatory factors for the re-distribution of authority common to all the cases: identity-related claims, economic imperatives, considerations of administrative efficiency, and political agency. Even as we identify these as the main causal threads, we are given pause by our difficulty in isolating them from each other or in classifying the cases as exemplifying one or the other. The discussion that follows treats these factors separately, but also inevitably considers their interaction.

FOUR EXPLANATORY FACTORS

Identity

In the post–Cold War era, the problem of identity, which was once thought to be a hallmark of traditional Asian and African societies, has come to light in every part of the world. Canada has its Quebec and the US its problems with racial minorities. Europe has been haunted by the specter of war in the Balkans over majority-minority relations and state identity. Africa's internal wars have seen the death and dismemberment of thousands in Rwanda, Somalia, and Ethiopia, to name only three locations. In Asia, apart from the apparent omnipresence of ethnic conflict, cultural identity is the key element in evolving doctrines on human rights, development, and political participation. Every major world region seems to have paid the price of intolerance in situations of diversity with the blood of innocent humans.

The "identity crisis" was defined by scholars of political development in terms of defining and building the identity of the state (for instance, Binder et al, 1975). For scholars of nationalism and ethnicity who do not necessarily use this term, "identity" and "identity-related issues" refer to problems arising from the need of ethnic, racial, and religious groups, within and across nation-state borders, to assert their distinctiveness or to claim privileges and rights, whether new or lost by virtue of their possessing that identity (Brass 1991). These are viewed here as two sides of the same coin and in the five cases in this volume where re-distribution of authority has followed identity-related problems, those problems meet both criteria (Breuilly 1993; Enloe 1986).

Side-stepping the essentialist (or primordialist) view of identity as intrinsically conflict-prone and therefore given to upsetting the status quo, we look at identity issues as expressive of a group's political aspirations within or outside a particular distribution of authority. Whether groups aspire for a place within or outside is determined by their location (within or across boundaries), their concentration or dispersal, and their historical relationship with those who manage the polity and with other constituents. Identity compounds economic problems and disparities when education and language policies empower or disempower sections of the population. Territorial imbalances that overlap with the regional distribution of identity groups can strengthen the hands of political leaders. At certain historical moments, the groundswell of popular resentment or nationalism can fuel an ambitious leadership to fight for a change in the way that authority is distributed. Sometimes, it just makes administrative sense to let local customary law prevail or to allow the use of a certain language in governmental offices.

In India, Pakistan, and Sri Lanka, the construction of a new state identity has made the identity of constituent communities problematic in a number of ways—through the creation and effacement of units that are discussed in this volume, and other inclusive and exclusive policies relating to education, employment, and even citizenship. On the other hand, this is a region in which the need of a group within the polity to assert its distinctiveness has twice partitioned states—once in 1947 with the partition of India and the creation of Pakistan, and then in 1971, with the secession of Bangladesh from Pakistan. Sri Lanka's insular location has not made it immune from this problem either. The definition of a Sri Lankan identity makes being Tamil difficult, and the now-militant Tamil response makes it impossible for Sri Lanka to seem anything but Sinhalese. In Spain, the creation of new autonomous regions that are home to the country's age-old ethnic communities may have addressed the needs and demands of those communities but it also amended the identity of the Spanish state. From a unitary state that was home to undifferentiated Spanish citizens, it was transformed into a unitary Spanish state in which several distinct communities of people ran a large part of their affairs locally. In Russia, Dowley tells us that more ethnic than nonethnic units seek autonomy from the center. Chechnya is a good example. Having been yoked to the Russian empire and then the Soviet federation, Chechnya declared itself independent in 1991. This declaration was not uncontested and Russian troops fought in the breakaway republic from 1994 to 1996.

All of these are examples of identity-pushed re-distribution in which authority is devolved. In each of these cases, a demand is articulated by a group of people who share an identity, and large numbers of whom occupy a particular territorial space. After a certain period of negotiation or fighting, the solution that is arrived at entails some measure of autonomy. Indeed, devolutionary re-distribution of authority is commonly considered a pragmatic solution to the problem of ethnic diversity (Horowitz 1985; Smith 1995).

However, there are instances in which authority may be centralized as a consequence of identity-related problems. Centralization may follow from at least four circumstances. First, where an ethnic majority seeks to consolidate its domination, it may either press for centralization or resist demands for decentralization. This is true in Sri Lanka, where the minority demand for devolution is adamantly resisted by members of the majority community. Second, situations of conflict, such as those in India's state of Kashmir, as in Pakistan's Sindh, strengthen the hands of those who argue that the security or law and order situation is not conducive to the normal functioning of the political system, let alone the granting of greater autonomy. Third, where the continued militancy of separatist groups (ETA in Spain, the Irish Republican Army in the United Kingdom, and the Liberation Tigers of Tamil Eelam in Sri Lanka) rallies all or a large part of the remaining public behind the central government's position, centralization results from the absence of dissent. Finally, where ethnic conflict, wars of self-determination, or other forms of internecine conflict leave a region awash with weapons and economically devastated, as we have seen in Afghanistan, Lebanon, and Chechnya, those regions become breeding grounds for narcotics and arms trafficking, the training of mercenaries, and simply, people who in search of sustenance will emulate the raiders and marauders of another time. Local authorities are often the worst equipped to cope, either militarily or economically, and must seek the protection and help of other levels of government, resulting in centralization. Autonomy may solve this problem theoretically, but the need of the hour is often effective government, i.e., the delivery of collective goods and services.

There is one case in this volume that begs the question. The United States is today a very diverse society, but the issues that Bowman raises as salient are economic and administrative considerations. The racial and ethnic groups within the states may be demanding specific protections and privileges but without seeking the kind of territorial representation or even electoral representation that minorities in other states have sought (the ethnic groups in Nigeria and Belgium, for example). This points to an important way in which identity is mediated by territorial factors. It seems as though, in the absence of a territorial base, the ability of an identity group to force change is considerably limited. In Taylor's terms, the group is able to ensure its place within a "politics of universalism," where it may enjoy to an equal extent the rights and access that others enjoy (1994). It is not able to assert, to the same extent as territorially concentrated groups, the rights that it might enjoy under a more particularistic framework.

While ethnic identity (construed in linguistic, racial or religious terms) is a powerful tool for political mobilization, it is the land-language combination that packs the greatest punch in dismantling the prevalent distribution of authority. When Pakistan was founded, the movement's leadership came not from the Muslim-majority regions of South Asia but elsewhere. However, right from the beginning, the idea of Pakistan was given a territorial home in these regions by the same leaders. A little over twenty years after the founding of the new state, East Pakistan broke away to form the state of Bangladesh—the combination of a Bengali-speaking majority localized in the Gangetic delta prevailed over the more intellectual notion of an Islamic nationality.

Whether as the rationale for demands of autonomy and separatism, or the rationale for centralization in the name of one statewide identity, re-distribution of authority appears to be a by-product of identity politics. The referent of the identity in dispute could be a substate group or the state itself, but the ongoing dialectic between them results intentionally or inadvertently in changing the distribution of power within the state.

Economic Imperatives

The "factor" of economic imperatives in reality encompasses several important elements that are, in turn, tightly intertwined. One of these is external pressure on states generated from the fact of globalization and interdependence. A second aspect is the economic development imperative. A third component is territorially based economic imbalances within states, regardless of their overall condition of development.

The concepts of interdependence and globalization are widely discussed and a variety of definitions for each may be identified (see, for example, Keohane and Nye 1989; Rosecrance and Stein 1973; Keohane and Ostrom 1995; Elazar 1998; Waters 1995). The general premise of these concepts relevant to this study is that of a world becoming increasingly "smaller" because of modernization and its accompanying developments in communications, transport, and information, a growing reliance (and pressure) on the planet's finite resources and the accompanying threat of environmental damage, and the progression of advanced destructive weaponry. Because of these developments, states, economies, societies, communities, and individuals are increasingly affected by each other. It is therefore not surprising that the re-distribution of authority within states is influenced by economic conditions and structures outside the state.

As demonstrated in the cases of Senegal, Russia, Spain, and South Africa, international governmental and nongovernmental organizations, as well as other states, may have an important influence on the re-distribution of authority. A major impetus for decentralization in Senegal comes from the international donor community. Likewise, Russian leaders' choices of governmental form are constrained by the need for development funding from international agencies and Western states, who may withhold such funding if certain conditions of "democratic development" are not met. The near collapse of the South African economy due to international pressure, particularly disinvestment and sanctions, was a major factor in the decision to dismantle the apartheid regime. Some regions in Spain are emboldened to make strong autonomy demands partly because they view themselves in the context of the larger single market of the EU. These demands, and the strengthening of substate authority more generally, are also promoted by EU institutions, through development programs that require substate input.

What may make the influence of external actors and processes so important is the economic conditions within states themselves. States with relatively low levels of economic development, such as Senegal, Russia, the South Asian cases, and Spain and Portugal relative to the rest of Europe, must conform to the wishes of these international actors in order to receive needed development funds. If, as in Senegal, Spain, and Portugal, receiving such funds depends partially on decentralizing reforms, the central state will feel enough pressure to at least give lip service to re-distributing authority downward.

Economic development imperatives are also quite important apart from the role of international actors. As illustrated in the recent debate over regionalization in Portugal and South Africa, and in the ongoing efforts in South Asia to build effective economic and political systems, pressures for both centralization and decentralization arise from different development strategies. Here, the central state has usually used the argument that it alone has the ability to understand the development problems in the state as a whole, particularly if there are territorial imbalances. The center is therefore the most efficient level at which to concentrate decision-making in economic matters. Substate actors counter that development will only be achieved by placing economic decision-making at lower levels, closer to the citizens and leaders who best understand their particular development problems.

Regarding territorial economic imbalances, either relative economic deprivation or relative economic strength may affect the demands made by substate actors on the center. Dowley shows that regions that are categorized by the center as "critically depressed" are more likely to demand autonomy. Conversely, Bukowski argues that it is the wealthier regions in the north of Spain (similarly to the case of the industrialized Italian North) that are more likely to mobilize their citizens in favor of further autonomy and to make effective demands on the center. These regional governments argue that their development is hindered by subsidization of the poorer regions, and that greater autonomy, particularly in the context of the wider European market, would further their development. Similarly, Patterson shows that the primary motivation for the separatist movement in the southern Casamance region in Senegal, which has relatively greater potential for economic development, is the fear that important resources such as offshore oil reserves will be squandered by the center.

The Exigencies of Administration

Administrative considerations also figure importantly in the rationale for re-distribution of authority. They take three forms. The first is an argument for rationalization of the functions of government at different levels and locations. The second is tied to the economic development imperative discussed above and may be deployed in a struggle mobilized around identity and/or democratization, illustrating how these factors interact. Finally, as administrative integration and institutionalization are important markers of state-building, re-distribution of authority occurs as a function of the latter.

In any state, under any political arrangement, authority is distributed—or delegated—to the agent in a location that usually makes sense. Seldom, for instance, is garbage collection the monopoly of the executive at the center. Likewise, responsibility for defense usually rests with central rather than local agencies. The re-distribution of authority can follow one of two lines: either allocating powers and functions away from where they rest in order to (or ostensibly to) make affairs run more smoothly, or appropriating them to a central office in order to streamline administrative procedures. The argument proffered for the partition of Bengal (in British India) in 1905 was that it would benefit not only the new province of Assam but also the streamlining of Bengal's unwieldy administration. This is once again the most important argument for the creation of smaller states. In Sri Lanka, where political devolution is so controversial, administrative decentralization was undertaken with less notice in the 1970s. In the US, the administrative needs of welfare and other social programs have often furthered the devolutionary process.

Rationalization may also take the form of load-shifting or blame-shifting, where the central authority parts with its more onerous or unpleasant functions through deconcentration or even devolution so that it neither has to undertake them nor take the blame for them. In their discussion of South Africa, Zeff and Pirro state that in post-apartheid South Africa, provinces have been created expressly to serve as a buffer insulating the federal government. In Portugal, the central government has also used this tactic in deconcentrating functions to local authorities.

A third form of rationalization is related to security concerns. When we associate the terms "security" and "authority," it is not difficult to think of centralization as the link between the two—centralization occurs as a response to insecurity. However, there are other linkages that are suggested by the cases here. First, in South Africa, in order to "rainbow" (that is, to improve the racial mix among those who work in) law enforcement agencies, the government has seen fit to centralize decision-making about recruitment and training. Thus, paradoxically, to improve power-sharing or to delegate responsibility for internal and external security, it may be essential to centralize responsibility for these functions. Second, setting up new units on the frontier with relative autonomy both reduces the dependence of the frontier areas on the center for defense and internal security and shortens the time for decision-making and response in the event of contentious frontiers. While this is not discussed in the chapter on unit demarcation in South Asia, this is a region where security considerations are often an important part of the calculations that accompany decision-making on the re-distribution of authority. Somewhat counter-intuitively, this re-distribution, which may take any form from deconcentration to federalization, strengthens the hands of the center rather than weakens it by enhancing the institutional presence of the state on the frontiers.

Finally, there is the impact of prolonged conflict on any actual distribution of authority. Civil wars can result in all kinds of changes, including the introduction of new players in the political arena. The need to pay for a conflict (including the costs of the campaign and the costs of reconstruction) may result in the levy of more taxes and the creation of new offices and agents to administer them. Further, as the civil administration is crippled, other forces fill the administrative vacuum as much as the political. As power is re-distributed, so is authority. The resettlement of the internally displaced creates new functions and therefore, new offices. Moreover, as the role of nongovernmental and international organizations in the relief and reconstruction area expands, so does their influence and ultimately, their authority. Finally, in the embattled zones, new causes for economic disparity are introduced. The flow of and trade in arms and drugs makes some sections of the local population very wealthy and they are now able to act politically where they may not have been able to before the conflict. Their influence grows in inverse proportion to that of local authorities. The creation of refugee camps and the distribution of relief monies to the refugees also alter economic equations where those payments exceed average local incomes. The Afghan crisis created both kinds of problems in the Peshawar area for Pakistan.

The association between the development imperative and re-distribution of authority has been discussed at length in the previous section. This imperative is acted on through administrative reforms—either centralizing or decentralizing. As the Senegal case study shows, efforts at administrative decentralization are tied to not only the development imperative but also to the closely related objective of democratization, through bringing decision-making closer to the citizen. While, in practice, this has not been achieved and Senegal may still be characterized primarily by "decentralized despotism," Senghor's attempts at African socialism, as well as more recent reform efforts, have been motivated by these related administrative, economic, and democratization concerns.

The relationship between state-building and re-distribution of authority is highlighted in the discussion of unit demarcation in South Asia. Defined in terms of the establishment and continued operation of a given institutional structure, the state-building process may be simply divided into three stages—the establishment and consolidation phase, the institutionalization phase, and finally, the decline and disintegration phase. Administrative integration and institutionalization are a central part of this process. In the first phase of establishment and consolidation, the experience of the colonial South Asian, Senegalese, and South African states suggests that re-distribution takes the form of centralization—from the effacement of units discussed in the South Asian cases, administrative centralism in the Senegalese, and disenfranchisement in the South African. Equally, one could place the Russian case in this category. In the second, institutional phase, the "pulling and tugging" continue, but as the US and Spanish cases show, it is possible for the result of the re-distribution to take both forms. While none of the case studies in this book can be identified as states in decline, one might argue that facing the threat of disintegration through secession, both Pakistan and Sri Lanka have responded by centralizing their administrations. The willingness to accommodate and delegate diminishes as the level of threat increases.

The exigencies of administration have the effect of driving changes in the distribution of authority, even as they, in turn, interact with and are affected by other structural processes—economic changes, cultural and identity issues, and finally, the inescapable demands of security and state-building. Often where debates may rage over re-distribution that is sought for other reasons, it is possible to usher in dramatic changes through administrative adjustments. Thus it is that we identify this as an important explanatory factor for the re-distributions of authority that have taken place historically in the nine cases in this book.

Political Agency

While many of the factors indicated in the case studies are structural, political agency also emerges as an important impetus to the re-distribution of authority. By agency we mean choices made and actions taken by political actors, both in response to, and outside of, the structural (economic, social, and legal) situation in which they find themselves. Agency here encompasses governmental and societal actors at all levels, from the suprastate to the individual. It becomes a factor in the re-distribution of authority when political actors make the decision to press for a change in the existing distribution. Which actors are involved in these decisions, how they arrive at their preferred choice, and what means they use to pursue their goals all affect how (or if) authority is re-distributed.

Political actors who decide to advocate and/or pursue a re-distribution of authority may be responding to the pressure of their constituents, in turn based on imperatives of economic development, democratization, security, and/or minority rights. Central government leaders in Portugal, Senegal, and Spain, for example, have responded, at least rhetorically, to general support among both elites and publics within those states for reforms to decentralize. In Russia, Spain, and India, territorially based support for decentralization was one factor influencing regional government leaders to demand greater autonomy from the center. Conversely, the centers in Sri Lanka, India, Spain, South Africa, and Russia have responded to public fears of violence, and internal or external threats to their security to pursue centralization, or to limit the transfer of autonomy to lower levels.

These actors may also be utilizing existing structural conditions to influence their constituencies in favor of their positions, and there is a reciprocal process of influence and pressure, as leaders and their constituents respond to each other. The cases of Russia, Spain, Sri Lanka, and the United States, for example, illustrate that substate leaders may "create" or promote regional unity and separateness from other state units (particularly based on ethnic and linguistic identity). These elites may also shift blame for the region's economic and political difficulties to the center, arguing that development would be better served at lower levels, in order to further their own political aspirations. In turn, favorable public response to these initiatives give the leaders' demands more legitimacy vis-à-vis the center. Likewise, as in Spain, Sri Lanka, and South Africa, central government leaders may promote public fears of separatist violence, external security threats, and/or dissatisfaction with economic inefficiencies in order to gain support for re-distribution of authority upward.

Once the various political actors across levels determine their stances on the distribution of authority, whose preferences win out (and if and how authority is re-distributed) depends largely on the strategies that the actors choose in their attempt to achieve their goals. From the cases presented here, it appears that the most successful strategy employed by substate actors (such as political parties) in pursuing their goal of greater autonomy is a combination of achieving strong public support from their constituents (importantly, business, labor, and other societal elites), and, if possible, gaining access and influence at the national bargaining table. The least successful strategy is the use of violence and/or separatist demands, particularly as illustrated by the case of Sri Lanka. Such actions and demands allow the center to appeal to the larger public's concerns for safety and state unity in limiting decentralization or promoting further centralization. As illustrated by the US case, however, the party in power in the national government does not always promote centralization. Particularly during the era of "New Federalism" of the 1980s, a coalition of political actors at the national, state, and local levels succeeded in shrinking the size of the national government and granting more responsibility to (and placing more burden on) state governments.

The outcomes resulting from these choices and strategies of the political actors (the re-distribution of authority) then set the stage for the next round of interactions that continues this dynamic process. If authority has been legally altered within the system (through reforms either centralizing or decentralizing competencies), then actors may find their ability to press their demands either constrained or enhanced. The creation of the Autonomous Communities in Spain, for example, has given regional actors a point of mobilization through which they are able to promote even greater autonomy. The failure of regionalization in Portugal deprives territorial elites of such points of mobilization. Increased centralization of government functions in South Africa also hinders the ability of substate or national elites to gain support for greater provincial autonomy.

Moreover, the outcomes may alter some of the structural factors, thus changing the ways in which actors at all levels are able to utilize these factors to promote their goals. As we see in the US case, how either centralizing or decentralizing reforms affect economic development and delivery of services is important in determining the future strategies of the political actors. The perceived excesses and inefficiencies of "creative federalism" allowed later administrations and their supporters to successfully argue for decreased authority and responsibility at the national level. In the South African case, if centralization fails to address the economic and security imperatives used to justify it, the ANC's opposition (such as the IFP) likely will have more ammunition, and public support, in their appeal for decentralization. The argument for further dividing the larger states in India is based on the rationale that smaller units better serve the purpose of economic development, given the apparent difficulties of the larger entities in achieving development goals.

CONCLUSIONS

The primary goal of this book has been to "glimpse the elephant." That is, we hoped at the outset of this project to cross theoretical, analytical, and geographic boundaries and to arrive at a more complete picture of the shifting of power and authority within, across, and beyond the nation-state. Our consciously inductive approach utilizes a diverse set of case studies, all asking the same two questions: Which are the factors that explain the re-distribution of authority? Under what conditions are some of these factors more important than others?

The nine states discussed here vary greatly in terms of geographic range and historical scope. In spite of this variation, their experiences yield remarkably similar insights, as the preceding discussion of explanatory factors demonstrates. We therefore conclude with two assertions regarding the convergence and interaction of factors most likely to lead to re-distribution either up or down (centralization or decentralization), which are potentially applicable to cases beyond those presented in this volume.

The re-distribution of authority downward, to substate institutions and elites, appears most likely when economic development and administrative efficiency imperatives coincide with strong ethnic-identity demands (especially language-based). Re-distribution downward is almost assured if the ethnic identity demands also have a territorial basis, and if territorial political leaders utilize these circumstances to demand autonomy (through means other than violence or threats of violence).

The re-distribution of authority upward to the central state government (or the maintenance of the centralized system), appears most likely when lower levels are (or appear to be) incapable of addressing economic and administrative efficiency issues, and where violence or threats thereof (particularly of the separatist variety) challenge the security and/or integrity of the state. Where there is no established territorial base for substate economic, administrative, and/or identity demands, and where central government leaders effectively focus the public's attention on these inefficiencies and/or challenges to security, decentralization becomes impossible.

These assertions illustrate the complexity of the ongoing processes of authority distribution and re-distribution, and link together many of the largely compartmentalized approaches to studying this phenomenon. The research and analysis presented here has been an important step in developing more complete, and realistic, explanations for the re-distribution of authority within and across the nation-state. Our hope is that it will serve as the basis for an ongoing effort in furthering knowledge in this area of study, which is important not only to the academic disciplines of political science, international relations, and comparative politics, but also, and more importantly, to the people who affect, and live out the consequences of, the re-distribution of authority.

Works Cited

Acosta España, R., ed. 1981. *La España de las Autonomías: Pasado, Presente y Futuro*, 2 vols. Madrid: Espasa-Calpe, S.A.

Africa Research Bulletin. 1994. April: 11385.

Agnew, John, ed. 1997. *Political Geography: A Reader*. London: Arnold.

Agranoff, Robert. 1996. Federal Evolution in Spain. *International Political Science Review* 17, no. 4: 385–401.

———. 1997. Toward Federal Democracy in Spain: An Examination of Intergovernmental Relations. *Publius: The Journal of Federalism* 27, no. 4 (Fall): 1–38.

Aizpeolea, Luis R. 1994. Aprobada la creación de una ponencia para la reforma constitucional del senado. *El País*, 29 September, Madrid edition.

———. 1998. El Gobierno suspende rasgos polémicos de la financiación autonómica. *El País*, 7 January, Internet edition (http://www.elpais.es/).

———. 1999. El final del desarrollo autonómico. *El País*, 6 May, Andalusia edition.

Alavedra, Maciá. 1993. Cuatro enfoques. *El País*, 4 January, Madrid edition.

Anderson, Barbara, and Brian Silver. 1984. Equality, Efficiency and Politics in Soviet Bilingual Education Policy: 1934–1980. *American Political Science Review* 78 no. 4: 1019–1039.

———. 1990. Some Factors in the Linguistic and Ethnic Russification of Soviet Nationalities. In *The Nationalities Factor in Soviet Politics*, edited by L. Hajda and Mark Beissinger. Boulder, CO: Westview Press.

Anderson, Benedict. 1991. *Imagined Communities: Reflections on the Origin and Spread of Nationalism*. London and New York: Verso.

Annadurai, C. N. 1975a. An Appeal to Conscience (May 1963). In *Anna Speaks: At the Rajya Sabha 1962–1966*, edited by S. Ramachandran, 45–50. New Delhi, India: Orient Longman.

———. 1975b. Secession and Sovereignty (January 1963). In *Anna Speaks: At the Rajya Sabha 1962–1966*, edited by S. Ramachandran, 31–45. New Delhi, India: Orient Longman.

———. 1985. *Ilatchiya Varalaaru*. Madras, India: Maruti Press.

Anti-Secession Bill Passed. 1963. *The Hindu*, 3 May, Madras, India.

Assembly of European Regions, the European Center for Regional Development (CEDRE). 1989. *Comparative Study of the Status and Powers of the Regions in Europe.* Strasbourg, France: Assembly of European Regions.

Aulestia, Kepa. 1993. *Días de viento sur: La violencia en Euskadi.* Barcelona: Antártida/Empúries.

Axelrod, Robert. 1984. *The Evolution of Cooperation.* New York: Basic Books.

Azar, Edward, and D. Ben-Dak, eds. 1973. *Theory and Practice of Events Research.* New York: Gordon & Breach.

Azarya, Victor. 1988. Reordering State-Society Relations: Incorporation and Disengagement. In *The Precarious Balance: State and Society in Africa,* edited by Donald Rothchild and Naomi Chazan. Boulder, CO: Lynne Rienner Publishers.

Bahry, Donna. 1987. *Outside Moscow: Power, Politics and Budgetary Policy in the Soviet Republics.* New York: Columbia University Press.

Baldassare, Mark. 1994. Regional Variations in Support for Regional Governance. *Urban Affairs Quarterly* 30 (December): 275–284.

Barnés Vazquez, Javier. 1994. Interview by Jeanie J. Bukowski and James J. Friedberg. Madrid and Seville, Spain, 18 and 19 November.

Barnes, William R., and Larry C. Ledebur. 1998. *The New Regional Economies.* Thousand Oaks, CA: Sage.

Barsenkov, A. S., ed. 1993. *Politicheskaia Rossiia Sevodnya: Ispolnitelnaia Vlast.* Moscow: Moskovskii Rabochii.

Basu, Durga Das. 1982. *Introduction to the Constitution of India.* New Delhi: Prentice-Hall of India.

Bates, Robert. 1981. *Markets and States in Tropical Africa.* Berkeley: University of California Press.

———. 1983. Modernization, Ethnic Competition, and the Rationality of Politics in Contemporary Africa. In *State vs. Ethnic Claims*, edited by Donald Rothchild. Boulder, CO: Westview Press.

Baum, Michael. 1998. Modernization and Cultural Homogenization: Political Culture(s) and Regionalization in Portugal. Paper presented at the Iberian Studies Group meeting, 6 March, at the Minda de Gunzberg Center for European Studies, Harvard University.

Baum, Michael, and André Freire. 1999. Political Parties and Cleavage Structures: The Portuguese Regionalization Referendum of 1998 in Comparative Perspective. Paper presented at the Mediterranean Studies Association Conference, 26–29 May, at the University of Coimbra, Coimbra, Portugal.

Bayart, Jean-Francois. 1986. Civil Society in Africa. In *Political Domination in Africa*, edited by Patrick Chabal. New York: Cambridge University Press.

Beer, Samuel H. 1993. *To Make a Nation.* Cambridge: Harvard University Press.

Behrman, Lucy. 1970. *Muslim Brotherhoods and Politics in Senegal.* Cambridge: Harvard University Press.

Beissinger, Mark. 1995. The Persisting Ambiguity of Empire. *Post-Soviet Affairs* no. 2: 149–84.

Belin, Laura. 1997. *OMRI Russian Regional Report* no. 2 (15 January).

Berg, Peter. 1983. Bioregions. *Resurgence* (May/June): 19–20.

Binder, Leonard, James S. Coleman, Joseph LaPalombara, Lucian W. Pye, Sidney Verba and Myron Weiner, eds. 1971. *Crises and Sequences in Political Development.* Princeton, NJ: Princeton University Press.

Birmingham, David. 1993. *A Concise History of Portugal*. Cambridge: Cambridge University Press.

Boone, Catherine. 1992. *Merchant Capital and the Rise of State Power in Senegal, 1930–1985*. Cambridge: Cambridge University Press.

Bouat, Marie-Claire, and Jean-Louis Fouillard. 1983. *Les finances publiques des communes et des communautées rurales au Sénégal*. Dakar, Senegal: Editions Clairafrique.

Boulding, Kenneth. 1989. *Three Faces of Power*. Newbury Park, CA: Sage.

Bowman, Ann O'M., and Michael A. Pagano. 1994. The State of American Federalism, 1993–1994. *Publius: The Journal of Federalism* 24 (Summer): 1–21.

Bowman, Ann O'M., and Richard C. Kearney. 1986. *The Resurgence of the States*. Englewood Cliffs, NJ: Prentice-Hall.

———. 1999. *State and Local Government* 4th ed. Boston: Houghton Mifflin.

Boyd, Rosalind. 1989. Empowerment of Women in Uganda: Real or Symbolic. *Review of African Political Economy*, no. 45: 106–117.

Brandeis, Louis. 1932. New York Ice Co. v. Liebmann, 285 U.S. 262, 311.

Brass, Paul. 1991. *Ethnicity and Nationalism*. New Delhi: Sage.

Bratton, Michael. 1989. Beyond the State: Civil Society and Associational Life in Africa. *World Politics* 41: 407–430.

———. 1998. After Mandela's Miracle in South Africa. *Current History* (May): 214–219.

Bratton, Michael, and Nicolas van de Walle. 1992. Toward Governance in Africa: Popular Demands and State Responses. In *Governance and Politics in Africa*, edited by Michael Bratton and Goran Hyden. Boulder, CO: Lynne Rienner Publishers.

———. 1997. *Democratic Experiments in Africa: Regime Transitions in Comparative Perspective*. New York: Cambridge University Press.

Breuilly, John. 1993. *Nationalism and the State*. 2nd ed. Manchester, England: Manchester University Press.

Buchanan, James M. 1995. Federalism as an Ideal Political Order and an Objective for Constitutional Reform. *Publius: The Journal of Federalism* 25 (Spring): 19–27.

Bukowski, Jeanie J. 1996. Governance Reconsidered: The Redistribution of Authority in the European Arena. Ph.D. diss., University of Illinois at Urbana-Champaign.

Bunker, Stephen. 1987. *Peasants Against the State: The Politics of Market Control in Bugisu, Uganda, 1900–1983*. Urbana: University of Illinois Press.

Burgess, Michael, and Allain Gagnon, eds. 1993. *Comparative Federalism and Federation*. Toronto: University of Toronto Press.

Callaghy, Thomas. 1984. *The State-Society Struggle: Zaire in Comparative Perspective*. New York: Columbia University Press.

Chazan, Naomi, Robert Mortimer, John Ravenhill, and Donald Rothchild. 1988. *Politics and Society in Contemporary Africa*. Boulder, CO: Lynne Rienner Publishers.

Clark, John. 1990. *Democratizing Development: The Role of Voluntary Organizations*. West Hartford, CT: Kumarian Press.

Clark, Robert P. 1987. The Question of Regional Autonomy in Spain's Democratic Transition. In *Spain in the 1980s: The Democratic Transition and a New International Role*, edited by Robert P. Clark and Michael H. Haltzel. Cambridge, MA: Ballinger Publishing Co.

———. 1990. *Negotiating with ETA: Obstacles to Peace in the Basque Country, 1975–1988*. Reno: University of Nevada Press.

Clegg, Thomas. 1987. Spain. In *Central and Local Government Relations: A Comparative Analysis of West European Unitary States*, edited by Edward C. Page and Michael Goldsmith. London: Sage Publications.

Club du Sahel. 1987. *Analyse des dynamiques d'organisation du monde rurale dans le Sahel: Le case du Sénégal.* Rapport de Mission. Paris: Club du Sahel.

Coates, Crispin. 1998. Spanish regionalism and the European Union. *Parliamentary Affairs* 51, no. 2 (May): 259–271.

Constantelos, John. 1995. Regional Interests and Economic Integration: Multi-Level Politics in the European Union. Paper presented at the International Studies Association Annual Meeting, 21–25 February, Chicago, IL.

Constitution of the Republic of South Africa. 1996. Chapters 5–7.

Conyers, Diana. 1983. Decentralization: The Latest Fashion in Development Administration? *Public Administration and Development* 3: 97–109.

Correia, Pedro. 1997. PS e PCP esticam a corda. *Diário de Noticias*, 25 July, Internet edition (http://www.dn.pt/).

Coulon, Christian. 1988. Senegal: The Development and Fragility of Semidemocracy. In *Democracy in Developing Countries*, edited by Larry Diamond, Juan Linz, and Seymour Martin Lipset. Boulder, CO: Lynne Rienner Publishers.

Council of Europe. 1993. *Structure and operation of local and regional democracy: Portugal.* Strasbourg, France: Council of Europe.

Covas, António. 1994. Interview by Jeanie J. Bukowski and James J. Friedberg, University of Evora, Portugal, 3 November.

———. 1997. *Integração Europeia, Regionalização Administrativa e Reforma do Estado-Nacional.* Lisbon: Instituto Nacional de Administração.

Cruise O'Brien, Donal. 1971. *The Mourides of Senegal.* Oxford, England: Clarendon Press.

Cuadrado Roura, Juan R. 1981. La política regional en los Planes de Desarrollo (1964–1975). In *La España de las Autonomías: Pasado, Presente y Futuro*, vol. 1, edited by R. Acosta España. Madrid: Espasa-Calpe, S.A.

Cuchillo, Montserrat. 1993. The Autonomous Communities as the Spanish Meso. In *The Rise of Meso Government in Europe*, edited by L. J. Sharpe. London: Sage Publications.

Daley, Suzanne. 1999a. Many hold second post-apartheid vote as dear as first. *New York Times*, 3 June.

———. 1999b. African National Congress wins re-election in a landslide. *New York Times,* 4 June.

———. 1999c. In South Africa, winner almost takes all. *New York Times,* 8 June.

de Silva, Chandra Richard. 1987. *Sri Lanka: A History.* Delhi, India: Vikas.

de Silva, Kingsley M. 1993. Regionalism and Decentralization of Power. In *Sri Lanka: Problems of Governance*, by K. M. de Silva. New Delhi, India: Konark.

Delgado, Christopher, and Sidi Jammeh, eds. 1991. *The Political Economy of Senegal under Structural Adjustment.* New York: Praeger Publishers.

Di Palma, Guiseppe. 1990. *To Craft Democracies: An Essay on Democratic Transitions.* Berkeley: University of California Press.

Diamond, Larry. 1988. Introduction: Roots of Failure, Seeds of Hope. In *Democracy in Developing Countries*, edited by Larry Diamond, Juan Linz, and Seymour Martin Lipset. Boulder, CO: Lynne Rienner Publishers.

Diamond, Larry, Juan Linz, and Seymour Martin Lipset, eds. 1989. *Democracy in Developing Countries.* 4 vols. Boulder, CO: Lynne Rienner Publishers.

Diamond, Larry, and Marc F. Plattner, eds. 1994. *Nationalism, Ethnic Conflict, and Democracy.* Baltimore: Johns Hopkins University Press.

Diamond, Martin. 1974. What the Framers Meant by Federalism. In *A Nation of States*, edited by Robert A. Goldwin. Chicago: Rand McNally.

Díaz, Anabel. 1992. Ceder el 15% del IRPF a las autonomías "quiebra la solidaridad regional," afirma el Gobierno andaluz. *El País*, 10 November, Andalusia edition.

DMK declared a State Party. 1958. *Homeland*, 9 March, Madras, India.

DMK to Strive for New Union in South. 1963. *The Hindu*, 4 November, Madras, India.

Donges, Juergen B., Christiane Krieger, Rolf J. Langhammer, Klaus-Werner Schatz, and Carsten S. Thoroe. 1982. *The Second Enlargement of the European Community: Adjustment Requirements and Challenges for Policy Reform.* Tubingen, Germany: J.C.B. Mohr.

Douglass, William. 1985. *Basque Politics: A Case Study in Ethnic Nationalism.* Reno: University of Nevada Press.

Dowley, Kathleen. 1998. Striking the Federal Bargain in Russia: Comparative Regional Government Strategies. *Communist and Post-Communist Studies* no. 4: 359–381.

Ehrenhalt, Allen. 1995. Cooperate or Die. *Governing* 8 (September): 29.

Elazar, Daniel J. 1984. *American Federalism: A View from the States* 3rd ed. New York: Harper & Row.

———. 1987. *Exploring Federalism.* Tuscaloosa: The University of Alabama Press.

———. 1994. *The American Mosaic.* Boulder, CO: Westview Press.

———. 1995. From Statism to Federalism; A Paradigm Shift. *Publius: The Journal of Federalism* 25 (Spring): 5–18.

———. 1998. *Constitutionalizing Globalism: The Postmodern Revival of Confederal Arrangements.* Lanham, MD: Rowman and Littlefield.

Ellwood, David T. 1998. Discussion. *New England Economic Review* (May/June): 44–47.

Emery, Anne. 1997. Social Movements and Democratization in South Africa. Paper presented, 28 July, at the Institute for Advanced Social Research, University of Witwaterstrand, South Africa.

Emizet, Kasangani, and Vicki Hesli. 1995. The Disposition to Secede: An Analysis of the Soviet Case. *Comparative Political Studies* no. 4: 493–536.

Enesco, M. 1996. Update on PP pact with CiU. *Agence France-Presse*, via Dow Jones News Retrieval Service, 28 April.

Engel, Christian, and Jef Van Ginderachter. 1993. *Trends in Regional and Local Government in the European Community.* Leuven, Belgium: Acco/Trans European Policy Studies Association.

Enloe, Cynthia H. 1986. *Ethnic Conflict and Political Development.* Lanham, MD: University Press of America.

Esman, Milton, and Norman Uphoff. 1984. *Local Organizations: Intermediaries in Rural Development.* Ithaca, NY: Cornell University Press.

European Report. 1995. Copyright European Information Service, via Dow Jones News Retrieval Service, 25 February.

Fatton, Robert. 1987. *The Making of a Liberal Democracy: Senegal's Passive Revolution, 1975–1985.* Boulder, CO: Lynne Rienner Publishers.

———. 1992. *Predatory Rule: State and Civil Society in Africa.* Boulder, CO: Lynne Rienner Publishers.

————. 1995. Africa in the Age of Democratization: The Civic Limitations of Civil Society. *African Studies Review* 38: 67–99.

Fleron, Frederic, and Eric Hoffman. 1993. *Communist Studies and Political Science.* Boulder, CO: Westview Press.

Friedman, Steven. 1995. South Africa: Divided in a Special Way. In *Politics in Developing Countries*, edited by Larry Diamond, Juan J. Linz, and Seymour Martin Lipset, 531–581. Boulder, CO: Lynne Rienner Publishers.

Friedrich, Carl J. 1968. *Trends of Federalism in Theory and Practice.* New York: Praeger.

Funky for a Day at Least. 1999. *The Economist*, 19 June, 41.

Gallagher, Thomas. 1979. Portugal's Atlantic Territories: The Separatist Challenge. *World Today* (September): 353–359.

García Añoveros, Jaime. 1993. Corresponsibilidad Fiscal. *El País*, 4 January, Madrid edition.

Garreau, Joel. 1981. *The Nine Nations of North America.* Boston: Houghton Mifflin.

Gaspar, Jorge. 1976. Regional Planning, Decentralization and Popular Participation in Post-1974 Portugal. *Iberian Studies* 5, no. 1 (Spring): 31–34.

Geertz, Clifford. 1963. *Old Societies and New States: The Quest for Modernity.* New York: Free Press.

Gellar, Sheldon. 1990. State Tutelage vs. Self-Governance: The Rhetoric and Reality of Decentralization in Senegal. In *The Failure of the Centralized State*, edited by James Wunsch and Dele Olowu. Boulder, CO: Westview Press.

Gellar, Sheldon. 1995. *Senegal: An African Nation Between Islam and the West.* 2d ed. Boulder, CO: Westview Press.

Gellar, Sheldon, Robert Charlick, and Yvonne Jones. 1980. *Animation Rurale and Rural Development: The Experience of Senegal.* Ithaca, NY: Cornell University Press.

Gerston, Larry N., and Peter J. Haas. 1993. Political Support for Regional Government in the 1990s. *Urban Affairs Quarterly* 29 (September): 162–173.

Giliomee, Hermann. 1998. South Africa's Emerging Dominant-Party Regime. *Journal of Democracy* 9, no. 4: 128–142.

Goldhagen, Erich. 1968. *Ethnic Minorities in the Soviet Union.* New York: Praeger Publishers.

Good, Kenneth. 1997. Accountable to Themselves: Predominance in Southern Africa. *Journal of Modern African Studies* 35, no. 4: 547–573.

Guibernau, Montserrat. 1995. Spain: a Federation in the Making? In *Federalism: The Multiethnic Challenge*, edited by Graham Smith. London and New York: Longman.

Gurr, Ted Robert. 1971. *Why Men Rebel.* Princeton, NJ: Princeton University Press.

————. 1993. *Minorities at Risk: A Global View of Ethnopolitical Conflicts.* Washington, DC: United States Institute of Peace.

Hajda, Lubomyr and Mark Beissinger. 1990. *The Nationalities Factor in Soviet Politics and Society.* Boulder, CO: Westview Press.

Handley, Antoinette, and Jeffrey Herbst. 1997. South Africa: The Perils of Normalcy. *Current History* (May): 222–226.

Harris, Charles Wesley. 1995. *Congress and the Governance of the Nation's Capital.* Washington, DC: Georgetown University Press.

Harvie, Christopher. 1994. *The Rise of Regional Europe.* London: Routledge.

Hayek, Freidrich. 1948. *Individualism and Economic Order*. Chicago: The University of Chicago Press.

Hebbert, Michael, and H. Machin, eds. 1984. *Regionalisation in France, Italy and Spain*. London: London School of Economics.

Heilbrunn, John. 1993. Social Origins of National Conferences in Benin and Togo. *The Journal of Modern African Studies* 31: 277–299.

Hofstadter, Richard. 1948. *The American Political Tradition*. New York: Vintage Books.

Hooghe, Liesbet. 1995. Subnational Mobilisation in the European Union. *West European Politics* 18, no. 3: 175–198.

Hooson, David, ed. 1994. *Geography and National Identity*. Oxford, England/Cambridge, MA: Blackwell.

Horowitz, Donald L. 1985. *Ethnic Groups in Conflict*. Berkeley: University of California Press.

How American Banks Suddenly Rushed to Curb Their Lending to South Africa. 1985. *Wall Street Journal*, 5 September.

Hueglin, Thomas O. 1986. Regionalism in Western Europe: Conceptual Problems of a New Political Perspective. *Comparative Politics* 18, no. 4: 439–458.

Huntington, Samuel. 1991. *The Third Wave: Democratization in the Late Twentieth Century*. Norman: University of Oklahoma Press.

Issues of Rugby and Race. 1996. *The Economist*, 24 August, 35.

Jackson, Robert, and Carl Rosberg. 1982. Why Africa's Weak States Persist: The Empirical and the Juridical in Statehood. *World Politics* 35: 1–25.

Jahan, Rounaq. 1972. *Pakistan: Failure in National Integration*. New York: Columbia University Press.

Jalal, Ayesha. 1995. *Democracy and Authoritarianism in South Asia*. New Delhi, India: Cambridge University Press.

Jatoi, Hyder Baksh. 1978. Sindhi and Karachi. *Sind Quarterly* 6, no. 2: 42–57.

Javeline, Debra. 1998. The Center-Region Power Divide: Views of Russia's Governors. *USIA Opinion Analysis* M-32–98.

Jillson, Calvin C. 1981. Constitution-Making: Alignment and Realignment in the Federal Convention of 1787. *American Political Science Review* 75 (December): 598–612.

Jones, Lilias. 1997. Neither Fish nor Fowl: Federalism, Native Americans, and United States Institutions. Paper presented at the Annual Meeting of the American Political Science Association, San Francisco.

Ka, Samba, and Nicolas van de Walle. 1992. *The Political Economy of Adjustment in Senegal: 1980–1991*. Dakar, Senegal: US Agency for International Development.

Kahan, James P., Mirjam van het Loo, Manuela Franco, João Gomes Cravinho, Vasco Rato, João Tiago Silveira, and Fátima Fonseca. 1999. A Seminar Game to Analyze Regional Governance in Portugal. Santa Monica, CA: Rand Corporation.

Kalansooriya, Ranga. 1998. Muslim Grievances Must Be Structurally Addressed: Interview with Rauf Hakeem (General Secretary, Sri Lanka Muslim Congress). *Daily News*, 3 April, Colombo.

Karl, Terry Lynn, and Philippe Schmitter. 1991. Modes of Transition in Latin America, Southern and Eastern Europe. *International Social Science Journal* 128: 269–284.

Keating, Michael. 1988a. Does Regional Government Work? The Experience of Italy, France and Spain. *Governance: An International Journal of Policy Administration* 1, no. 2: 184–204.

―――. 1988b. *State and Regional Nationalism: Territorial Politics and the European State.* New York, London: Harvester-Wheatsheaf.

―――. 1996. *Nations against the State: The New Politics of Nationalism in Quebec, Catalonia and Scotland.* New York: St. Martin's Press.

Keller, Bill. 1990. Yeltsin's Response to the Separatists: Feel Free. *The New York Times*, 3 September: 2, col. 1.

Kenyon, Daphne A., and John Kincaid. 1991. *Competition among States and Local Governments.* Washington, DC: Urban Institute Press.

Keohane, Robert, and Joseph Nye. 1989. *Power and Interdependence.* Boston: Scott, Foresman and Co.

Keohane, Robert, and Elinor Ostrom. 1995. *Local Commons and Global Interdependence: Heterogeneity and Cooperation in Two Domains.* London: Sage Publications.

Khan, A. Sattar. 1993. The Role of Sindh in the Pakistan Movement. *Journal of the Research Society of Pakistan*, XXX:1.

Khuhro, Hameeda. 1978. *The Making of Modern Sind: British Policy and Social Change in the Nineteenth Century.* Karachi, Pakistan: Indus Publications.

Khuhro, Hamida. 1982. Separation of Sind and the Working of an Autonomous Province. *Sindhological Studies* (Summer): 43–66.

Kincaid, John. 1995. Values and Value Tradeoffs in Federalism. *Publius: The Journal of Federalism* 25 (Spring): 29–44.

―――. 1998. The Devolution Tortoise and the Centralization Hare. *New England Economic Review* (May/June): 13–40.

Kymlicka, Will. 1998. Is Federalism a Viable Alternative to Secession? In *Theories of Secession*, edited by Percy B. Lehning. London/New York: Routledge.

Kynoch, Gary. 1996. The Transformation of the South African Military. *Journal of Modern African Studies* 34, no. 3: 441–457.

Lapidus, Gail, and Edward Walker. 1995. Nationalism, Regionalism and Federalism: Center-Periphery Relations in Post-Communist Russia. In *The New Russia: Troubled Transformation*, edited by Gail Lapidus. Boulder,CO: Westview Press.

The Laputan Flapper. 1959. New State of Singapore Is Born! *Homeland*, 7 June, Madras, India.

Lari, Suhail Zaheer. 1994. *A History of Sind.* Karachi, Pakistan: Oxford University Press.

Leavitt, Michael O. 1995. Restoring States to Their Historic, Rightful Role. *Governing* 8 (February): 11.

Leonard, David, and Dale Rogers Marshall, eds. 1982. *Institutions of Rural Development for the Poor.* Berkeley: University of California Press.

Levi, Margaret. 1988. *Of Rule and Revenue.* Berkeley and Los Angeles: UCLA Press.

Lewis, Stephen R., Jr. 1989. *The Economics of Apartheid.* New York: New York Council on Foreign Relations Press.

Lijphart, Arend. 1977. *Democracy in Plural Societies.* New Haven, CT: Yale University Press.

Linden, Carl, and Dimitri Simes, eds. 1977. *Nationalities and Nationalism in the USSR: A Soviet Dilemma.* Washington, DC: Georgetown Center for Strategic and International Studies.

Linz, Juan, and Alfred Stepan. 1996. *Problems of Democratic Transition and Accommodation: Southern Europe, South America, and Post-Communist Europe*. Baltimore: Johns Hopkins University Press.

Lodge, Tom. 1996. State Formation and State Consolidation in Post Colonial South Africa. Paper presented, 19 August, at the Institute for Advanced Social Research, University of Witwatersrand, South Africa.

———. 1997. Political Corruption in South Africa. Paper presented, 18 August, at the Institute for Advanced Social Research, University of Witwatersrand, South Africa.

Loganathan, Ketheshwaran. 1996. *Sri Lanka: Lost Opportunities*. Colombo, Sri Lanka: Centre for Policy Research and Analysis, University of Colombo.

Lorca Corrons, Alejandro V., Aurelio Martínez Estévez, and Leandro García Menéndez. 1981. Una evaluación de la política de "polos de desarrollo." In *La España de las Autonomías: Pasado, Presente y Futuro*, vol. 1, edited by R. Acosta España. Madrid: Espasa-Calpe, S.A.

Lyman, Princeton N. 1996. South Africa's Promise. *Foreign Policy* 102 (Spring): 105–119.

Majumdar, R. C. and Kali Kinkdar Datta. 1963. Administrative System. In *The History and Culture of the Indian People: British Paramountcy and Indian Renaissance*, vol. 9, part I, edited by R.C. Majumdar. Bombay: Bharatiya Vidya Bhavan.

Malik, Iftikhar H. 1993. Ethnicity and Political Ethos in Sindh: A Case Study of the Muhajireen of Karachi. In *Ethnicity, Identity, Migration: The South Asian Context*, edited by Milton Israel and N. K.Wagle. Toronto: Centre for South Asian Studies, University of Toronto.

Malleret, Thierry. 1992. *Conversion of the Defense Industry in the Former Soviet Union*. New York: Institute for East-West Studies.

Mamdani, Mahmood. 1996. *Citizen and Subject: Contemporary Africa and the Legacy of Colonialism*. Princeton, NJ: Princeton University Press.

Mandela's Heir. 1999. *The Economist*, 29 May, 21.

Mann, Michael. 1986. The Autonomous Power of the State. *Archives Européennes de Sociologie* XXV (1): 185–213.

Manuel, Paul Christopher. 1998. The Process of Democratic Consolidation in Portugal, 1976-1996. *Portuguese Studies Review* 7, no. 1: 33–47.

Maphai, Vincent T. 1996. A Season for Power Sharing: The New South Africa. *Journal of Democracy* 7, no.1: 67–81.

Maravall, José María. 1993. Economic Reforms in New Democracies: The Southern European Experience. Working Paper #3, East-South System Transformation, Occasional Papers. Chicago: Department of Political Science, University of Chicago.

Maravall, José María, and Julián Santamaría. 1986. Political Change in Spain and the Prospects for Democracy. In *Transitions from Authoritarian Rule: Southern Europe*, edited by Guillermo O'Donnell, Philippe Schmitter, and Laurence Whitehead. Baltimore: Johns Hopkins University Press.

Mardones, Inmaculada G. 1994. Bono pierde la guerra del agua pese a entrevistarse in La Moncloa con González. *El País*, 22 July, Andalusia edition.

Markovitz, Irving Leonard. 1991. Animation Rurale: Biography of an African Administrative Agency. In *The Political Economy of Senegal under Structural*

Adjustment, edited by Christopher Delgado and Sidi Jammeh. New York: Praeger Publishers.

Marks, Gary. 1993. Structural Policy and Multilevel Governance in the EC. In *The State of the European Community: The Maastricht Debates and Beyond*, vol. 2, edited by Alan W. Cafruny and Glenda G. Rosenthal. Boulder, CO: Lynne Rienner Publishers.

Marks, Gary, Liesbet Hooghe, and K. Blank. 1996. European Integration from the 1980s: State-Centric v. Multi-level Governance. *Journal of Common Market Studies* 34, no. 3: 341–378.

Marks, Gary, François Nielsen, Leonard Ray, and Jane E. Salk. 1996. Competencies, Cracks, and Conflicts: Regional Mobilization in the European Union. *Comparative Political Studies* 29, no. 2 (April): 164–192.

Martín-Retortillo, Sebastián, ed. 1989. *Pasado, presente y futuro de las Comunidades Autónomas*. Madrid: Instituto de Estudios Económicos.

Martins, Hermínio. 1998. Federal Portugal: A Historical Perspective. *Portuguese Studies Review* 7, no. 1: 13–32.

Mason, W. Dale. 1999. Tribal-State Relations: A New Era in Intergovernmental Relations. Paper presented at the Annual Meeting of the Southwestern Political Science Association, San Antonio.

Mateke, P. 1982. Curzon and the Idea of Transfer of Sind to Punjab. *Sindhological Studies* (Summer).

Mattes, Robert, and Hermann Thiel. 1998. Consolidation and Public Opinion in South Africa. *Journal of Democracy* 9, no. 1: 95–110.

Maxwell, Kenneth. 1986. Regime Overthrow and the Prospects for Democratic Transition in Portugal. In *Transitions from Authoritarian Rule: Southern Europe*, edited by Guillermo O'Donnell, Philippe Schmitter, and Laurence Whitehead. Baltimore: Johns Hopkins University Press.

Mbeki's South Africa. 1999. *The Economist*, 29 May, 14.

McArthur, S. 1996. Portuguese Regional Plan May Exact Political Toll. Reuters News Service, via Clarinet, 10 May.

Merchant, Carolyn. 1992. *Radical Ecology*. London: Routledge.

Meriwether, Robert L. 1959. *The Papers of John C. Calhoun*. Columbia: University of South Carolina Press.

Misra, B. B. 1990. *The Unification and Division of India*. Oxford, UK: Oxford University Press.

Monongahela River Valley Steering Group. 1986. *An Interstate River Valley in Economic Transition*. Unpublished paper.

Montville, Joseph V., ed. 1990. *Conflict and Peacemaking in Multiethnic Societies*. Lexington, MA: Lexington Books.

Morata, Francesc. 1991. Spanish Regions and the 1992 Community Challenge. Working Paper 34. Barcelona: Institut de Ciències Polítiques i Socials.

Mutizwa-Mangiza, Naison, and Diana Conyers. 1996. Decentralization in Practice, with Special Reference to Tanzania, Zimbabwe, and Nigeria. *Regional Development Dialogue* 17: 77–93.

Nakashima, Ellen. 1996. 100-Year-Old Cause Spurs Sovereignty Vote. *Washington Post*, 27 August.

Ndoye, Kader, Ibrahima Gaye, and Philippe Tersiguel, eds. 1994. *La decentralization au Senegal: L'etape de la régionalisation*. Dakar, Senegal: École Nationale d'Economie Appliquée.

Nefedova, Tatiana, and Andre Trevish. 1994. *Raiyoni Rossii I Drugikh Evropyeskikh Strans Perekhodnoi Ekonomikoi.* Moscow: Institute Geography RAN.

Nehru, Jawaharlal. 1985. *Letters to Chief Ministers, 1947–1964.* General editor, G. Parthasarathi. Delhi, India: Oxford University Press.

Nekrich, Aleksandr. 1978. *The Punished Peoples: The Deportation and Fate of Soviet Minorities at the End of the Second World War.* New York: W.W. Norton and Company.

Neumann, Franz L. 1955. Federalism and Freedom: A Critique. In *Federalism: Mature and Emergent*, edited by Arthur W. MacMahon. New York: Russell & Russell.

Nice, David C., and Patricia Fredericksen. 1995. *The Politics of Intergovernmental Relations.* 2nd ed. Chicago: Nelson-Hall.

Norton, Alan. 1994. *International Handbook of Local and Regional Government: A Comparative Analysis of Advanced Democracies.* Hants, England: Edward Elgar Publishing.

Nugent, John D. 1999. The New Rhetoric of State-Governmental Interests: States' Rights Revisited? Paper presented at the Annual Meeting of the Western Political Science Association, Seattle.

Nunes Silva, Carlos. 1993. Os Municípios e o Desenvolvimento Local: Associacões de Municipios e Regiões Administrativas. Paper presented at the conference, First Encounter for a Development Perspective and Future without Losing Identity, 18–19 June, in Figueiró dos Vinhos, Portugal.

———. 1994. Interview by Jeanie J. Bukowski and James J. Friedberg. Humanities Faculty, University of Lisbon, Lisbon, Portugal, 3 November.

Nzouankeu, Jacques Mariel. 1994. Decentralization and Democracy in Africa. *International Review of Administrative Sciences* 60: 213–227.

O'Donnell, Guillermo, Philippe Schmitter, and Laurence Whitehead, eds. 1986. *Transitions from Authoritarian Rule.* 4 vols. Baltimore: Johns Hopkins University Press.

Olowu, Dele, and Paul Smoke. 1992. Determinants of Success in African Local Governments: An Overview. *Public Administration and Development* 12: 1–17.

Opello, Walter. 1978. The Second Portuguese Republic: Politico-Administrative Decentralization since April 25, 1974. *Iberian Studies* 8, no. 2 (Autumn): 43–48.

———. 1993. Portuguese Regionalism in the Transition from the *Estado Novo* to the Single Market. In *The Regions and the European Community: The Regional Response to the Single Market in Underdeveloped Areas*, edited by Robert Leonardi. London: Frank Cass.

Ordeshook, Peter. 1996. Russia's Party System: Is Russian Federalism Viable? *Post-Soviet Affairs*, no. 3: 195–223.

Ostrom, Elinor. 1990. *Governing the Commons.* New York: Cambridge University Press.

Ostrom, Vincent. 1991. *The Meaning of American Federalism.* San Francisco: Institute for Contemporary Studies.

Ottaway, Marina. 1993. *South Africa: The Struggle for a New Order.* Washington, DC: The Brookings Institute.

Oye, Kenneth, ed. 1986. *Cooperation under Anarchy.* Princeton, NJ: Princeton University Press.

Paddison, Ronan. 1983. *The Fragmented State: The Political Geography of Power.* Oxford, England: Basil Blackwell.

Pagano, Michael A., and Ann O'M. Bowman. 1995. The State of American Federalism, 1994–1995. *Publius: The Journal of Federalism* 25 (Summer): 2.

Panhwar, M.H. 1990. Economic Plight of Sindh under Pakistan. *Sind Quarterly* 18, no. 2.

Patterson, Amy. 1996. *Participation and Democracy at the Grassroots: A Study of Development Associations in Rural Senegal.* Ph.D. diss., Indiana University.

———. 1998a. External Influences and Democracy: The Case of Donors and Local Development Associations in Senegal. Paper presented at the annual conference of the African Studies Association, 29 October–1 November, Chicago, Illinois.

———. 1998b. A Reappraisal of Democracy in Civil Society: Evidence from Rural Senegal. *The Journal of Modern African Studies* 36: 423–441.

———. 1999. The Dynamic Nature of Citizenship and Participation: Lessons from Three Rural Senegalese Case Studies. *Africa Today* 46: 3–27.

Pereira, Armando. 1991. The System of Local Government in Portugal. In *Local Government in Europe: Trends and Developments*, edited by Richard Batley and Gerry Stoker. New York: St. Martin's Press.

———. 1995. Regionalism in Portugal. In *The European Union and the Regions*, edited by Barry Jones and Michael Keating. Oxford, England: Clarendon Press.

Pérez-Díaz, Víctor. 1990. Governability and the Scale of Governance: Mesogovernments in Spain. Working Paper 1990/6. Madrid: Instituto Juan March de Estudios e Investigaciones.

Peterson, Paul E. 1995. *The Price of Federalism.* Washington, DC: Brookings Institution.

Power to the States. 1995. *Business Week*, 7 August, 49–50.

Przeworski, Adam, ed. 1996. *Sustainable Democracy.* Cambridge: Cambridge University Press.

Putnam, Robert. 1993. *Making Democracy Work.* Princeton, NJ: Princeton University Press.

Raby, David L. 1988. *Fascism and Resistance in Portugal: Communists, Liberals and Military Dissidents in the Opposition to Salazar, 1941–1974.* Manchester, England: Manchester University Press.

Rajagopalan, Swarna. 1997. National Integration in India, Sri Lanka and Pakistan: Constitutional and Elite Visions. *Nationalism and Ethnic Politics* 3, no. 4:1–38.

———. 1998. *National Integration: The State in Search of Community.* Ph.D. diss., University of Illinois at Urbana-Champaign.

Rajayyan, K. 1982. *History of Tamil Nadu, 1565-1982.* Madras, India: Raj Publishers.

Rakowska-Harmstone, Therese. 1974. The Dialectics of Nationalism in the USSR. *Problems of Communism*, no. 23: 1–22 (May-June).

Raz, Joseph. 1990. *Authority.* Oxford, England: Basil Blackwell Ltd.

Regional Disparities, Coastal Area. 1994. Lisbon: Ministry of Planning and Territorial Administration, Directorate General of Regional Development.

Ribot, Jesse. 1995. From Exclusion to Participation: Turning Senegal's Forestry Policy Around? *World Development* 23: 1587–1600.

———. 1999. Decentralization, Participation and Accountability in Sahelian Forestry: Legal Instruments of Political-Administrative Control. *Africa* 69: 23–65.

Riker, William H. 1964. *Federalism: Origin, Operation, Significance.* Boston: Little, Brown & Co.

Rivlin, Alice. 1992. *Reviving the American Dream.* Washington, DC: Brookings Institution.

Robinson, Richard Allen Hodgson. 1979. *Contemporary Portugal: A History.* London: George Allen & Unwin.

Rocha, José Manuel. 1999. Novo modelo de descentralização: um milhão para as ADR. *Público,* 13 July.

Roeder, Philip. 1991. Soviet Federalism and Ethnic Mobilization. *World Politics,* no. 2: 196–232.

Romero, Ana. 1994. Los partidos aprueban por unanimidad el estudio para reformar la Constitución. *El Mundo,* Madrid edition, 29 September.

Rosecrance, Richard, and Arthur Stein. 1973. Interdependence: Myth or Reality? *World Politics* 26, no. 1 (October): 1–27.

Rosenau, James N. 1990. *Turbulence in World Politics: A Theory of Change and Continuity.* Princeton, NJ: Princeton University Press.

Rossiiskii Statisticheskii Yezhegodnik. 1995. Moscow: Goskomstat Rossii.

Rudolph, Joseph R., Jr., and Robert J. Thompson. 1989. *Ethnoterritorial Politics, Policy and the Western World.* Boulder, CO: Lynne Rienner Publishers.

Salamat, Zarina. 1992. *Pakistan, 1947–1958: A Historical Review.* Islamabad, Pakistan: National Institute of Historical and Cultural Research.

Samaraweera, Vijaya. 1973. The Colebrooke-Cameron Reforms. In *The University of Ceylon, The History of Ceylon,* vol. III, edited by K. M. de Silva. Peradeniya: University of Ceylon.

Sanford, Terry. 1967. *Storm over the States.* New York: McGraw Hill.

Saunders, Cheryl. 1995. Constitutional Arrangements of Federal Systems. *Publius: The Journal of Federalism* 25 (Spring): 61–79.

Schaffer, Frederic. 1998. *Democracy in Translation: Understanding Politics in an Unfamiliar Culture.* Ithaca, NY: Cornell University Press.

Schraeder, Peter. 1995. From Berlin 1884 to 1989: Foreign Assistance and French, American, and Japanese Competition in Francophone Africa. *Journal of Modern African Studies* 33: 539–567.

Schumacher, Edward. 1975. *Politics, Bureaucracy, and Rural Development in Senegal.* Berkeley: University of California Press.

Shah, Sayid Ghulam Mustafa. 1983. An Urdu Conference is Patriotic, a Punjabi Conference is Patriotic, but a Sindhi Conference is Unpatriotic. Sind: Causes of Present Discontent. *Sind Quarterly* 11, no. 4.

Shanahan, Eileen. 1996. Devolution and the Blame Game. *Governing* 9 (January): 13.

Sharlet, Robert. 1994. The Prospects for Federalism in Russian Constitutional Politics. *Publius,* no.1: 115–127.

Sharpe, Laurence J. 1988. The Growth and Decentralisation of the Modern Democratic State. *European Journal of Political Research* 16: 365–380.

———. 1993a. The European Meso: An Appraisal. In *The Rise of Meso Government in Europe,* edited by L. J. Sharpe. London: Sage Publications.

———, ed. 1993b. *The Rise of Meso Government in Europe.* London: Sage Publications.

Sheehy, Ann. 1991. Ethnographic Developments and the Soviet Federal System. In *Soviet Federalism, Nationalism and Economic Decentralization,* edited by Alastair McAuley. Leicester and London, England: Leicester University Press.

Shils, Edward A. 1960. The Intellectual in the Political Development of the New States. *World Politics* XII (April): 329–368.

Silver, Brian. 1974. Social Mobilization and the Russification of Soviet Nationalities. *American Political Science Review,* no. 1 (March): 45–66.

Simkins, Charles. 1996. Problems of Reconstruction: the New South Africa. *Journal of Democracy* 7, no. 1: 82–95.

Sindhi as the Official Language of the Province of Sind. 1982. *Sind Quarterly* 10, no. 1:22–34.

Singh, L. P. 1989. *National Integration.* New Delhi, India: Centre for Policy Research.

Sisk, Timothy D. 1995. *Democraticization in South Africa.* Princeton, NJ: Princeton University Press.

Sivathamby, Karthigesu. 1987. The Sri Lankan Ethnic Crisis and Muslim-Tamil Relationships—A Socio-Political Review. In *Facets of Ethnicity in Sri Lanka*, edited by Charles Abeysekera and Newton Gunasinghe. Colombo, Sri Lanka: Social Scientists Association.

Sklar, Richard. 1987. Developmental Democracy. *Comparative Studies in Society and History* 29: 531–552.

Skocpol, Theda. 1985. Bringing the State Back In: Strategies of Analysis in Current Research. In *Bringing the State Back In*, edited by Peter Evans, Dietrich Rueschemeyer, and Theda Skocpol. New York: Cambridge University Press.

Slider, Darrell. 1996. Elections to Russia's Regional Assemblies. *Post-Soviet Affairs*, no. 3: 243–264.

Smith, Graham, ed. 1995. *Federalism: The Multiethnic Challenge.* London and New York: Longman.

South Africa and the EU, Lemon Squeezer. 1996. *The Economist*, 13 July, 41.

South Africa's Profligate Provinces. 1998. *The Economist*, 28 February, 49.

Stadler, A.W. 1997. The Rise and Decline of Party Activism in South Africa. Paper presented, 6 October, at the Institute for Advanced Social Research, University of Witwaterstrand, South Africa.

Stalin, Josef. 1950. *The National Question and Leninism.* Moscow: Foreign Language Publishing House.

Stanfield, Rochelle. 1995. Holding the Bag? *National Journal* 27 (September 9): 2206–2209.

Stohr, Walter B., and D. R. F. Taylor, eds. 1981. *Development from Above or Below? A Radical Reappraisal of Spatial Planning in Less Developed Countries.* Sussex, England: John Wiley.

Stoner-Weiss, Kathryn. 1997. *Local Heroes: The Political Economy of Russian Regional Governance.* Princeton, NJ: Princeton University Press.

Sullivan, John. 1999. Forty Years of ETA. *History Today* 49, issue 4 (April): 34.

Sullivan, Stefan. 1995. Interethnic Relations in Post-Soviet Tuva. *Ethnic and Racial Studies*, no. 1: 64–88.

Sy, Cheikh Tidiane, ed. 1988. *Crise du développement rural et désengagement de l'état au Sénégal.* Dakar, Senegal: Les Nouvelles Editions Africaines.

Tahir, Tanvir Ahmad. 1990. Pakistan Resolution and Politics in Sind. In *Pakistan Resolution Revisited*, edited by Kaneez F. Yusuf, M. Saleem Akhtar, and S. Razi Wasti. Islamabad, Pakistan: National Institute of Historical and Cultural Research.

Takougang, Joseph. 1997. Cameroon: Biya and Incremental Reform. In *Political Reform in Francophone Africa*, edited by John Clark and David Gardinier. Boulder, CO: Westview Press.

Tannenwald, Robert. 1998. Devolution: The New Federalism—An Overview. *New England Economic Review* (May/June): 1–12.

Tannenwald, Robert, and Jonathan Cowan. 1997. Fiscal Capacity, Fiscal Need, and Fiscal Comfort among U.S. States: New Evidence. *Publius: The Journal of Federalism* 27 (Summer): 113–125.

Taylor, Charles. 1994. The Politics of Recognition. In *Multiculturalism: Examining The Politics of Recognition*, edited by Amy Gutmann. Princeton, NJ: Princeton University Press.

Tendler, Judith. 1997. *Good Government in the Tropics*. Baltimore: Johns Hopkins University Press.

Thomas, Gerald B. 1995. The Politics of Hope: An Eclectic Vision of the Future. In *Environmental Politics and Policy*, 2nd ed., edited by James P. Lester. Durham, NC: Duke University Press.

Thompson, Leonard. 1995. *A History of South Africa*. New Haven, CT: Yale University Press.

Thompson, Robert J., and Joseph R. Rudolph, Jr. 1989. The Ebb and Flow of Ethnoterritorial Politics in the Western World. In *Ethnoterritorial Politics, Policy, and the Western World*, edited by Joseph R. Rudolph, Jr. and Robert J. Thompson. Boulder, CO: Lynne Rienner Publishers.

Thompson, Tommy. 1995. Devolution Blues. *The Economist*, 22 July, 27.

Tiebout, Charles M. 1956. A Pure Theory of Local Expenditures. *Journal of Political Economy* 64 (October): 416–435.

Tilly, Charles. 1978. *From Mobilization to Revolution*. Englewood Hills, NJ: Prentice Hall.

Tolz, Vera. 1993. The Role of the Republics and Regions. *Radio Liberty Research Reports*. April 9.

Tordoff, William. 1994. Decentralisation: Comparative Experience in Commonwealth Africa. *The Journal of Modern African Studies* 32: 555–580.

Treisman, Daniel. 1997. Russia's Ethnic Revival: The Separatist Activism of Regional Leaders in a Post Communist Order. *World Politics*, no. 2: 212–249.

Tripp, Aili Mari. 1998. Decentralization and Women's Local Participation in Uganda. Paper presented at the annual conference of the American Political Science Association, 3-6 September, Boston.

US Advisory Commission on Intergovernmental Relations. 1993. *State Laws Governing Local Government Structure and Administration*. Washington, DC: US ACIR.

Under Threat. 1998. *The Economist*, 10 October, 50–51.

United Nations. 1992. *Cooperation au développement: Sénégal 1991*. Dakar, Senegal: United Nations.

Vale, Peter. 1999. Dominion and Discourse in the Making of South Africa's Security. Paper presented at the International Studies Association meeting, Washington D.C., February.

Valles, Josep María, and Montserrat Cuchillo Foix. 1988. Decentralization in Spain: A Review. *European Journal of Political Research* 16: 395–407.

van de Walle, Nicolas. 1998. Managing Aid to Africa: The Rise and Decline of the Structural Adjustment Regime. Paper presented at the AERC-ODC Collaborative Research Workshop on Managing the Transition from Aid Dependence in Sub-Saharan Africa, 21–22 May, Nairobi, Kenya.

van de Walle, Nicolas, and Timothy Johnston. 1996. *Improving Aid to Africa*. Baltimore: Johns Hopkins University Press.

Van der Merwe, Basil. Economic Counselor, South African Embassy, Washington, D.C. 1999. Interview by Ellen Pirro and Eleanor Zeff, Des Moines, Iowa, 18 September.

Van Son, Victoria. 1993. *CQ's State Fact Finder.* Washington, DC: Congressional Quarterly.

Vengroff, Richard. 1989. *Decentralization and the Implementation of Rural Development in Senegal.* Lewiston, NY: Edwin Mellen Press.

———. 1993. The Transition to Democracy in Senegal: The Role of Decentralization. In *Establishing Democratic Rule: The Re-emergence of Local Governments in Post-Authoritarian Systems,* edited by Ilpyong Kim and Jane Shapiro Zacek. Washington, DC: In Depth Books.

Vengroff, Richard, and Lucy Creevey. 1997. The Evolution of a Quasi-Democracy. In *Political Reform in Francophone Africa,* edited by John Clark and David Gardinier. Boulder, CO: Westview Press.

Vengroff, Richard, and Alan Johnston. 1987. Decentralization and the Implementation of Rural Development in Senegal: The Role of Rural Councils. *Public Administration and Development* 7: 273–88.

———. 1989. *Decentralization and the Implementation of Rural Development in Senegal.* Lewiston, NY: The Edwin Mellen Press.

Vengroff, Richard, and Momar Ndiaye. 1998. The Impact of Electoral Reform at the Local Level in Africa: The Case of Senegal's 1996 Local Elections. Paper presented at the Annual Meeting of the American Political Science Association, September 3–6, Boston.

Verney, Douglas V. 1995. Federalism, Federative Systems and Federations: The United States, Canada, and India. *Publius: The Journal of Federalism* 25 (Spring): 81–97.

Villalón, Leonardo. 1994. Democratizing a (Quasi) Democracy: The Senegalese Elections of 1993. *African Affairs* 93: 163–93.

———. 1995. *Islamic Society and State Power in Senegal.* New York: Cambridge University Press.

Walker, David B. 1981. *Toward a Functioning Federalism.* Cambridge, MA: Winthrop.

———. 1995. *The Rebirth of Federalism.* Chatham, NJ: Chatham House.

Walker, Jennone. 1993. European Regional Organizations and Ethnic Conflict. In *Central and Eastern Europe: The Challenge of Transition,* edited by Regina Cowen Karp. New York: Oxford Press.

Wallich, Christine. 1994. *Russia and the Challenge of Fiscal Federalism.* Washington, DC: World Bank Regional and Sectoral Studies.

Waseem, Mohammed. 1997. Ethnicity and Religion in South Asia: The Pakistan Experience. Lecture at the Regional Centre for Strategic Studies Workshop on Ethnicity, Migration and Environment, 7 March, in Kandy, Sri Lanka.

Washbrook, D.A. 1989. Caste, Class and Dominance in Tamil Nadu: Non-Brahmanism, Dravidianism and Tamil Nationalism. In *Dominance and State Power in Modern India,* vol. I, edited by Francine Frankel and M.S.A. Rao. Delhi, India: Oxford.

Waters, Malcolm. 1995. *Globalization.* London, New York: Routledge.

Watts, Ronald. 1993. Contemporary Views on Federalism. Paper presented at the Centre for Constitutional Analysis, Republic of South Africa. Quoted in Douglas V. Verney, Federalism, Federative Systems and Federations: The United States, Canada, and India. *Publius: The Journal of Federalism* 25 (Spring): 81–97.

Weissert, Carol S., and Sanford F. Schram. 1998. The State of American Federalism, 1997–1998. Paper presented at the Annual Meeting of the American Political Science Association, 5 September, Boston.

Wheare, Kenneth C. 1946. *Federal Government.* London: Oxford University Press.

White South Africa on the Wing. 1998. *The Economist*, 6 June, 43–44.

Wight, Martin. 1952. *British Colonial Constitutions 1947.* London: Oxford University Press.

Wills, Garry. 1981. *Explaining America: The Federalist.* New York: Penguin Books.

Wilson, A. Jeyaratnam. 1988. *The Break-Up of Sri Lanka: The Sinhalese-Tamil Conflict.* Honolulu: University of Hawaii Press.

Your Friends, the Police. 1997. *The Economist*, 15 February, 44.

Zimmerman, Joseph F. 1992. *Contemporary American Federalism.* New York: Praeger.

Index

About the Contributors

ANN O'M. BOWMAN is a professor of political science in the Department of Government and International Studies at the University of South Carolina. She was co-editor of the *Annual Review of Federalism* issue of *Publius: The Journal of Federalism* from 1989 to 1995. She is co-author of *State and Local Government: The Essentials* (2000). Her current research involves local governments and vacant land.

JEANIE J. BUKOWSKI is an assistant professor of international studies at Bradley University in Peoria, Illinois. She is the author of "Decentralization in Spain: A Re-examination of Causal Factors" (*South European Society and Politics*, 1998) and is co-editor, with Marc Smyrl and Simona Piattoni, of *Between Globalization and Local Society: The Space for Regional Governance in Europe* (2001). Her current research examines multilevel policy networks in the European Union and decision making in substate regional governments.

KATHLEEN M. DOWLEY is an assistant professor of political science at SUNY New Paltz. She is the author of "Striking the Federal Bargain in Russia: Comparative Regional Government Strategies" *(Communist and Post-Communist Studies*, 1998) and is co-author of "Post-Materialism in World Societies" *(American Journal of Political Science*, 1999) and "Measuring Political Culture in Multi-Ethnic Societies" (*Comparative Political Studies*, 2000). She continues research on the relationship between politics and ethnicity, and institutional attempts to reconcile multiple and competing sources of politicized identity.

AMY PATTERSON is assistant professor of political science at Elmhurst College, a small liberal arts institution in the Chicago area. She received her Ph.D. from Indiana University and has published in *The Journal of Modern African Studies* and *Africa Today* on democracy in civil society and citizenship in Senegal. Her current research examines the role of power in the construction of local development organizations in Africa.

ELLEN B. PIRRO is co-inventor of the Wordsmith™ content analysis system and has specialized in Research Methodology, Developing Areas and Africa. She has taught at a number of universities, most recently Iowa State University. She currently heads an international research and consulting firm based in Des Moines, Iowa. Author of a number of books and articles, her recent work includes "Analysis of the Tiananmen Square Crisis: A Methodological Approach," presented to the Midwest Sociological Society Annual Meeting, April 1991 (with Mack C. Shelley, II, Liangfu Wu, and Xia Li) and "Contextual Content Analysis," (*Quality and Quantity*, 24: 245–265, Kluwer Academic Publishers, 1990), with Donald G. McTavish.

SWARNA RAJAGOPALAN is a Post-doctoral Fellow at Michigan State University and holds degrees from the University of Illinois at Urbana-Champaign, Syracuse University, and the University of Bombay. Her research interests include nationalism, political development, security, and conflict resolution, and her work has been in the South Asian context. She has published articles in *Nationalism and Ethnic Politics* and *Nethra* and is currently revising a book manuscript comparing the national integration processes in India, Pakistan, and Sri Lanka.

ELEANOR E. ZEFF is adjunct associate professor at Drake University in Des Moines, Iowa and specializes in the politics of developing areas, especially Africa, and in European politics. She has taught at both Iowa State and Drake Universities. Her recent publications include "Stumbling Toward Union: Policy Making in the European Union," with Ellen B. Pirro (*Policy Studies Journal*, 1998), and she is currently editing a book on the European Union. She has also published in *Journal of African Studies* and in the *African Studies Review*.

ISBN 0-275-96377-2

HARDCOVER BAR CODE